D1711886

CONTEMPORARY
Black
Biography

ISSN-1058-1316

CONTEMPORARY

Black

Biography

Profiles from the International Black Community

Volume 51

THOMSON

━━━ ✦ ━━━ ™

GALE

ST. PHILIP'S COLLEGE LIBRARY

Detroit • New York • San Francisco • San Diego • New Haven, Conn. • Waterville, Maine • London • Munich

Contemporary Black Biography, Volume 51

Sara and Tom Pendergast

Project Editor
Pamela M. Kalte

Image Research and Acquisitions
Robyn V. Young

Editorial Support Services
Nataliya Mikheyeva

Rights and Permissions
Emma Hull, Lisa Kincade, Andrew Specht

Manufacturing
Dorothy Maki, Rhonda Williams

Composition and Prepress
Mary Beth Trimper, Gary Leach

Imaging
Lezlie Light, Mike Logusz

ISBN 0-7876-7923-2
ISSN 1058-1316

Printed in the United States of America
10 9 8 7 6 5 4 3 2 1

Advisory Board

Contents

Introduction

Contemporary Black Biography provides informative biographical profiles of the important and influential persons of African heritage who form the international black community: men and women who have changed today's world and are shaping tomorrow's. Contemporary Black Biography covers persons of various nationalities in a wide variety of fields, including architecture, art, business, dance, education, fashion, film, industry, journalism, law, literature, medicine, music, politics and government, publishing, religion, science and technology, social issues, sports, television, theater, and others. In addition to in-depth coverage of names found in today's headlines, Contemporary Black Biography provides coverage of selected individuals from earlier in this century whose influence continues to impact on contemporary life. Contemporary Black Biography also provides coverage of important and influential persons who are not yet household names and are therefore likely to be ignored by other biographical reference series. Each volume also includes listee updates on names previously appearing in CBB.

Designed for Quick Research and Interesting Reading

- **Attractive page design** incorporates textual subheads, making it easy to find the information you're looking for.

- **Easy-to-locate data sections** provide quick access to vital personal statistics, career information, major awards, and mailing addresses, when available.

- **Informative biographical essays** trace the subject's personal and professional life with the kind of in-depth analysis you need.

- **To further enhance your appreciation** of the subject, most entries include photographic portraits.

- **Sources for additional information** direct the user to selected books, magazines, and newspapers where more information on the individuals can be obtained.

Helpful Indexes Make It Easy to Find the Information You Need

Contemporary Black Biography includes cumulative Nationality, Occupation, Subject, and Name indexes that make it easy to locate entries in a variety of useful ways.

Available in Electronic Formats

Diskette/Magnetic Tape. Contemporary Black Biography is available for licensing on magnetic tape or diskette in a fielded format. Either the complete database or a custom selection of entries may be ordered. The database is available for internal data processing and nonpublishing purposes only. For more information, call (800) 877-GALE.

On-line. Contemporary Black Biography is available on-line through Mead Data Central's NEXIS Service in the NEXIS, PEOPLE and SPORTS Libraries in the GALBIO file and Gale's Biography Resource Center.

Disclaimer

Contemporary Black Biography uses and lists websites as sources and these websites may become obsolete.

We Welcome Your Suggestions

The editors welcome your comments and suggestions for enhancing and improving Contemporary Black Biography. If you would like to suggest persons for inclusion in the series, please submit these names to the editors. Mail comments or suggestions to:

The Editor
Contemporary Black Biography
Thomson Gale
27500 Drake Rd.
Farmington Hills, MI 48331-3535
Phone: (800) 347-4253

Anthony Anderson

1970—

Actor

One of the fastest-rising African-American comic actors of the early 2000s was Anthony Anderson, who broke through to fame in 2000 with roles in the hit films *Big Momma's House* and *Me, Myself & Irene.* Following in the footsteps of other modern comedians such as Bernie Mac, he created comic situations modeled closely on his own life and experiences; his television series *All About the Andersons* (2003) drew on his relationship to his family. With his friendly, quick-witted image and his strong feel for the comedy inherent in family relationships, Anderson became a familiar face even to casual film and television fans.

Anderson, Anthony, photograph. Kevin Winter/Getty Images.

Born in Los Angeles on August 15, 1970, Anderson grew up in the tough but culturally fertile suburb of Compton, California. He was born into the acting life; his mother Doris was a telephone operator and an aspiring actress who had roles as an extra in such films as *Uptown Saturday Night,* and she put her son on stage in a play while he was still a baby. The strong male figure in Anderson's life was his stepfather Sterling Bowman, the owner of a chain of stores with clothes for plus-sized women. "For my sixth birthday my biological father said he was going to bring me a

bike but never did," Anderson recalled to Jeannine Amber of *Essence.* "So my real daddy went out and got me one. That's my dad."

Saw Mother Perform in Play

Anderson appeared in a television commercial at the age of five, and soon his mother inspired him to pursue acting as a career. "I remember sitting in Compton Community College...in their theater at nine years old and my mother was doing a production of *A Raisin in the Sun*...man, and it just hit me," he told interviewer Tavis Smiley of National Public Radio. "I was like, you know what, that's what I'm going to do for the rest of my life." Anderson attended a performing arts high school and went on with the help of a scholarship to Howard University in Washington, D.C. One of his classmates at Howard was comedian Marlon Wayans.

After graduating from Howard, Anderson returned to the Los Angeles area and moved back in with his mother and stepfather—much to their displeasure, for they had told Anderson and his siblings that they needed to plan to be out on their own after they turned 18. Anderson's stepfather pushed him gradually in the

At a Glance . . .

Born August 15, 1970, in Los Angeles, CA; married; children: two daughters and one son. *Education:* Howard University, Washington, DC.

Career: Actor, 1996–.

Selected awards: Acapulco Black Film Festival, Rising Star Award, 2001.

Addresses: *Agent*—William Morris Agency, 151 El Camino Dr., Los Angeles, CA 90212.

direction of independence, providing him with a rich source of future comic material in the process. He installed a pay telephone and a coin-operated washer and dryer in his own home, forcing the young graduate to end his freeloading when it came to phone calls and laundry. The hope was that Anderson would join the family clothing business, but when he refused and got a job in a mall instead, his stepfather padlocked the household refrigerator. "That's how my father systematically tried to get me out of the house," Anderson explained to *TelevisionWeek.*

Television Career Grew

Gradually, Anderson got his life in gear and began pursuing performance opportunities. His career began with small television roles, including one on the UPN series *In the House* in 1995. He had a recurring role as Theodore "Teddy" Brodis on NBC's *Hang Time* from 1996 to 1998, and he garnered roles in episodes of such top-rated series as *NYPD Blue* and *Ally McBeal.* In 1999 Anderson broke into films with a small role in the Martin Lawrence-and-Eddie Murphy comedy *Life.* Film roles followed thick and fast after that, with the actor showing his range by appearing in non-comic roles like one in the martial-arts Shakespeare adaptation *Romeo Must Die.* He had his first starring role in the Martin Lawrence comedy *Big Momma's House* (2000).

Top-notch slapstick turns in several huge comedy hits over the next few years made Anderson a familiar face among both industry people and audiences. He appeared opposite Jim Carrey as one of triplet sons of Carrey's split-personality character in *Me, Myself & Irene,* and in *Barbershop* (2002) he played one of a hapless pair of thieves who steal an automatic teller machine but then find that it becomes an enormous millstone as they struggle to move it from place to place. Anderson functioned well in the flourishing African-American ensemble film genre, taking a turn in the funeral-themed comedy-drama *Kingdom Come.*

The year 2003 brought Anderson, whose friends call him "Ant," no fewer than four film parts, including his first lead role, in *Kangaroo Jack.* That comedy featured Anderson as one of a pair of friends who try to recover $50,000 in an envelope lost to an aggressive kangaroo in Australia; it received generally lukewarm reviews but topped American box-office lists for a week. Anderson also appeared that year in *Cradle 2 the Grave, Scary Movie 3,* and the hip-hop spoof *Malibu's Most Wanted.*

Pay Phone Resurfaced as Gag

Meanwhile, Anderson and writing partner Adam Glass had been working on a big leap back into the world of television for the portly 270-pound actor: an idea and then a pilot episode for a weekly sitcom, starring Anderson and based in large part on his own experiences after he moved back in with his parents after college. Finally, after three years of meetings, the WB network signed on and premiered *All About the Andersons* in 2003. The pay phone and padlocked refrigerator resurfaced as plot elements in the show, although new characters (such as an eight-year-old son) were introduced and other details altered. Critics and audiences gravitated toward Anderson's enthusiastic personality, but the series suffered from uneven scripts. *People* opined that "the show gets close to a kind of truth that it's not really brave enough to confront," and it was canceled after a year.

Anderson bounced back easily, starring in the films *Hustle & Flow* and *My Baby's Daddy,* and signing on to appear in at least 10 episodes of a crime drama, *The Shield,* on the FX cable network in 2005. That marked a new challenge for the actor; he was set to take on his first dramatic television role, as a former drug dealer whose claims to have reformed were questionable. Happily married with two daughters and a son, Anderson was an unlikely candidate for the Hollywood rumor mill, and a rape charge leveled against the actor by a Memphis woman in 2004 was thrown out by a judge who termed the accuser's testimony some of the most suspicious he had ever heard. Continuing to expand his reach and hone his technique, Anderson seemed set to remain a fixture of both large and small screens in years to come.

Selected works

Films

Life, 1999.
Liberty Heights, 1999.
Romeo Must Die, 1999.
Big Momma's House, 2000.
Me, Myself & Irene, 2000.
Kingdom Come, 2001.
Two Can Play That Game, 2001.
Exit Wounds, 2001.

Barbershop, 2002.
Kangaroo Jack, 2002.
Scary Movie 3, 2003.
Malibu's Most Wanted, 2003.
Cradle 2 the Grave, 2003.
My Baby's Daddy, 2003.
Hustle & Flow, 2004.
Agent Cody Banks 2: Destination London, 2004.
King's Ransom, 2005.

Television

Hang Time, 1996-98.
All About the Andersons, 2003.
The Shield, 2005.

Sources

Periodicals

Chicago Sun-Times, January 22, 2003, p. 50.

Daily News (Los Angeles), September 12, 2003, p. U30.
Essence, March 2004, p. 128.
Jet, February 3, 2003, p. 54; October 25, 2004, p.35.
People, October 27, 2003, p. 36; November 17, 2003, p. 120.
TelevisionWeek, April 28, 2003, p. 10.
Toronto Sun, October 23, 2003, p. 78.
Variety, January 12, 2005, p. 14.

On-line

"Anthony Anderson," *All Movie Guide,* http://www.allmovie.com (March 1, 2005).

Other

The Tavis Smiley Show, National Public Radio, October 24, 2003, transcript.

—James M. Manheim

Regina Belle

1963—

Singer

Belle, Regina, photograph. Frederick M Brown/Getty Images.

Singer Regina Belle has dazzled critics and fans alike since her debut album, *All By Myself*, was released in 1987. Acclaimed as one of the most exciting new singers to emerge on the rhythm and blues scene, the New Jersey songstress boasts a style that recalls some of the most successful black pop female singers in the industry, yet is nonetheless distinctive. Jim Miller in *Newsweek* heralded Belle's entry onto the music scene in 1987: "Move over, Anita Baker—and make way for Regina Belle, who may be the most electrifying new soul singer since Baker herself…. Imagine a singer who simultaneously recalls Aretha Franklin, Sade and Anita Baker, and you'll get a fair idea of Belle's singular style." Belle's subsequent albums solidified her place on the American music scene, with reviewers comparing her favorably to jazz great Billie Holiday.

Belle's wide vocal range has particularly impressed reviewers. "She has a strong, expressive voice and she's versatile, dealing well with sultry ballads ('Baby Come to Me') or sassy jump-ups ('When Will You Be Mine')," wrote David Hiltbrand in *People* of *Stay With Me*, Belle's follow-up to *All By Myself*. Steve Bloom commented in *Rolling Stone* that Belle's "full-throated, pop-gospel vocal style brings to mind Anita Baker, Patti LaBelle, and Stephanie Mills." A number of critics have similarly compared Belle's vocals to those of soul-jazz phenomenon Baker. Hiltbrand noted that, like Baker, Belle "displays a voice of tantalizing quality…. She can sound both promisingly intimate and world-weary without sacrificing vibrancy."

Belle has remarked, however, that comparisons to Baker are off-target. She told Bloom: "Because Anita Baker is prominent right now, Regina Belle sounds like Anita Baker…. I've been singing since I was three years old. By the time [Baker's 1986 album] *Rapture* came out, my style was already developed. People say I got certain inflections from Anita, but I got them from Phyllis Hyman. *That* was my girl." In addition to Hyman, Belle lists other musical influences as Billie Holiday, Donny Hathaway, and Nancy Wilson; she refers to the latter as her "show business mother." Belle met famous song stylist Wilson at a music convention in Los Angeles. "When I met her she told me that Billie Holiday did it for Dinah [Washington], Dinah did it for her and she has to do it for me," Belle was quoted as saying in *Jet*. Belle told *Essence* that she considers Billie Holiday her musical mentor, calling her

At a Glance . . .

Born on July 17, 1963; in Englewood, NJ; daughter of Eugene and Lois Belle; married Horace A. Young III (divorced); married John Battle (professional basketball player), 1991; children: Tiy (daughter), Jayln (son) and Sydni Milan (daughter, second marriage). *Education*: Attended Rutgers State University.

Career: The Manhattans, singer, 1985-87; solo singer and recording artist, 1987–. Feed the Homeless (charitable organization), Atlanta, GA, cofounder, c. 1999.

Awards: Nomination for best rhythm and blues female singer, American Music Awards, 1991.

Addresses: *Record company*—Peak Records, 100 N. Crescent Drive, Suite 275, Beverly Hills, CA 90210. *Home*—Atlanta, GA.

"the total epitome of femininity." Although reviewers comment on the similarities between Belle's and Holiday's sultry style, Belle stated in *Essence* that "I don't want people to think that I want to be Billie Holiday. But through my music, I can keep her alive—through zamani. As long as you can remember a person and escalate that memory, that person lives. That's called zamani in Swahili."

Belle's musical roots are in gospel, which she grew up singing in church with her family. She told an *Ebony* contributor that she was raised in a house where music was "something…involuntary." Her mother's specialty was gospel, and she learned rhythm and blues from her father. "The music was the same, just the message was different," she told Bloom. Belle sang during high school and on weekends attended classes at New York City's Manhattan School of Music, where she studied opera and classical music. Belle did not study jazz until college, when she enrolled in the Jazz Ensemble at Rutgers University. Belle told Bloom that with jazz she learned "to listen for colors, as opposed to trying to sing just notes. For the longest time, I couldn't figure out what that meant."

Not sure that music would be her career, Belle majored in accounting and history at Rutgers. She soon discovered that economics and accounting were not her strong suit, but that African-American history was. "Learning my history was the beginning of Regina Belle—knowing who she is and where she fits in life," she told *Essence*. She would go on to incorporate her understanding of history into her music.

Her big break as a singer came when disc jockey Vaughn Harper heard her open a concert on the Rutgers campus. Impressed, Harper introduced Belle to the manager of the singing group The Manhattans, who were looking for a female backup singer. Shortly thereafter Belle was touring with the group; a recording contract from the group's label, Columbia, soon followed.

Belle's 1987 debut, *All By Myself*, was an instant success; *Stay With Me*, her 1989 effort, established Belle as a major singer on the rhythm and blues scene. Both albums generated a string of solo hits, including "Show Me the Way," "Make It Like It Was," and "When Will You Be Mine." Belle has been primarily popular on the black charts, something she hoped would eventually change. "It's insulting to me when somebody says, 'You're Number One on the *black* charts.' It suggests that nobody appreciates my music but black people," she told Bloom. "I'd love to have a Number One pop single, but I'm not at the point where I *have* to. It doesn't plague me."

Belle soon gained wider recognition, however. In 1989 she scored back-to-back number one singles with "Baby Come to Me" and "Make It Like It Was." Belle then earned her first Grammy award with a track from her *Passion* album. "A Whole New World (Aladdin's Theme)" her duet on that album with Peabo Bryson won four Grammy Awards in 1993. While admitting to *Billboard* that neither she nor Bryson had not expected the Grammy, Belle added that "it sure made us happy." Her 2002 album *This Is Regina* was nominated for a Grammy.

Over her two-decade career, Belle has combined the sounds of R&B with jazz. And with her 2004 album *Lazy Afternoon,* Belle realized her own sound. She related on the Peak Records Web site that she hopes when her fans hear the album, they'll think: 'We always knew she was going to do this.'

In addition to receiving acclaim as a recording artist, Belle is also considered an outstanding live performer who is not afraid to take chances musically. "Her gifted voice and stage presence make her a tough 'opening' act," noted *Ebony*. "She is said to hold her own on any given night, and on others make the 'headliner' acts sweat for their star-status." Peter Watrous of the *New York Times* reviewed a show-stealing opener by Belle in 1989, noting that "Ms. Belle, who has an extraordinary voice, dug deep into gospel and blues melodies, letting the grit of her voice show, often tearing apart the original impulse of a song." The following year Watrous reviewed Belle as a headliner at New York's Avery Fisher Hall, commenting that "though she's not working as a jazz singer, she is an exceptional improviser." Belle's shows, Watrous continued, are "expansive and improvisatory, old-fashioned qualities that make her one of the most exciting pop singers working." In 2005 Belle was a featured artist at the eleventh annual Essence Festival, the premier R&B festival in America.

Selected discography

(With the Manhattans) *Back to Basics,* 1986.
All by Myself, Columbia, 1987.
Stay with Me, Columbia, 1989.
Passion, Columbia, 1993.
Reachin' Back, Columbia, 1995.
Believe in Me, MCA, 1998.
This Is Regina, Peak Records, 2002.
Lazy Afternoon, Peak Records, 2004.

Sources

Periodicals

Billboard, May 16, 1998; October 20, 2001; July 24, 2004.

Ebony, June 1990; November 1993.
Essence, May 1990; August 1993; October 1995.
Jet, May 14, 1990; December 12, 1994; September 4, 1995; January 17, 2005.
Newsweek, June 22, 1987.
New York Times, September 16, 1989; June 30, 1990; July 27, 1998.
People, June 22, 1987; October 2, 1989.
Rolling Stone, April 5, 1990.

On-line

"Biography: Regina Belle," *Peak Records,* www.peak-records.com/bios/reginabio.htm (April 26, 2005).

—Michael E. Mueller and Sara Pendergast

Albert Black

1940—

Sociologist, principal lecturer

Albert Black's parents taught him about hard work and responsibility when he was very young, and he took their lessons to heart. He not only worked throughout his childhood to help support his family, but he worked persistently to gain a higher education when it often seemed impossible that he would succeed. When he finally did earn his doctorate and become a university lecturer, he took his responsibilities as a teacher very seriously. He has consistently placed more value on being an attentive and caring teacher than on advancing his career, and in addition has taken on the responsibility of making the academic journey less difficult for African-American students at all levels. In university classes with names like "Race Relations" and "Afro-American Political Thought," Black has explored social issues which have often been overlooked or avoided within largely white institutions. Outside of class, he has taught sociology in a different way, working in the community and in public schools to help solve the problems that often prevent poor students and students of color from doing well in school.

Encouraged Early to Get an Education

Albert Wesley Black, Jr., was born in Chicago on April 25, 1939. His father, Albert Wesley Black, Sr., had run away from his Missouri home at the age of fourteen and ended up in Detroit, Michigan. A few years later he met Grace Green, who had left her parents' farm in South Carolina to live with her aunt in the big city of Detroit. Albert and Grace married and had four chil-

dren, two boys and two girls. Albert Senior supported his family by working two jobs. During the day, he was a maintenance worker for Children's Hospital, while in the evenings he ran a janitorial business. From an early age, Albert Junior and his brother worked with their father every evening cleaning office buildings. When the boys complained about scrubbing toilets, their father gave them the same answer so often that it became a private joke between them: "If you don't like cleaning the white man's toilets, get an education." Though they laughed, both boys followed their father's advice.

However, even with Albert Senior's two jobs, Grace Black's work as a beautician, and the help of the children, the Blacks knew real poverty. Winters are icy cold in Detroit, and when there was not enough money to pay for the gas heat, the water froze in the toilets and the children slept in their coats. The lack of money caused stress within the family, simply because it made life very difficult.

The Black family lived in a working-class neighborhood populated by Polish immigrants and blacks. There was little tension between the two groups, but they lived separately and had very little social contact. Black grew to respect his hardworking immigrant neighbors, whose yards were like immaculate fenced islands within an otherwise close-knit African-American community. Church and family were the most important institutions in young Black's world. His playmates were most often his brother, sisters, and cousins, and each Saturday evening boys and girls alike ironed their best clothes to wear to church on Sunday morning.

At a Glance . . .

Born Albert Wesley Black, Jr., on April 25, 1939, in Detroit, Michigan; married Varetta Jones, 1963 (divorced 1975); married Linda Thompson, 1977; children: children: Allison and Angela (first marriage); Alia and Nicole (second marriage). *Education:* University of Michigan, BS, zoology, 1963; Wayne State University, MA, sociology, 1967; University of California at Berkeley, PhD, sociology, 1976.

Career: California School of Arts and Crafts, Oakland, California, Sociology Department, lecturer, 1969-70; University of California at Davis, Sociology Department, lecturer; 1971-2; University of Washington, Sociology Department and Black Studies Department, assistant professor, lecturer, senior lecturer, and principal lecturer, 1973–.

Selected memberships: National Association of Black Sociologists, American Society of Criminology, American Sociological Association.

Selected awards: University of Washington, Distinguished Teaching Award, 1977; Alpha Kappa Alpha Sorority, Inc. and Kappa Alpha Psi Fraternity, Inc., Seattle Alumnae Chapters, "Talented Tenth Award," 1993; Washington Alliance of Black School Educators, Certificate of Appreciation for Distinguished Service on behalf of Children, 1998; University of Washington, Outstanding Public Service Award, 1999; University of Washington, Office of Minority Affairs and Educational Opportunity Programs, Charles E. Odegaard Award, 1999.

Addresses: *Office*—Department of Sociology, Box 353340, University of Washington, Seattle, WA 98195-3340.

Success in High School Led to College

School was another important institution in young Albert Black's life. Detroit schools were racially segregated during the 1950s, and, while most of the students were African American at Black's school, almost all of the teachers were white. He did well in school and in sports, where he played football and ran track. In his senior year, he was elected president of his class, president of student council, and president of the citywide student council. Upon graduation he received many awards and was salutatorian of his class, which means that he had the second-highest grade point average.

Even though he did well in high school, Black did not at first consider college a possibility. No one in his family, or even in his neighborhood, had gone to college. However, he received assistance from an African-American doctor whose office was in one of the buildings he helped his father clean every night. Dr. Collins took an interest in Black's education and helped him obtain a scholarship to the University of Michigan.

The University of Michigan is a high-prestige, and at the time, a largely white, university. The level of skill expected from him both in the classroom and on the athletic field came as something of a shock to Black. Unlike his high school experience, he did not do well. He soon dropped out of athletics to focus all of his energies on his academic studies. Even then, he only managed to get average grades in his pre-medical program.

After graduating from Michigan in 1963, Black got married, started his own family, and went to work as a factory foreman at the Ford Motor Company. The dirty, noisy factory work was made even harder by the fact that the workers he supervised were mostly white immigrants from Eastern Europe or the Southern United States, who were not happy to be working for a black boss. He soon left that job and went to work at Children's Hospital as a diener. Diener comes from the German word for servant and means an assistant who helps with autopsies, or medical examinations of dead bodies.

Became Interested in Sociology

His work as a diener reawakened Black's interest in medicine. He had begun to think that he wanted to be a "social doctor," or sociologist. Sociology is the study of how and why people form societies, and the effect those societies have on the people who live within them. Black's mother-in-law knew a dean at nearby Wayne State University, and with her encouragement and assistance, Black took some extra courses to bring his grades up and was accepted into the master's program in sociology at Wayne State.

As he reached the end of his master's program, Black saw a notice that the University of California at Berkeley was seeking students of color for their doctoral program in sociology. When one of his professors expressed doubt that Black could succeed in a difficult program at an elite school like Berkeley, Black worked even harder to do well in his master's work. He wrote such a good final paper that his professor relented and wrote him a letter of recommendation to Berkeley. In 1967 Black headed for California.

The late 1960s was a time of political protest and social movement in the United States, and Berkeley, California, was a major center of youthful unrest. Within weeks of Black's arrival in California he had joined a Young Socialist Party protest and had been arrested. He managed to convince university authorities that he was a dedicated and responsible young man, however, and continued his studies at Berkeley.

In 1973 Black was offered a job teaching sociology at the University of Washington in Seattle. Except for a brief period in 1976 when he returned to Berkeley to finish work on his Ph.D., he would remain in Seattle for the rest of his career. He not only became one of the most beloved and awarded teachers on the university campus, but he also took his commitment out into the community, speaking and teaching at countless workshops and public events over the years.

Taught Inside and Outside the Classroom

Black had learned from his own experience how difficult it could be for poor students and students of color to learn and succeed in school. When he did achieve success in the form of a teaching job at a respected university, he did not stop his efforts, but continued to devote a large part of his time to helping and encouraging students and their parents, in the Seattle area and throughout the country. Among his many contributions have been organizing a mentor program in which university students work in high schools assisting younger students, starting a Father's Group at Seattle's Franklin High School to involve fathers in their children's education, and developing programs to help student athletes deal with the special pressures they face in college.

Black has also left his home state to spread his message in other areas of the country. During the mid-1990s, he was contracted to lecture on minority issues for the Detroit Public School System and the Detroit Juvenile Justice System. In 1994, he worked as a consultant for foster care providers in Wayne County, Michigan. He conducted workshops and classes for at-risk youth in Yonkers, New York, Gilroy, California, and Santa Clara County, California. In addition to these, he found time to host a weekly talk show on a Seattle African-American radio station, titled, *Community Potpourri: A Conversation with Dr. Al Black,* where he discusses a wider range of topics.

Success in academic institutions is often measured in terms of granting an employee "tenure." Tenure is a promise of lifetime employment, granted to a professor by the university where he or she works. When a professor is given tenure, it is not only the guarantee of

a job, but also an acknowledgement of excellence in that professor's work. Most colleges and universities grant tenure based not only on a teacher's performance in class, but also on outside work, such as writing and publishing books and articles in his/her field. Because Alfred Black devoted his energies to working directly with students and the community, he did not do the sorts of theoretical research or publish the kind of works that would allow the university to grant him tenure. Black and his supporters argued that educators who dedicate themselves to teaching should be regarded as highly as those who commit their time and energies to research and writing. Though many university officials were sympathetic to Black and admired his work, they could not grant him tenure in the usual way. Instead they gave him the title of "principal lecturer" with the guarantee of employment at the university for the rest of his career.

Sources

Periodicals

Seattle Post-Intelligencer (WA), July 12, 2003.

On-line

"Albert Black," *Columns: The University of Washington Alumni Magazine,* http://www.washington.edu/alumni/columns/june99/black.html (March 23, 2005).
"Black's Goal: Better Life for All Children" *University Week,* http://depts.washington.edu/uweek/archives/1999.06.JUN_03/article15.html (February 25, 2005).
"Black Named Principal Lecturer," *University Week,* http://admin.urel.washington.edu/uweek/archives/issue/uweek_story_small.asp?id=1220 (March 23, 2005).
"Black Named UW's First Principal Lecturer," *A&S Perspectives,* http://www.artsci.washington.edu/newsletter/Autumn03/Awards.htm#Black (March 23, 2005).
"Black Parents' Fragile Link to Schools," *Seattle Post-Intelligencer,* http://seattlepi.nwsource.com/disciplinegap/61941_parents12.shtml (March 23, 2005).

Other

Information for this profile was obtained through an interview with Albert W. Black, Jr., on February 25, 2005.

—Tina Gianoulis

Tom Burrell

1939—

Advertising executive

Tom Burrell was first directed toward a career in advertising by a high school aptitude test. However, it was his own independent spirit, creativity, and courage that guided him from a working-class childhood on the south side of Chicago to a position as chairman and chief executive officer of the company that would bear his name, Burrell Communications. Though for much of his life, Burrell was unsure of his own abilities, he not only worked his way up from the mailroom to the head office, but he also pioneered an advertising philosophy that acknowledged the economic power of youth and communities of color, and showed an understanding of the unique cultural characteristics of both.

Thomas Jason Burrell was born on March 18, 1939, in Chicago, Illinois. His father Thomas was an entrepreneur who had come to the large Midwestern city from Tennessee during the 1920s. Because he had little faith in banks, he did not deposit his money in bank accounts; instead, he saved it on his own. When many banks failed in 1929 at the beginning of the Great Depression that would ravage the country throughout the 1930s, Thomas Burrell Sr. did not lose his money as so many others did. With cash on hand, he found himself able to make money by buying buildings while prices were low. Soon he owned and operated his own tavern, a "blues joint," which featured famous musicians such as Muddy Waters and B.B. King.

Young Thomas' mother Evelyn had also come to Chicago from the South. One of ten children, she had left her family in Alabama, following her other sisters and brothers who had sought opportunity in the North. Evelyn Burrell had attended beauty school, and while she cared for her children, she worked as a beautician in her home.

Created Jobs as a Child

Tom Burrell spent much of his childhood working. He found many ways to earn extra money, developing the creativity that would later bring success to his advertising agency. An aunt who worked at a soap factory brought home damaged bars of soap for free and young Tom sold them door to door. He also shined shoes, set up pins in bowling alleys, washed windows, and rode public transit mornings and evenings to deliver newspapers before and after school.

Burrell's experience at school was often difficult. Though he liked his classes when his teachers were interesting and attentive, he often found himself the victim of bullies in the schoolyard. He felt that he did not fit in and, in an effort to keep out of trouble, he stayed apart, watching and learning. This role of observer taught him a lot about human nature, and he would put that knowledge to work later in his adult life and career.

When Burrell was a teenager, one of his friends was killed while fleeing police in a stolen car. This tragic event affected him deeply, in part because it showed him his own possible future. In his junior year of high school Burrell decided to put his future on a better track. He changed high schools, switching from Englewood High to Parker High, a more academic school with fewer tough kids. The decision was his alone. He

At a Glance . . .

Born Thomas Jason Burrell on March 18, 1939, in Chicago, Illinois; married Barbara Aldridge, 1968 (divorced 1979); married Joli Owens, 1989 (divorced 2005); children (first marriage): Alexandra, Jason. *Education:* Roosevelt University, BA, English, 1962.

Career: Wade Advertising, Chicago, copywriter, 1961-64; Leo Burnett Company, Chicago, copywriter, 1964-67; Foote Cone and Belding, London, copy supervisor, 1967-68; Needham Harper & Steers, New York, copy supervisor, 1968-71; Burrell Communications Group, Chicago and Atlanta, founder and chief executive officer, 1971-2004, chairman emeritus, 2004–.

Selected memberships: American Advertising Federation Foundation, Standing Committee on Diversity and Taskforce on Diversity and Multi-cultural Advertising; Chicago Lighthouse for the Blind, board of governors, Chicago Urban League, board of directors and Business Advisory Council; Howard University, School of Communications, Advisory Council.

Selected awards: Albert Lasker Award for Lifetime Achievement in Advertising, 1986; University of Missouri School of Journalism Honors Medal for Distinguished Service, 1990; Chicago Lighthouse for the Blind, Lifetime Achievement Award, 1998; Rainbow/PUSH Coalition, Living Legend Award, 2003; American Advertising Federation, Advertising Hall of Fame, 2005.

Addresses: *Office*—Burrell Communications Group, 233 N. Michigan Avenue, Chicago, IL 60602.

with characteristic determination, he set his sights on a career in advertising.

Struggled for Success in College

College was the first step, and after his graduation from high school in 1957, Burrell entered Chicago's Roosevelt University. College was not easy for him. He had little guidance when he entered the university, and his first year he took a very heavy course load and joined both the staff of the college newspaper and an advertising fraternity. By his second semester he was so stressed from work and activities that he began to have health problems. He related in an interview with *Contemporary Black Biography* (*CBB*) that when one of his advisors told him bluntly that he was "just not intelligent enough to graduate from college, " he became discouraged and left school to work at a paint factory.

However, Burrell hated factory work and decided to give the university another try. More experienced now, and having sampled the sort of job he might get without a degree, he began to do better in school, getting As and Bs. He graduated from Roosevelt University in 1962.

During his senior year, Burrell had gone to work in the mailroom of Wade Advertising, a Chicago agency. Within a year, he had been promoted to writing advertising copy on such well-known accounts as Alka Seltzer and Robin Hood Flour. He continued to move up in the field, getting jobs in other prestigious agencies, and even living in London for a year working for the agency of Foote Cone and Belding. Even as he worked at some of the best agencies in advertising, Burrell knew that he was preparing himself to start his own business. Like his father, he did not want to spend his life working for someone else. As he performed his job, he constantly observed and learned how every aspect of an advertising agency worked.

Finally, in 1971, he was ready. He left his job as copy supervisor in the Chicago office of the New York firm of Needham Harper & Steers to open his own agency with a partner, Emmett McBain. Burrell McBain, as it was called then, decided to focus on a largely ignored audience, African-American consumers. One of their earliest successes was a black urban Marlboro man for a Phillip Morris tobacco advertising campaign.

Developed Self-Confidence in Business

During the first six months of running his own agency, Burrell had many moments of nervousness and fears of failure. As he had in college, he almost became ill from the stress, but he persevered because he had decided that he needed the independence of running his own

had grown used to making his own decisions about his life, because his mother had always treated him with respect for his opinions. He had learned early that if he really thought he could do something, his mother would encourage him to try it.

It was at Parker High School that Burrell took the aptitude test that would affect the course of his life. The test determined that Burrell was "artistic and persuasive," and a teacher suggested that writing copy for an advertising company might be a good career for someone with those qualities. The idea interested him, and, business. Even if his advertising agency did not succeed, he determined that he would never return to a corporate advertising job. He had even thought of other businesses he might try, but he did not need to use those ideas. In 1972, after his firm's initial success with Marlboro, Burrell landed the national McDonald's restaurant chain as a client, and, a year later, Coca-Cola. In 1974, McBain left the agency, and the firm name was changed to Burrell Advertising.

Perhaps Burrell's biggest business success was in learning to trust his own skills and intelligence. Having convinced himself by bad school experiences that he was not intelligent, Burrell had felt that he needed other people to help him run his agency. Once he was on his own, however, his confidence in his abilities grew, and the success of his business increased. Burrell told *CBB* that "it took him many years of success at work to rebuild his confidence after the college advisor's disheartening warning." To guard others against his experience, he told *CBB* that in the future he made it a point "to advise young African Americans to respect those in authority, but to maintain their belief in themselves."

Burrell's agency continued to prosper and gain new clients, winning awards for some of its innovative commercials. By 1979 Burrell's client billings reached more than $10 million. In 1983 the company opened an office in Atlanta, Georgia, and in 1992 the firm name was changed to Burrell Communications Group and billings approached $100 million. The agency has created successful campaigns for such products targeted specifically at African Americans, including Johnson Products' Afrosheen and Ultrasheen, to brands and services used by everyone, like Verizon, Kmart, Sears, Tide, Crest Toothpaste, and Sprite, among many others.

Though Burrell has always wanted his agency to represent all kinds of products and to appeal to all sorts of people, most advertisers continue to view Burrell Communications as a way to reach youth and urban markets and people of color. Before Burrell entered the business, there were very few people of color in commercials. Those that were seen were usually stereotyped. Burrell's commercials gave a very human face to blacks in advertising, focusing on families and relationships. When Toyota received criticism for another agency's ad that was perceived by many as racist, they turned to Burrell for a more positive campaign. Burrell also invented the advertising term "yurban," a combination of young and urban, that describes an important target market. Burrell advertisements treat their young audience with respect, using humor, music, and honesty to sell products.

In the summer of 2004, Burrell announced his retirement from Burrell Communications. The agency continues to be one of the top advertising companies, and Burrell still maintains a role as chairman emeritus. However, he considers himself, as he told CBB, "more rewired than retired," and continues to try new adventures, such as performing as a singer.

Sources

Periodicals

Advertising Age, June 3, 1996, pp. C1-16.
Advertising Age (Midwest Region Edition), June 14, 1999, p. 36.
ADWEEK (Midwest Edition), November 12, 2001, pp. 5-6.
Crain's Illinois Business, Spring 1986, pp. 45-7.
Jet, December 21, 1998, pp. 8-11; July 5, 2004, p. 48.

On-line

Burrell Communications Group, www.burrell.com (March 5, 2005).
"Tom Burrell Biography," *The History Makers,* www. thehistorymakers.com/biography/biography.asp? bioindex=62&category=businessmakers (March 5, 2005).
"Tom Burrell's Cultural Anthropological Route to Hip-Hop Marketing." *Ethnographic Solutions,* www. ethnographic-solutions.com/pages/tomburrell.htm (March 5, 2005).
"Tom Burrell To Receive Advertising Industry's Highest Honor," *Forbes,* www.forbes.com/businesswire/ feeds/businesswire/2005/01/19/ businesswire20050119005663r1.html (March 5, 2005)

Other

Information for this profile was obtained through an interview with Tom Burrell on February 25, 2005.

—Tina Gianoulis

Robert L. Carter

1917—

Judge, civil rights activist

Robert L. Carter was stung by the treatment he suffered as a young black man, but the pain was an incentive, not a discouragement. Carter grew up to be one of the key architects in the 1954 Supreme Court case *Brown v. the Board of Education,* which outlawed racial segregation in public schools. Despite the achievements made in civil rights in the 50 years since that landmark ruling, Carter told the *New York Times,* "I am not satisfied. This country is still dedicated to white supremacy, and I am black."

Prompted to Activism by Pool Ban

Carter was born on March 11, 1917 in Careyville, Florida. His parents moved to New Jersey with his seven sisters and brothers when Robert was a baby, and Carter's father died soon after. His mother worked as a maid to put her children through school. Carter grew up far from the segregated South and was an exceptional student at his school in East Orange, New Jersey—he skipped two grades to graduate early. Nevertheless, he was barred from his school's all-white boys' swim team.

At the time, the school's swimming pool was drained and cleaned after black students used it. Carter's sense of injustice was riled. Early in his senior year, armed with a newspaper article detailing the New Jersey Supreme Court ruling that prohibited public schools from banning blacks from school facilities, Carter burst into a "whites only" swim practice and demanded to be included. The coach tried threats, then pleas, but Carter was not to be deterred. For the rest of the school year he was allowed to join the white students in the pool. It was a lonely victory. The white students avoided him, and as he could not swim, he hovered alone at the shallow end of the pool. "None of the other black students joined me," Carter recalled in a 1996 speech to the Federal Bar Council recorded in *Vital Speeches of the Day.* "In view of the school's intimidating environment, that should not surprise." Carter credited that early experience as crucial in his decision to become a civil rights activist and lawyer.

At the age of 16, Carter landed a scholarship to Lincoln University. He graduated *magna cum laude* with a political science degree in 1937. Three years later he earned a law degree from Howard University in Washington, D.C. He finished his studies with a master's in law from Columbia University in 1941. By that time World War II was on, and upon graduation Carter was promptly drafted as an officer into the then-segregated Air Force. He was greeted by a captain who routinely told well-schooled black recruits that he did not believe in "education for niggers" and warned them against "getting uppity," Carter recalled to the Federal Bar Council. Again his anger rose. Just as he had tried to integrate his high school swimming pool, young Lieutenant Carter tried to make the Air Force give its black officers the same privileges as whites. He barely escaped with an honorable discharge. The "raw, vicious, and pervasive" racism Carter experienced during his military service "made a militant of me," Carter said to the Federal Bar Council. "It instilled in me a fierce determination to fight against racism with all my intellectual and physical strength."

At a Glance . . .

Born on March 11, 1917, in Careyville, FL; married Gloria Pamela Spencer (deceased); children: John, David. *Education*: Lincoln University, BA, political science, 1937; Howard University, JD, 1940; Columbia University, LLM, 1941. *Military Service*: Army Air Corps, second-lieutenant, 1941-44.

Career: NAACP Legal Defense Fund, New York, NY, assistant special counsel, 1944-56; NAACP Legal Defense Fund, New York, NY, general counsel, 1956-68; Poletti, Freidin, Prashker, Feldman and Gartner, New York, NY, senior partner, 1969-72; US District Court, Southern District of New York, federal judge 1972–.

Memberships: World Assembly on Human Rights, delegate, 1968; New York City Mayor's Judiciary Committee, 1968-72; National Conference of Black Lawyers, co-chairman, 1968-82; National Committee Against Discrimination in Housing, board member; American Civil Liberties, board member.

Awards: Presidential Medal of Freedom, 1995; Federal Bar Council, Emory Bucknor Medal for Outstanding Public Service, 1995; Harvard Law School, Medal of Freedom, 2000; NAACP, Spingarn Medal, 2004; NAACP Legal Defense Fund, Thurgood Marshall Lifetime Achievement Award, 2004.

Addresses: *Office*—United States Courthouse, 500 Pearl Street, Room 2220, New York, NY 10007-1312.

Forged Legal Fighting for Civil Rights

The fight for equal treatment for black Americans had remained on the back burner throughout World War II, but African-American soldiers who had fought for American ideals were not willing to settle back into second-class citizenship when they returned home. The civil rights movement was fueled in part by these veterans. Carter was at its forefront, and his career took off as the movement did.

In 1944 Carter joined the National Association for the Advancement of Colored People (NAACP) Legal Defense and Educational Fund as a legal assistant to the famed civil rights lawyer Thurgood Marshall. Marshall would later become the first African American appointed as a justice on the United States Supreme Court. Though the two men would make history to-

gether in *Brown vs. the Board of Education*, they never became close. "I don't recall that Thurgood and I ever developed a personal friendship," Carter told the *New York Times*. Many civil rights historians point out that Carter was as vital to the *Brown* case as Marshall, yet had never received due credit. Carter shrugged those claims off, telling the *New York Times*, "I'm not one of those people to toot my horn well." He also pointed out the positive working relationship they shared. "Thurgood always wanted me to go for the outer edges of the law," Carter told the *Boston Herald*. "He kept me out of politics. But he let me have my say. He wouldn't let anyone shut me off. So if I stood up and argued, he would back me up." Carter was also proud to receive the Thurgood Marshall Lifetime Achievement Award in 2004.

Carter served with the NAACP from 1944 until 1968. During that time he tried cases in every state of the former southern Confederacy. He won 21 of the 22 cases he presented before the U.S. Supreme Court. He helped defeat racism in colleges, labor unions, voting laws, housing, and hiring. According to a newsletter of the Organization of American Historians, Carter was a model for black youngsters who may never have seen an educated African-American professional stand up to white authority.

Laid Groundwork for Brown v. the Board of Education

Carter's crowning achievement was masterminding the strategy behind *Brown vs. the Board of Education*. It was Carter's idea to use social science and psychology to prove that state-sponsored separation of black and white children did terrible harm to black youngsters. Carter used dolls to illustrate his point, pointing to studies that revealed that little black girls chose to play with white dolls over black dolls. Carter's argument drew skepticism from NAACP colleagues; however, Carter won them over. "My argument was real simple," Carter recalled to the *Boston Herald*. He asked them, "'Do you have anything better?'" Carter's dolls worked and history was made. "Judge Carter's goading and pivotal role in *Brown vs. the Board of Education* serve to demonstrate his tremendous and long-lasting impact in the fight to bring equality to school children and poor people of all colors throughout this country," Kweisi Mfume, former president of the NAACP, said in an article on the NAACP Web site.

After Thurgood Marshall joined the United States judiciary in 1956, Carter assumed the role of head of the NAACP Legal Defense Fund. Carter's important cases during that time included a 1958 Alabama ruling that protected the NAACP membership lists from publication—removing a subtle weapon employers and governments used against black activists. Carter also sued and argued to strike down laws that segregated colleges and carved-up voting districts according to race. Carter's office also oversaw many cases that stemmed directly from *Brown*. "We had a whole new world of litigation ahead of us," one of Carter's NAACP colleagues told the *New York Times*. "Shortly after the [*Brown*] decision we represented students who sat in at North Carolina lunch counters, an action that led to the Civil Rights Act of 1964, ending segregation in businesses that engaged in interstate commerce. It was another huge development: the ability of blacks to eat in local restaurants in the south, to stay in hotels."

In a move reminiscent of his youthful activism, Carter decided to personally test the implications of the Civil Rights Act of 1964. He and a group of African-American activists spent a week traveling through Mississippi in January of 1965, desegregating restaurants, hotels, and other public facilities previously delineated by "White Only" and "Colored" signs. "We had only one scary incident in the infamous town of Philadelphia," Carter recalled in his Federal Bar Council speech. "When we left an establishment we were testing, white men not looking too friendly and carrying guns were lined up on each side of the path we had to traverse to get to our vehicle. You can be sure I was frightened, but fortunately, the men apparently were there only to try to intimidate us by their presence and not to do any physical harm." Carter concluded, "The Mississippi exercise was an exhilarating experience because it seemed to us that if the Civil Rights Act could effect such a drastic change in Mississippi, success was assured nationwide."

Moved from the Trenches to the Bench

Carter left the NAACP in 1968 for a try at teaching and practicing labor law with a private firm, but in 1972 he re-entered public service when President Richard Nixon appointed him a federal judge in New York City. He continued his pioneering—often controversial—work in interpreting the rights of individuals. In 1986 he made headlines when he cited all 350 of the country's Roman Catholic bishops for contempt of court, fining them $100,000 per day until they complied with a court order demanding documentation of their anti-abortion politicking.

In 1986 Carter reached senior judge status. Through the years he married and was widowed, raised two children, taught law at a long list of colleges, was a United States delegate to United Nations conferences, and co-founded the National Conference of Black Lawyers. He wrote dozens of articles and studies on discrimination and race in America and had plans to complete an autobiography. In 1995 President Bill Clinton awarded Carter the Presidential Medal of Freedom, America's highest civilian honor.

In 2004, on the 50th anniversary of *Brown*, Carter was widely celebrated, receiving several prestigious awards and giving dozens of interviews. Despite the accolades, the disappointment over what he saw as the lack of progress made by black Americans was evident. "Black children aren't getting equal education in the cities," he told the *New York Times*. "The schools that are 100 percent black are still as bad as they were before *Brown*." In an interview with the *Boston Herald* he blamed part of the problem the very thing that he and so many civil rights activists had fought so hard to obtain—equal opportunity. He believed that blacks had simply become too comfortable. "We can't have faith in any white institutions," he warned. "We have to push on our own. No one wants to give up privilege. We have to be on the edge, complaining, pushing, not accepting." Carter felt that the overwhelming number of young blacks in the prison, the loss of Affirmative Action programs, and schools still effectively segregated by the urban-suburban divide were all a result of middle-class black complacency. But as a man who not only witnessed, but helped orchestrate, the greatest changes American society had lived through, he still held out hope. "In the United States, we make progress in two or three steps, then we step back," he told the *New York Times*. And blacks are more militant now and will not accept second-class citizenship as before."

Sources

Books

Vital Speeches of the Day, March 1, 1996, p290.

Periodicals

Boston Herald, August 17, 2004.
Journal of Blacks in Higher Education, August 31, 2001.
New York Times, May 5, 2004.
Time, May 19, 1986.

On-line

"NAACP Awards 2004 Spingarn Medal too Judge Robert L. Carter," *NAACP*, www.naacp.org/news/ 2004/2004-06-15.html (February 25, 2005).
"Judge Carter and the Brown Decision," *Organization of American Historians*, www.oah.org/pubs/nl/ 2004feb/sullivan.html (February 25, 2005).

—Candace LaBalle

Sekou Damate Conneh, Jr.

1960—

Liberian rebel leader

As leader of the rebel group Liberians United for Reconciliation and Democracy (LURD), Sekou Damate Conneh Jr. takes credit for bringing about the removal of dictator Charles Taylor from his position as president of Liberia. Taylor's resignation on August 11, 2003, came after 13 years of civil war. Taylor left office for exile in Nigeria only when LURD forces laid siege to the Liberian capital of Monrovia; he was later placed on Interpol's "Most Wanted" list. In his attempts to wrest political control from Taylor, Conneh is also thought to have overseen some of the most bloody and destructive battles ever enacted on African soil. Thousands of "child soldiers" served on both sides in the civil war, and LURD forces were responsible for rape, torture, and other atrocities as they fought in the name of democracy and freedom.

Conneh's determination to remove Taylor from power, and his willingness to risk his own life in doing so, made him a popular rebel leader, but his links to massacres and extreme violence weighed heavily against him in the run-up to Liberia's long-hoped-for elections in 2005. In January 2004 his continuing attacks on the capital led his wife Asha Keita-Conneh to declare herself leader of LURD in the first of a series of challenges to Conneh's authority that suggested deep divisions in the organization and eventually led to its collapse as a unifying opposition force. Despite his stated aims to bring peace and democracy to Liberia, observers feared that if Conneh was to take power his hold over the country would be both authoritarian and divisive. Nevertheless without his determination and strength of will, Charles Taylor's tenure as one of

Africa's most brutal leaders would not have come to an end.

Sekou Damate Conneh Jr. was born in 1960 in Gbarnga, Liberia. His father, Sekou Damate Conneh Sr., and his mother, Margaret (Makay) Conneh, owned a rubber plantation and farmstead in Bong County. His wealthy father was a chieftain of the Mandingo ethnic group. Though the family was Muslim, Conneh started his education at the St. Martin's Cathedral School in 1966, going on to the William V.S. Tubman Methodist High School, where he graduated with a high school diploma in 1979. Conneh's political allegiances forced him to flee Liberia in the early 1980s, but he returned in 1985 and began studying for a Bachelor of Arts in Business Administration (BBA) at the University of Liberia in 1986. His studies ended the same year when he became a revenue agent working for the Liberian Ministry of Finance. He held this position, working in Rivercess and later Montserrado Counties, until the assassination of President Samuel K. Doe in 1990 and the outbreak of civil war.

Joined the Armed Struggle

Conneh began his active political life at the age of 19 when he joined the Progressive People's Party (PPP), founded in 1978, which campaigned for the democratic government and was at the time the only legal opposition party in the country. Much of the violence and destruction that ravaged Liberia between 1990 and 2004 stems from the uneasy relationship between the indigenous African Liberians and the minority

At a Glance . . .

Born Sekou Damate Conneh Jr. in 1960; married Asha Keita-Conneh (separated). *Education:* William V.S. Tubman Methodist High School, graduated 1979.

Career: Revenue agent for Ministry of Finance, 1985-90; founder and managing director of Damate Corporation, 1990–; revenue agent, 1997-99; leader of LURD forces in northern Liberia, 1999-2003; president of the LURD national executive committee, 2003-04; LURD factional leader, 2004–.

Memberships: Progressive people's Party, 1979–; Liberians United for Reconciliation and Democracy (LURD), 1999–.

"Americo-Liberians," descended from freed American slaves for whom the country was founded in 1847. But for most of its history Liberia enjoyed peace, prosperity, and stability. President William V.S. Tubman—an Americo-Liberian—took office in 1944 and remained in place until his death in 1971, presiding over improving trade relations, low unemployment, and relative wealth; his successor, William R. Tolbert Jr., was less successful. A sharp rise in food prices in the 1970s led to unrest among African Liberians, who saw the Americo-Liberians as holding power unjustly. Tolbert's government cracked down on the emerging rebel PPP in 1979 and it was banned in 1980. By then Conneh was serving as the party's senior coordinator in the Kokoyah District of Bong County and fled to Uganda. Tolbert was murdered by a rebel military group in 1980 and Samuel K. Doe, an army sergeant, was installed as president of the Interim National Assembly.

Conneh returned to Liberia in 1985 to stand in the forthcoming election. But the PPP remained an illegal party and he was forced to give up his political ambitions for a while. Doe later won the 1985 presidential election, though he was actually ineligible because of his age; he changed his birth date from 1951 to 1950 to qualify. After losing his job at the Ministry of Finance when Doe was assassinated, Conneh founded the Damate Corporation, a company that specialized in importing used cars from Europe.

The killing of Doe by the National Patriotic Front of Liberia (NPFL), led by Charles Taylor, triggered civil war that lasted until 1996. Divisions existed not only between African and Americo-Liberians, but between ethnic groups within the country. Deepening poverty caused by destruction of crops, a major refugee crisis, and escalating violence, made those divisions wider. In

1997 Taylor was elected president of Liberia and at first it seemed his election might bring stability to the country. Conneh resumed his work for the Ministry of Finance but quit soon after and moved to Conakry, the capital of neighboring Guinea, where he resumed his used-car trading, this time exporting cars from Guinea into Liberia. In 1998 he was arrested on the Liberian border by intelligence officers who accused him of smuggling and was moved to a jail in Monrovia, the Liberian capital. He was released when his wife, Aisha Keita-Conneh, petitioned the Guinean President Lansana Conteh to put pressure on Taylor. Conneh returned to Conakry on his release because Taylor's forces had begun to target various ethnic groups, including Conneh's own Mandingo people.

Became a Rebel Leader

In the years leading up to Taylor's election it is estimated that 150,000 people were killed and at least 850,000 became refugees. After a brief respite, when it became clear that Taylor's regime was tightening its grip on power, civil war broke out again. By then Conneh was a member of Liberians United for Reconciliation and Democracy (LURD), a rebel group that entered Liberia in 1999 with support from neighboring Guinea to the north. Much of the support for LURD from President Conte of Guinea depended on his friendship with Conneh's wife, Asha Keita-Conneh, a self-proclaimed prophet and sorceress, whom he adopted as his daughter when she correctly predicted and foiled an assassination plot. Conneh became president and chairman of the national executive committee of LURD in 2003 largely because of his contacts at the highest levels of the Guinean government, but in fact it was his wife who wielded the most influence with President Conteh. Conneh's promotion to chairman significantly enhanced her power over Liberia's largest rebel group.

Between 1999 and 2003 Conneh established himself as a powerful army commander, expanding from territory in the north to share almost two thirds of the country with another rebel group, Movement for Democracy in Liberia (MODEL) which moved in from the south. Significantly, LURD forces laid siege to the capital, Monrovia, and with outside pressure from the United States, Taylor was forced to resign the presidency on August 11, 2003. This was achieved despite LURD's aims remaining unclear; the organization's uncertain identity is summed up by BBC journalist James Brabazon, who described the LURD rebels in 2003 as "a bizarre mixture of partly uniformed irregular soldiers and LA gangster chic."

With a peace deal brokered and 15,000 United Nations peacekeeping troops arriving in the country the following October, Conneh was in line to be a candidate for president in elections planned for 2005. But in October 2003 as he and his followers entered the capital they were shot at by government militia, an action that spurred Conneh's troops to continue their attacks on the capital and against areas of the country where Taylor's supporters were thought to be hiding. In many cases LURD militia were reported to have destroyed villages and towns, murdering and raping men, women, and children as they went. By the end of 2003 the fragile peace deal signed in August was under threat, but Conneh showed no sign of ending the violence, despite spending a great deal of time touring African and European capitals discussing the situation with heads of government and aid agencies.

Then on January 20, 2004, Conneh's wife declared to the world's media that she was the new leader of LURD, and that she had seized control because she believed her husband was putting the peace process at risk. Long thought to be the power behind her husband, Aisha Keita-Conneh, who gave birth to a daughter only a month earlier, told the press that she was the "boss lady," and in particular her husband's "double boss." Setting aside worries that her move might trigger factional fighting she declared: "I am here as a peacemaker and mother for all." Keita-Conneh's strategy paid off and her husband was persuaded to stop his forces attacking the capital, Monrovia, at least for a while. In the longer term the dispute caused a split in LURD that threatened the chances of holding elections. Despite a reconciliation that seemed to have settled the dispute by February, Conneh's authority was once again challenged in July when he was suspended as leader of the rebel group. LURD disbanded as a fighting force soon after.

Conneh's achievement as leader of Liberia's biggest rebel movement is indisputable. His determination, drive, and military skill led to the removal from power of one of Africa's most brutal and dangerous dictators. His dedication to the causes of democracy and freedom has often been stated and his record suggests a willingness to take huge personal risks for the sake of the rebel cause. But from the late 1990s onwards Conneh's reputation was marred by accusations, including using excessive military force against civilians, and by the behavior of many of the military units under his control. Despite the power-sharing agreement and elections planned for October 11, 2005, Liberia remained in a state of unrest and political uncertainty. In February 2005 Conneh called for an amnesty for all those involved in the civil war in the interests of reconciliation, including his enemy Charles Taylor, who is wanted for war crimes. Conneh, whose own organization has been accused of serious human rights abuses, has said he would favor this approach rather than a commission to investigate war crimes in Liberia along the lines of the South African Truth and Reconciliation Commission.

Sources

Periodicals

Jet, February 9, 2004.
The Guardian (London and Manchester), January 21, 2004.
The Independent (London, England), Oct 2, 2003, p. 17.
The Scotsman, Jan 21, 2004.
The Seattle Times, Jan 21, 2004, p. A7.
The Washington Times, August 13, 2003, p. A01.

On-line

"Crisis Profile: West Africa Teeters Between War and Peace," *Reuters Alertnet*, www.alertnet.org/the facts/reliefresources/110987057530.htm (March 4, 2005).
"Liberia: Profile of LURD Leader, Sekou Conneh," *UN Office for the Coordination of Humanitarian Affairs*, www.irinnews.org/report.asp?ReportID=36 075 (March 4, 2005).
"Profile: Liberia's Rebels," *BBC News*, http://news.bbc.co.uk/2/hi/africa/2979586.stm (February 28, 2005).
"Rebel leaders' marital spat raises fears of violence in Liberia," *CNN.com*, www.cnn.com/2004/WORLD/africa/01/21/liberia.lurd.split.ap/ (February 28, 2005).
"The Search for Eddie Peabody," *Houston Chronicle Online*, www.chron.com/cs/CDA/ssistory.mpl/special/04/peabody/2402773 (February 28, 2005).
Sekou Damate Conneh Liberation Center, www.damate.org/start.html (February 28, 2005).

—Chris Routledge

Joseph Mason Andrew Cox

1930—

Writer, educator, poet, playwright

Joseph Mason Andrew Cox spent his adult life in New York City, working primarily as a writer, poet, and educator. Best known for his poetry, Cox also published a three-act play, two novels, and contributed to literary journals and anthologies. He also taught for over a decade in the City University of New York system.

Cox was born on July 12, 1930, in Boston, Massachusetts, to Hiram and Edith (Henderson) Cox. His mother was a nurse. Cox was educated at Columbia University in New York City, where he received a bachelor's degree in 1945 and a law degree in 1953. He completed his education at World University in Hong Kong, where he earned a doctorate in art psychology in 1972.

In 1955 Cox began his career as a reporter and feature writer for the black political newspaper, the *New York Age*. In 1958 he became a reporter and feature writer for the *New York Post*. After working at the *Post* for two years, he took the position as president of the Afro-American Purchasing Commission, based in New York City, where he remained from 1961 to 1968. From 1969 to 1971 he served as a consultant for the New York City Board of Education in Brooklyn.

In 1972 Cox took his first teaching job, spending a year as a lecturer at Manhattan Community College of the City University of New York, and the follow school year, he began serving as an assistant professor of English at Medgar Evers College of the City University of New York in Brooklyn. In 1974 he became president of Cox & Hopewell Publishers, Inc. in New York City.

Cox also continued to teach, and between 1975 to 1983 he taught courses at City University of New York, Manhattan Community College, Bronx Community College, Medgar Evers College, and the New York City University Research Center. From 1983 to 1988 Cox worked for the Federal Government Crime Insurance. He also served as producer and moderator for the television program *Focus on Profound Thought*.

In 1963, while working at the Afro-American Purchasing Commission, Cox published his first book, a novel titled *The Search*, which was published by Freedom Press. Soon thereafter Cox began receiving recognition for his writing skills. In 1964 he was presented with the International Essay from the Daniel S. Mead Agency, and in 1965 he was given the Great Society Writer's Award from President Lyndon B. Johnson. In 1967 Cox served as the U.S. representative to the World Poetry Conference, Expo 67, in Montreal, Quebec.

Although Cox did not produce another full-length work until 1970, he contributed to four editions of the *Golden Quill Anthology,* published by Golden Quill, from 1968 to 1971. He also served as a columnist for the *Caribbean Echo*, a weekly newspaper directed to the West Indian community, from 1969 to 1971, and he contributed articles to numerous periodicals, including *Poetry Review*, *West Review*, and London's *The Spring Anthology.*

Cox's first and only play to be produced and published, the three-act *Ode to Dr. Martin Luther King, Jr.*, was

At a Glance . . .

Born on July 12, 1930, in Boston, MA; son of Hiram and Edith (Henderson) Cox. *Education:* Columbia University, BA, 1945: Columbia University, LLB, 1953; World University, Hong Kong, PhD, art psychology, 1972. *Religion:* Unitarian-Universalist. *Politics:* Democrat.

Career: *New York Post,* reporter and feature writer, 1958-60; Afro-American Purchasing Commission, New York City, president, 1961-68; New York City Board of Education, Brooklyn, NY, consultant, 1969-71; *Caribbean Echo,* columnist, 1969-71; Manhattan Community College of the City University of New York, lecturer, 1972-73; Medgar Evers College of the City University of New York, assistant professor of English, 1973-74; Cox & Hopewell Publishing, Inc., New York City, president, 1974-200(?); City University of New York, Manhattan Community College, Bronx Community College, Medgar Evers College, and the New York City University Research Center, lecturer, 1975-83; Federal Government Crime Insurance, 1983-88.

Selected memberships: International Poetry Society; International Poets Shrine; Poetry Society of America; United Poets Laureate International; World Literature Academy.

Selected awards: "Great Society" writer's award, President Lyndon B. Johnson, 1965; Master Poets Award, American Poet Fellowship Society, 1970; World Poets Award, World Poetry Fellowship Society, 1972; Humanitarian Award and Gold Medal for poetry, International Poets Shrine, both 1974; "Statue of Victory" World Culture Prize, Accademia Italia, 1985.

Addresses: *Home*—Bronx, NY.

first staged at the University of Pittsburgh's Creatadrama Theatre in 1970. In the same year it was also published by Philadelphia publisher J. Brook Dendy.

In 1970, while working for the New York City Board of Education, Cox published the first collection of his poetry, aptly titled *The Collected Poetry of Joseph Mason Andrew Cox,* published by Golden Quill. In that same year he was given the Master Poets Award from the American Poet Fellowship Society. He also continued to contribute to a number of anthologies. Cox's

poetry appeared in World of Poets Publishing's *World Poets Anthology* in 1971 and in two volumes of South and West Publishers' serial anthology, *Poems by Blacks,* in 1971 and 1972. His poetry can also be found in *Moon Age Poets* and *New and Better World Poets,* both published by Prairie Press in 1971 and 1972, respectively, and *Lincoln Log,* published by the Illinois State Poetry Society in 1973.

Cox was presented with the World Poets Award from the World Poetry Fellowship Society in 1972, and in that same year he received a PEN grant. In 1973 he was honored with the International Poet Laureate Award. In 1974, having formed his own Cox & Hopewell Publishers, Cox produced his second collection of poetry, the 188-page *Shore Dimly Seen.* In the same year he also published another collection, *Bouquet of Poems,* and the novel *Indestructible Monument.* Once again recognized for his work, Cox received the Humanitarian Award and the Gold Medal for poetry from the International Poets Shrine, both in 1974, and the United Poet Laureate International Gold Crown in 1976. *New and Selected Poems, 1966-1978,* for which Cox received a nomination for an American Book Award, was published in 1979 by Blue Diamond Press.

Cox took a break from his poetry to write *Great Black Men of Masonry: Qualitative Black Achievers Who Were Freemasons, 1723-1982,* published by Blue Diamond Press in 1982. A member of the Most Worshipful Prince Hall Grand Lodge in New York, Cox provided an enlightening account of 269 black men who belong to the Masonic Lodge. The list included Ralph Abernathy, William "Count" Basie, Thurgood Marshall, Edward "Duke" Ellington, Richard Pryor, Booker T. Washington, Andrew Young, and Rev. Jesse Jackson. Cox was awarded the Medal of Distinction by the Asbury Park Neptune NAACP in 1984, the "Statue of Victory" World Culture Prize by Accademia Italia and the Bronze Statue by the Academy of Arts, Science and Letters, both in 1985, and a Gold Medal from the American Biographical Association in 1987 and in 1988. In 1993 he published his final work, *Unfolding Orchid, 1847-1993.*

According to *Black American Writers Past and Present,* Cox wrote to make an impact: "My art…is a sword to fight the dehumanizer and best of civilization and for a one world concept. Therefore, I must make it plain with the whole truth. Half-truths have proven inadequate to awaken a mass of unaware people." Cox retired and remained in New York City. A Democrat and a Unitarian-Universalist, he is also a member of numerous literary organizations.

Selected writings

Poetry

The Collected Poetry of Joseph Mason Andrew Cox, Golden Quill, 1970.

Beetlecreek's black section, and a black teenager sent from his hometown of Pittsburgh to live with relatives in Beetlecreek. The novel received international acclaim and quickly placed Demby among the elite of contemporary African-American authors.

It would be 15 years before Demby's next important work, the novel *The Catacombs,* was published. *The Catacombs*, which takes place in Rome and features a character who bears a striking resemblance to the author himself, is about the process of writing, tracking an author's progress from a germ of an idea to an all-consuming spell. The main character, like Demby—an African American author living in Italy—is attempting to write a novel that contrasts the lives of a sexy actress/model and an African nun. *The Catacombs* met with mixed reactions from critics. Its avant-garde style confused some readers, while others considered it a modernist masterpiece and compared Demby to the likes of Gertrude Stein. Critic Helen Jaskoski wrote in the journal *Critique* that the novel "draws on significant formal and thematic traditions with a long history in Western literature. Within the specifically African-American tradition, Demby engages the themes of freedom and literacy,…the recurring hallmark of African American tradition; however, modernist Demby recasts the quest in light of the expatriate intellectual's relationship to a worldwide struggle for national independence."

Between novels, Demby wrote shorter pieces for publication, including a series of magazine essays with such titles as "The Geisha Girls of Ponto-cho," and "Blue-blood Cats of Rome." In 1969 Demby returned to the United States and took a teaching job at the College of Staten Island, part of the City University of New York (CUNY) system. His third novel, *Love Story Black,* came out in 1978. Like *The Catacombs, Love Story Black* features a Demby-like character, an expatriate African American novelist teaching in a New York City College. This time, the Demby alter ego is attempting to unravel the mysterious past of Mona Pariss, an elderly entertainer, for a magazine article he is writing. According to some sources, Demby published another book, *Blue Boy,* shortly after *Love Story Black,* but it is unclear whether it was actually made available to the public in any legitimate way. In fact, as Demby told *Contemporary Black Biography,* he has never seen a copy of it, and does not really remember what it was about.

Upon his return from Italian exile, Demby settled in Sag Harbor, New York, a site of great importance in African-American history. Blacks have lived in Sag Harbor since the time before the American Revolution, trading freely with both colonial Americans and the British. Some early black residents relocated to England and eventually moved to Sierra Leone.

Demby retired from CUNY in 1987, and has lived a relatively quiet life since then. In 1987 he worked with noted feminist author Betty Friedan to organize the Sag Harbor Initiative, a three-day gathering of leading writers and intellectuals to discuss important social and political issues of the time. While Demby continues to maintain a residence in Sag Harbor, he has lived primarily in Italy since retiring. His Italian wife died in 1995. In April of 2004, Demby married Barbara Morris, a lawyer and civil rights activist who had, among other things, played a key role in the Medgar Evers case. Demby and Morris had been friends at Fisk University back in the 1940s, but had fallen out of touch when Demby moved to Italy. They reestablished contact only recently. The couple spends most of their time in Florence, Italy, where their activities include running a music festival. Demby told *CBB* that he is working on a novel called *King Comus,* which he expects to finish in 2006 or so, though he has not set a rigid deadline for himself. As with his other novels, it will be done when he decides it is done. Even if he never decides that his next novel is finished, William Demby's position as a key figure in the history of African-American literature is secure.

Selected writings

Novels

Beetlecreek, Rinehart, 1950.
The Catacombs, Pantheon, 1965.
Love Story Black, Reed, Cannon & Johnson, 1978

Periodicals

"The Geisha Girls of Ponto-cho," *Harpers,* December 1954, pp. 41-47.

"They Surely Can't Stop Us Now," *Reporter,* April 5, 1956, pp. 18-21.

"A Walk in Tuscany," *Holiday,* December 1957, pp. 141-145.

"Blueblood Cats of Rome," *Holiday,* April 1960, pp. 203-206.

Sources

Books

Dictionary of Literary Biography, Vol. 33: Afro-American Fiction Writers After 1955, Gale, 1984.

Margolies, Edward, *Native Sons: A Critical Study of Twentieth-Century Negro American Authors,* Lippincott, 1968, pp. 173-188.

Oxford Companion to African American Literature, Oxford University Press, 1997, pp. 208-209.

Periodicals

Critique: Studies in Contemporary Fiction, Spring 1994, p. 181.

Triquarterly, Spring 1969, pp. 127-141.

On-line

"William Demby," *Annie Merner Pfeiffer Library* (West Virginia Wesleyan College), www.wvwc.edu/lib/wv-authors/a_demby.htm (March 1, 2005).

"William Demby," *Biography Resource Center,* www.galenet.com/servlet/BioRC (March 1, 2005).

Other

Additional information for this profile was obtained through an interview with William Demby on March 8, 2005.

—Bob Jacobson

Herman Edwards

1954—

Football coach

Edwards, Herman, photograph. Chris Trotman/Getty Images.

New York Jets coach Herman Edwards became only the fifth African-American leader of a National Football League (NFL) franchise when he took over as head coach in 2001. Known for his calm coaching style, Edwards has been hailed as a new generation of coaches who bring a leadership ethos culled from the business management theories to professional sports.

Born in 1954 in Monmouth, New Jersey, Edwards grew up in Seaside, California, a coastal community near Monterey. His parents were an interracial couple at a time when such unions were rare and even illegal in some American states. They had met in Germany, where Edwards's African-American father had been stationed while in the U.S. Army. Back in civilian clothes, his father worked as a construction supervisor in the Seaside area, while Edwards devoted himself to football from an early age. He was an outstanding athlete at Monterey High School, and went on to play for Monterey Peninsula College. Eventually he transferred to San Diego State University, where he earned a degree in criminal justice in 1975. Bypassed in the NFL draft pick, he was signed as a free agent by the Philadelphia Eagles in 1977.

Edwards arrived at the Eagles' training camp along with 20 other rookies hoping for a defensive-back slot on the team. Advancing far past the others, he won a rookie starting spot and was signed to the team, then under the helm of legendary coach Dick Vermeil. Edwards went on to a 135-straight game record as a starter, with 38 career interceptions. He also entered the annals of football legend during the last 30 seconds of a 1978 Eagles game against the New York Giants played at the Meadowlands, the Giants' home field. Edwards picked up a fumble from Joe Pisarcik and made the touchdown that won the game. He was hailed in the press as the "Miracle of the Meadowlands," a nickname that would regularly be invoked again when he took over the Jets, whose home field was also at Meadowlands.

Edwards spent a decade on the NFL player roster, nine of those years with the Eagles. When he was cut during his tenth season, he went on to positions with the Los Angeles Rams and Atlanta Falcons before realizing it was time to retire. "I decided as a player it was better to move on because I didn't want to hinder the opportunity of the younger guy," he told *New York Times*

At a Glance . . .

Born on April 27, 1954, in Monmouth, NJ; son of Herman Edwards Sr. (a U.S. Army sergeant and construction foreman); married second wife, Lia, 2000; children: (first marriage) Marcus. *Education:* Attended Monterey Peninsula College, 1970s; San Diego State University, BA, criminal justice, 1975.

Career: Philadelphia Eagles, professional football player, 1977-86; Los Angeles Rams, professional football player, late 1980s; Atlanta Falcons, professional football player, late 1980s; San Jose State University football team, coaching staff, 1987-90; Kansas City Chiefs, talent scout and defensive backs coach, 1990-95; Tampa Bay Buccaneers, assistant head coach, 1996-2001; New York Jets, head coach, 2001–.

Addresses: *Office*—c/o New York Jets, 1000 Fulton Ave., Hempstead, NY 11550-1099.

writer Judy Battista. "There's this little window of opportunity. Before you move on, you've got to set a standard for the next person. I always knew my limitations. But I always knew my strengths. You play the cards you're dealt. In life, you get four cards. You've got to play them. God doesn't deal bad hands."

Edwards moved on to training that next generation, taking a coaching job with San Jose State University in 1987. Hired by the Kansas City Chiefs three years later, he served as a scout and then a defensive coach for the team. In 1996 he joined the Tampa Bay Buccaneers as assistant head coach and defensive backfield coach, thanks in part to head coach Tony Dungy, an old friend. Edwards and Dungy met at the 1974 Hula Bowl game during their college careers and had remained close over the years. Dungy was, at the time, the NFL's only black head coach, and Edwards later credited his friend with teaching him much about the art of leading a group of well-compensated, overly feted, and physically imposing players. "Watching him work and watching him earn the respect of the players, I realized you didn't have to be boisterous and you didn't have to holler," Edwards told *Philadelphia Daily News* sportswriter Paul Domowitch.

Edwards gained a reputation with the Bucs as a skilled manager of players with impressive motivational skills, and was predicted to one day hold a head-coach job himself. That day came a bit more quickly than expected, when the Jets announced in January of 2001 that Edwards would succeed the retiring coach, Bill Parcells. Some of the credit may have come from

another longstanding association that Edwards enjoyed, this one with new Jets general manager Terry Bradway, whom he knew from his Kansas City days.

Edwards became only the fifth African American head coach in NFL history, joining a roster that included Dungy and Dennis Green of the Minnesota Vikings by then. He was also the first black to coach a pro football team in New York. In recent years, Dungy and others had spoken out about the dearth of coaching positions held by minorities in the league, in an era when nearly 70 percent of the players were African American. NFL brass had recently taken measures to remedy the imbalance, but pundits conceded that despite the political significance of the offer, Edwards seemed to have won the job because of his impressive record with the Bucs.

Edwards enjoyed a terrific first season, with the Jets finishing with ten wins and six losses, and he became the tenth rookie head coach in NFL history to lead his team to the playoffs. But the Jets have checkered history and are known for their spotty years combined with playoff-berth seasons, and had not even appeared in a Super Bowl since their 1969 win. They finished the 2002 season with a record of nine-wins, seven-losses, but sank to a record of six-wins and ten-losses in 2003 and failed to make the playoffs for the first time since Edwards took over. The team enjoyed a much better season in 2004, finishing with ten wins and six losses.

Edwards earns $850,000 a year, but puts in a long, intense day during the football season. One of the final duties of what often turn out to be 15-hour days is making calls to the team trainer. "The trainers and the equipment guys—they know more about the team than half the coaches," Edwards explained to *Newsweek* writer Devin Gordon. "The players see them as men, not as coaches. So they hear how the team's doing. Are they tired? Are they happy?" The team's star quarterback, Chad Pennington, who helped lead the team to that impressive 2004 season after coming back from a wrist injury a year earlier, was one of Edwards's biggest fans. "You'll never see Coach Edwards tight or nervous on the sideline," Pennington told *Sports Illustrated*'s Michael Silver. "He has confidence in our preparation and enjoys watching his players perform. That's why he's so calm."

Sources

Periodicals

Ebony, December 2003, p. 82.
Newsweek, September 2, 2002, p. 48.
New York Daily News, January 19, 2001; January 4, 2003.
New York Post, January 19, 2001, p. 100.
New York Times, January 18, 2001, p. D1; January 21, 2001, p. 3; December 1, 2003, p. D2; January 14, 2005, p. D4.

Philadelphia Daily News, August 28, 2001.
Sports Illustrated, October 25, 2004, p. 52.

—Carol Brennan

James Forman

1928-2005

Civil rights leader

James Forman was "a strong pillar of the modern-day civil rights movement," his former colleague Rep. John Lewis told the *Sacramento Observer*. In April of 1969, when James Forman presented the *Black Manifesto*, a public call for reparations to the African-American community for years of oppression, he made national headlines as an outspoken black radical. This moment captured why Forman was eulogized in *Jet* as "the most independent and fearless in his desire to promote ideas fostering black equality."

As executive secretary of the Student Nonviolent Coordinating Committee (SNCC; often pronounced "snick") from 1961 to 1966, Forman worked as a frontline organizer in nearly every major civil rights campaign of the era. His revolutionary vision, based upon socialist doctrine and militant black nationalism, had a profound influence on the structure and philosophical outlook of SNCC, which was one of the most significant civil rights organizations of the 1960s. Forman espoused more vigorous protest tactics than Martin Luther King, Jr., but his legacy would be bringing "down one of the most violent and dehumanizing systems without firing a shot," Ruby Nell Sales, civil rights leader and director of SpiritHouse, related to *Sojourners*.

Forman was born in Chicago, Illinois, on October 4, 1928. When he was only eleven months old, his parents took him to live on his grandmother's 180-acre farm in Marshall County, Mississippi. Though he lived in a state of severe poverty, Forman enjoyed the company of his grandparents, two subsistence farmers who worked their "poor and hilly" land by a mule-drawn plow. Receiving his education at home from his Aunt Thelma, a schoolteacher, Forman developed an early interest in books.

Upon returning to Chicago to live with his parents, Forman attended St. Anselm's Catholic School. A member of the Protestant faith, he was torn by the clash between his own beliefs and Catholic religious doctrine. At age twelve, Forman enrolled in a public grammar school. As he recalled in his autobiography *The Making of Black Revolutionaries*, "It was a huge relief to not have to take religion, not to be weighed down by the conflict over Catholicism."

Awakened to Racial Discrimination

Outside the classroom, Forman sold the *Chicago Defender*, one of the most prominent black newspapers in the country. The stories of lynching, discrimination, and injustices awakened him to the need for people of color to struggle against white racist oppression. By reading the works of W. E. B. Du Bois and Booker T. Washington, Forman became aware of the two leading ideologies guiding the progress of African Americans. Opposed to Washington's conciliatory program, Forman embraced Du Bois's call for black people to seek political power and higher education in order to adapt to the rapid changes of industrial society.

After graduating from high school in 1947 as a *Chicago Tribune*-sponsored honor student, Forman attended Wilson Junior College, where he studied English, French, and world history. Disillusioned by the

At a Glance . . .

Born on October 4, 1928, in Chicago, IL; died on January 10, 2005, Washington, DC; son of Jackson and Octavia (Allen) Forman; married Mary Forman (date unknown, divorced); Mildred Thompson (date unknown, divorced); married Constancia Ramilly (date unknown, divorced); children: Chaka (son), James. *Education*: Attended Wilson Junior College and University of Southern California; Roosevelt University, BA, 1957; attended African Research and Studies Program, Boston University, 1958, and Chicago Teachers College, 1959-60; Cornell University, MA, African-American studies, 1980; Union of Experimental Colleges and Universities with the Institute for Policy Studies, PhD, 1982. *Military*: U.S. Air Force, early 1950s.

Career: *Chicago Defender*, journalist covering events in Little Rock, AR, 1958-59; Chicago Public Schools, teacher, 1960; *Chicago Defender*, reported while working with the Emergency Relief Committee, Fayette County, TN, 1960; Student Nonviolent Coordinating Committee (SNCC), executive secretary, 1961-66, SNCC, administrator of the national office, Atlanta, GA, 1967; SNCC, director of International Affairs Commission, New York City, 1967; Black Panther Party, minister of foreign affairs, 1968; Unemployment and Poverty Action Committee, Washington, DC, president, mid-1970s-1980s; *Washington Times*, founder, 1981; Black American News Service, founder, early 1980s(?).

Awards: National Conference of Black Mayors' Fannie Lou Hamer Freedom Award, 1990.

lack of employment opportunities available to educated African Americans, Forman joined the U.S. Air Force. He explained in his book *The Making of Black Revolutionaries* that while stationed at segregated military bases in the Deep South and on the Pacific island of Okinawa, he "came to see the Armed Forces in broad terms, as a dehumanizing machine which destroys thought and creativity in order to preserve the economic system and political myths of the United States."

Following his discharge from the Air Force in 1952, Forman lived in Oakland, California. To escape the pressure of his military experience, he periodically supported himself by gambling in pool halls and betting on card games. While attending the University of Southern California that same year, Forman was arrested by two white policemen who falsely accused him of participating in a robbery. Forman was taken to the police station, incarcerated, and then beaten; after several days of questioning he was finally freed without charges. Unable to deal with the shock of this experience, he suffered a breakdown and was placed in a state hospital.

Back in Chicago in 1954, Forman enrolled at Roosevelt University. Unlike his earlier college experiences, Roosevelt turned out to be an exciting and stimulating learning institution that helped to shape Forman's worldview. He became president of the "brotherhood," a small student group that gathered to discuss politics, racism, and the merits of integration. He spent many hours studying anthropology, sociology, history, and economics, and aside from the assigned textbooks, he read works by American theologian Reinhold Niebuhr and novelist John Steinbeck. The Montgomery bus boycott of 1955-56 further heightened Forman's growing concern about the advancement of civil rights. As he related in *The Making of Black Revolutionaries*, "The boycott woke me to the real—not the merely theoretical—possibility of building a nonviolent mass movement of southern black people to fight segregation."

Soon after his graduation from Roosevelt in 1957, Forman received a grant to attend the African Research and Studies Program at Boston University. The next year, he obtained a press assignment from the *Chicago Defender* to cover the civil rights struggle in Little Rock, Arkansas. Inspired by his trip to Little Rock, Forman began a novel based upon the exploits of northern civil rights workers in the South. Finishing the final draft in the fall of 1959, Forman subsequently took education courses at Chicago's Teachers College and, by the spring of 1960, began to teach in the Chicago public schools.

Dedicated Life to Fighting Oppression

That summer, Forman went to Middlebury College in Vermont to study French. As the student sit-in movement swept the South, and African countries struggled for independence, Forman decided that upon his return to Chicago he would become a full-time member of the fight for civil rights. On the invitation of the Emergency Relief Committee, a subcommittee of the Chicago branch of the Congress of Racial Equality (CORE), Forman worked among dispossessed black tenant farmers in Fayette County, Tennessee. Writing press releases for the *Chicago Defender*, he recorded personal accounts of black farmers who had been evicted for taking part in a local voter registration campaign. In 1961 Forman went to Monroe, North Carolina, to visit Robert F. Williams, the chairman of the Monroe NAACP whose advocacy of "meeting violence with violence" created massive opposition within the black and white communities. During his short stay at Williams's home in Monroe, Forman discussed the positive role of armed self-defense in the struggle against white oppression.

Although Forman returned to the North to teach in a Chicago elementary school, he soon resigned from his teaching position to join SNCC, becoming executive secretary of the operation in 1961. From his small Atlanta office, Forman struggled to bring order to an organization that he found to be lacking in discipline and a "clearly defined code of staff ethics."

At first mocked by younger members of SNCC, Forman and his administrative zeal proved indispensable. As Taylor Branch wrote in *Parting the Waters*, "Forman's aggressive competence filled a vacuum in SNCC." Through telephone and press releases, Forman worked to keep close communications with SNCC volunteers throughout the South. In *The Student Nonviolent Coordinating Committee: The Growth of Radicalism in a Civil Rights Organization*, SNCC member Jane Stembridge explained that if "Forman had not been on the phone" to SNCC members in southwest Mississippi "there was no way they would have ever come out of those counties at all."

Worked as SNCC Organizer

Forman's first involvement as a frontline organizer with SNCC began when he traveled to Albany, Georgia, on December 10, 1961. Arriving by "freedom train," Forman, along with six others, was arrested for attempting to challenge the segregated seating policy of Albany's Union Railway Terminal. When released from jail, Forman spoke out against the effort to invite Martin Luther King, Jr., to Albany. He warned that King's leadership would influence the local populace to throw its support behind one monolithic leader, thus causing the demise of Albany's student-led "people's movement." Mass media coverage of King's visit to Albany brought Forman national attention as one of the highest ranking and most militant members of the civil rights movement.

With funds raised through the Voter Registration Project, Forman worked with SNCC in 1962 to desegregate the cities of Cairo, Illinois, and Charleston, Missouri. Not long after, he traveled to Cleveland, Mississippi, to help organize a voter registration campaign. His incessant activity, however, resulted in severe health problems. In January of 1963, he fell ill with a bleeding ulcer and was hospitalized for several weeks. Soon afterward, he was arrested in Alabama for taking part in another march to Jackson, Mississippi.

After being released from jail once more, Forman drove to Birmingham, Alabama, where King and his supporters were in the midst of a massive civil rights campaign. Although Forman urged SNCC members to cooperate with King's Southern Christian Leadership Conference (SCLC), he advocated that demonstrators exhibit a heightened sense of militancy. He criticized King for remaining behind the scenes, while students faced the wrath of police dogs, fire hoses, and armed police officers. Forman viewed King's negotiations with the city of Birmingham as a sell-out between the SCLC and then-Attorney General Bobby Kennedy. "People had become too militant for the government's liking and Dr. King's image," wrote Forman in *The Making of Black Revolutionaries*. "I felt the masses of young people who had been the backbone of the protest had been cheated once more. The mighty leader had proven to have feet of clay."

Traveled to Washington and Selma

On August 28, 1963, Forman participated in the March on Washington, a mass civil rights campaign that brought more than 200,000 demonstrators to the nation's capital. Along with SNCC chairman John Lewis and several others, Forman helped prepare a speech expressing "bitter criticism" of American society. Upon reading the first draft, various civil rights leaders demanded that Lewis and his staff omit passages from the speech that contained blatant revolutionary rhetoric. After much debate, SNCC leaders agreed to make several changes. "The rewriting took place at the Lincoln Memorial," stated Forman in the documentary *Eyes on the Prize*. "It was done out of a spirit of unity. We wanted the SNCC participation to be very visible; we were certainly not interested in withdrawing from the March on Washington."

About a year and a half later, in March of 1965, Forman traveled to Selma, Alabama, where he voiced opposition to King's 50-mile march to Montgomery, the state's capital. King had staged the march to protest the denial of voting rights to African Americans. Forman, however, was anxious to see a more aggressive display of black dissatisfaction, and he influenced many local civil rights activists while he was in Selma. In *Black in Selma*, J. L. Chestnut, Jr., described Forman's role in motivating Selma's black population: "He talked about what black people were sick and tired of taking at the hands of the white man; he told the black folk in the audience to come out in the open with their views on freedom and get themselves down to the registration office the next week to hasten the day of reckoning."

Increasing disputes with SNCC chairman John Lewis led Forman to resign as executive secretary of the organization in 1966. After his resignation, he held an administrative position in SNCC's Atlanta office; then, in 1967, he served as director of SNCC's Internal Affairs Commission in New York City. By urging SNCC members to study the revolutionary works of Chinese statesman Mao Tse-tung and Caribbean-born activist Frantz Fanon, Forman hoped to promote a revolutionary black nationalist consciousness—one that paralleled the freedom movements for cultural independence on the African continent. While serving as the minister of foreign affairs in the Black Panther Party in 1968, Forman worked to promote an alliance between SNCC and the Panthers. Faced with personal opposition and internal disputes, however, Forman left the party shortly afterward.

Called for Reparations

On April 26, 1969, in Detroit, Michigan, Forman presented the *Black Manifesto* at the National Black Economic Development Conference. Sponsored by the Interreligious Foundation for Community Organizations, the conference adopted a manifesto that demanded Protestant and Jewish organizations pay $500 million in reparations to the African American community. In his speech, Forman called upon blacks to join in a black-socialist-led armed struggle to overthrow the United States government.

A month later, Forman interrupted services at New York City's Riverside Church to demand that the congregation pay reparations for the past damage inflicted upon people of color by white America. According to Larry Neal in *The Black Seventies*, this act not only made national front-page news, but marked "one of the high points of nonviolent action" during the conservative years of U.S. president Richard M. Nixon's administration.

As his involvement in SNCC activities decreased, Forman turned his attention to writing and academic study. Published in 1968, his first work, *Sammy Younge, Jr.: The First Black College Student to Die in the Black Liberation Movement*, is a biographical account of a young SNCC volunteer who was murdered by a white man in Tuskegee, Alabama. Aside from penning several other works, including his autobiography *The Making of Black Revolutionaries*, Forman earned a master's degree in professional studies in African and African American history from Cornell University in 1980 and a doctorate from the Union Institute. In spite of the ravages of cancer that initially appeared in the early 1990s, Forman continued to work from his Washington, D.C., office. He and Constancia Romily, his divorced wife, had two sons—James Jr., a public defender in Washington, D.C., and Chaka, a member of the Screen Actor's Guild.

In the December 2000 issue of *The Progressive* magazine, political scientist Adolph L. Reed, Jr. revisited Forman's notion that white America might owe reparations to black Americans for slavery and its legacy. As recounted by Reed, after James Forman presented his demand for $500 million in reparations at the Riverside Church in 1969, the idea of reparations smoldered until Jesse Jackson brought it to life again during the 1972 presidential campaign with his demand for a $900 million "freedom budget." Nothing came of the idea, however, and over the next two decades it was largely forgotten. But in 2000, thirty-one years after Forman delivered his "Black Manifesto," Randall Robinson published *The Debt: What America Owes to Blacks*, and the reparations issue again was on the front burner. Although yet to be resolved, the issue continues to intrigue and puzzle legal scholars and policy makers alike.

Remained Dedicated to Civil Rights Movement

Although he has often been overshadowed by some of the more famous figures of the civil rights movement, Forman possessed an indisputable facility for organization and leadership and is widely recognized among activists and scholars. In her work *The Student Nonviolent Coordinating Committee*, Emily Stoper pointed out that the leadership of SNCC from 1961 to 1966 rested primarily "in the hands of Forman at the Atlanta office." And Julian Bond, chairman of the National Association for the Advancement of Colored People was quoted in the *Times* as saying that Forman had "imbued the [SNCC] organization with a camaraderie and collegiality that I've never seen in any organization before or since." In tribute to the former SNCC executive secretary, Cleveland Sellers wrote in *The River of No Return*: "The movement was not a job to Jim Forman: it was a way of life."

Forman never lost his drive to improve the lives of black Americans. In 1982 he participated in the organization of a second March on Washington. He also founded a short-lived newspaper and the Black American News Service in Washington in the early 1980s. He also imbued his sons with a sense the "you attained fulfillment through service to others," according to his son, social activist and legal scholar James Forman, Jr., in *Black Issues in Higher Education*.

Forman died of colon cancer on January 10, 2005. Congressional delegate Eleanor Holmes Norton related to the *Sacramento Observer* on the occasion of Forman's death that: "Americans may not know Jim's name as a household word, but if they look around them at the racial change in our country, they will know Jim by his work." He left a "blueprint" that she predicted will "continue to be used for civil, social, and human rights."

Selected writings

Sammy Younge, Jr.: The First Black College Student to Die in the Black Liberation Movement, Open Hand Publishing, 1968.

Liberation viendra d'une chose noir, Maspero, 1968.

The Political Thought of James Forman, Black Star Press, 1970.

The Making of Black Revolutionaries, Open Hand Publishing, 1972.

Self-Determination: An Examination of the Question and Its Application to the African American People, Open Hand Publishing, 1984.

Sources

Books

Ashmore, Harry S., *Hearts and Minds: A Personal Chronicle of Race in America*, Seven Locks Press, 1988.

Black Protest Thought in the Sixties, edited by August Meier and Elliott Rudwick, Quadrangle Books, 1970.

Black Protest Thought in the Twentieth Century, edited by August Meier, Elliott Rudwick, and Francis L. Broderick, Bobbs-Merrill, 1971.

The Black Seventies, edited by Floyd B. Barbour, Extending Horizon, 1970.

Branch, Taylor, *Parting the Waters: America in the King Years, 1954-1963*, Simon & Schuster, 1988.

Chestnut, J. L., Jr., and Julia Cass, *Black in Selma: The Uncommon Life of J. L. Chestnut, Jr.—Politics and Power in a Small American Town*, Farrar, Straus, 1990.

The Eyes on the Prize Civil Rights Reader: Documents, Speeches, and Firsthand Accounts from the Black Freedom Struggle, 1954-1990, Viking Press, 1991.

Forman, James, *The Making of Black Revolutionaries,* Open Hand Publishing, 1985.

Haines, Herbert H., *Black Radicals and the Civil Rights Mainstream, 1954-1970*, University of Tennessee Press, 1988.

King, Richard H., *Civil Rights: The Idea of Freedom*, Oxford University Press, 1992.

Lawson, Steven F., *Running for Freedom: Civil Rights and Black Politics in America since 1941*, Oxford University Press, 1992.

Marable, Manning, *Race, Reform, and Rebellion: The Second Reconstruction in Black America, 1945-1990, 2nd edition*, University Press of Mississippi, 1991.

Schuchter, Arnold, *Reparations: The Black Manifesto and Its Challenge to White America*, J. B. Lippincott, 1970.

Sellers, Cleveland, and Robert Terrell, *The River of No Return: The Autobiography of a Black Militant and the Life and Death of SNCC*, University Press of Mississippi, 1990.

Stoper, Emily, *The Student Nonviolent Coordinating Committee: The Growth of Radicalism in a Civil Rights Organization*, Carlson, 1989.

Walter, Mildred Pitts, *Mississippi Challenge*, Bradbury Press, 1992.

Zinn, Howard, *The New Abolitionists*, Beacon Press, 1964.

Periodicals

Black Issues in Higher Education, January 13, 2005, p. 24.

First Things: A Monthly Journal of Religion and Public Life, June-July 2002, p. 32.

Guardian (London), January 14, 2005, p. 29.

Jet, January 31, 2005, p. 51.

Sacramento Observer, January 22, 2005.

Sojourners, April 2005, p. 10.

Times (London), January 17, 2005, p. 50.

Washington Post, January 11, 2005, p. B6.

On-line

"The Case Against Reparations," *Progressive,* www.progressive.org/reed1200.htm (April 28, 2005).

Other

Additional information for this profile was taken from the PBS video series *Eyes on the Prize: America's Civil Rights Years*; segments consulted include "Ain't Scared of Your Jails, 1960-1961" and "No Easy Walk, 1961-1963," both narrated by Julian Bond.

—John Cohassey and Sara Pendergast

Reggie Fowler

1959—

Entrepreneur

Arizona entrepreneur Reggie Fowler created a stir in 2005 when he nearly became the first African American to own the majority stake in a National Football League (NFL) team, the Minnesota Vikings. His impending purchase was hailed as a milestone in professional sports, and it was hoped that it would eradicate some of the imbalance in a league where nearly three-quarters of the players are minorities, while the ranks of coaches and front-office staffers have yet to become fully integrated. From the beginning, however, questions about Fowler's finances, and a minor stir about inaccuracies on his resume, raised questions. By mid-2005, the bid had fallen through and Fowler backed away from his efforts to buy the team. Minneapolis-area activist Spike Moss was quoted in the San Jose Mercury News as saying, "Everybody was looking forward to him being the first, but first you have to have the money to be considered."

Born in February, 1959, Fowler was one of five children in a family headed by a father who had been an officer in the U.S. Air Force. When Al Fowler settled in the Tucson, Arizona, area, he opened Al's Pit Bar-B-Que, a successful eatery whose original location was used as the diner in the 1974 Martin Scorsese film, *Alice Doesn't Live Here Anymore*. Fowler's first job was as a dishwasher at the restaurant. Midway through middle school, his parents moved the family to another section of Tucson, and from then on Fowler and his siblings attended schools that were predominantly white. At Saguaro High School, he was an outstanding athlete and was elected to homecoming court; his father cooked the pre-game meals for him and his

football teammates. After graduating in 1977, he entered the University of Wyoming on a football scholarship, starting out as a running back but then switching to wide receiver and linebacker positions.

Tried Out for Bengals

Though Fowler led the University of Wyoming Cowboys in unassisted tackles during his senior year, the changes in his position likely harmed his prospects with the NFL, and he was not drafted. Several months after his December, 1981, graduation, however, he was able to join the Cincinnati Bengals' pre-season training camp, but was cut before the regular season started. He was also on the roster for a short-lived United States Football Team in Arizona in 1983, but played no games with the Wranglers. Returning to school, he took business courses at Arizona State University in the mid-1980s and joined a training program with Mobil Oil's chemical division. He worked in sales for the company before striking out on his own in 1989.

Fowler founded his firm, Spiral Inc., originally as a company that sold the food containers used by grocery stores—the plastic tubs at the deli counters, for example, and the foam trays used in meat packaging. He named the company after a football term that players use to describe the perfectly thrown pass, and his initial investment in it was allegedly just $1,000. The company, which was based in Chandler, Arizona, expanded over the years to include several other divisions, including real-estate development and an aviation-simulator business. Fowler went on to own a cattle ranch as well as a financial institution, the Bank of the Southwest, and he and Spiral, Inc., made their first appearance on the annual *Black Enterprise* rankings list of the top African-American-owned companies in 1993 as No. 98 in the Industrial/Service sector. Six years later, it had jumped to the No. 22 spot, and was at No. 11 in 2004, after posting previous-year sales of $314 million. The *Arizona Republic* newspaper estimated Fowler's net worth at around $400 million by then.

Met the Press

Rumors first surfaced in August of 2004 that a relatively unknown Arizona businessman was interested in buying the Minnesota Vikings. The team was owned by Red McCombs, who had tried for several years to strike a deal with Minneapolis-St. Paul-area civic authorities to build a new stadium to replace the Vikings' home turf at the Metrodome. There was intense local opposition in the Twin Cities for a taxpayer-subsidized deal, especially since the Vikings had proven to be one of the most profitable teams in NFL. There were even hints that the team might pack up and move to Los Angeles. But after their 2004 season began, rumors of a sale died down, since teams rarely change hands during the NFL season. The rumors surfaced again in January, and on Valentine's Day of 2005, Fowler wired McCombs's office a $20 million deposit.

Later that day, Fowler and McCombs appeared at a press conference to discuss the pending sale, which was subject to clearing several other hurdles before it could be finalized. The team's price tag was thought to be $625 million, and the Vikings franchise had been valued at $604 million in 2004 by *Forbes* magazine. Fowler was not the only buyer, though he was the majority owner, or general partner. His limited partners were a pair of real-estate developers from the New York area: Alan B. Landis, once the part-owner of the National Basketball League Association's New Jersey

Nets; Zyggi Wilf, whose Garden Commercial Properties firm had expressed some interest in a potential stadium construction project for the Vikings; and David Mandelbaum, a real estate attorney, also from the New York area.

At the press conference announcing Fowler's agreement to buy the team, he stressed there were no plans to relocate the Vikings to Los Angeles or anywhere else. In fact, he said, it would be he that moved to the Twin Cities. "I want you all to know that this is probably the greatest day of my life," *Saint Paul Pioneer Press* writer Sean Jensen quoted him as saying that day. "I'm excited to be here in the Twin Cities, the state of Minnesota, to let you know that we are here to, No. 1, acquire your team and hopefully put the team back into the hands of the state of Minnesota and let you know that we're committed to being here." There were many questions put to Fowler about potentially becoming the first black owner of an NFL team, but he deflected attention away from the issue. "I think it's a great thing," *New York Times* writer Richard Lezin Jones quoted him as saying in response to a question about the historic first. "I'm happy that I'm black. As James Brown says, 'Say it loud, I'm black and I'm proud.' That really doesn't play a big part to me, I just happen to be black."

Admitted Errors in Biography

The journalists assembled at that news conference were handed a biographical fact sheet on Fowler, and it was subsequently found to contain a few inaccuracies. It claimed he had played in the Little League World Series, had a bachelor's degree in business administration and finance, and had played with the Cincinnati Bengals and the Canadian Football League's Calgary Stampeders. It asserted that his company was ranked eleventh on the *Black Enterprise* list of African American-owned firms in 2004. In reality, the "world series" was the name used for a Tucson all-star event for youth teams in which Fowler had played, and his undergraduate degree from the University of Wyoming had been in social work, not business. He had been released during training camp for the Bengals as well as the Canadian Football League tryout. Finally, his company was No. 11 only in the *Black Enterprise* Industrial/Service category, not in the overall rankings.

The press, especially in the Twin Cities, had a field day with the errors, and Fowler flew back to Minnesota to deal with the matter himself just four days later. He explained that the biography released had been a mere draft copy done by a Twin Cities public-relations firm he hired, and had not been ready for release; the rudimentary details had apparently been supplied by Spiral, Inc.'s Chandler headquarters. Fowler was quick to accept blame, however, and released a formal statement. "I realized that there was some confusion surrounding my background, and I wanted to make perfectly clear the facts of who I am and what I have done," it read, according to a Knight Ridder/Tribune News Service report. "I regret that a draft copy of my biography was issued, and I want to make sure the facts on my background are clear."

Black Coaches Voted Their Approval

Some media pundits raised questions about whether or not Fowler could actually afford to buy the Vikings. NFL ownership rules specify that the majority owner must put up 30 percent of the purchase price from his own holdings, but Fowler deflected questions about his net worth at the earlier press conference by reminding reporters that "Mr. McCombs is a very astute business-man," the *Saint Paul Pioneer Press*'s Jensen quoted him as saying. "I don't think we would be sitting here together if we didn't have the ability to come up with that 30 percent."

Fowler faced more serious tests on his quest to become the Vikings' newest owner. He had to meet with the NFL finance committee in March, and answer detailed questions about his net worth and company holdings; then, 32 other NFL team owners had to vote their approval for the transfer. In early May of 2005, however, Fowler withdrew his ownership bid, acknowl-edging that he could not provide adequate proof of his financial stake in the ownership group. Fowler held out the possibility that he might be a limited partner in an ownership group, which might help him avoid the possibility of losing his $20 million deposit if the deal collapses. Sports sociologist Harry Edwards told the *Mercury News* "This is not a race issue or double standard. These [financial issues] should have been uncovered and dealt with before he was introduced. There was tremendous hope in Fowler. The NFL wants to get past this historic discrepancy, but hope is a very, very poor strategy."

Sources

Periodicals

Arizona Daily Star, February 20, 2005, p. A1.
Grand Rapids Press, February 15, 2005, p. D5.
Houston Chronicle, February 19, 2005, p. 7.
Knight-Ridder/Tribune News Service, February 18, 2005; February 27, 2005.
Mercury News (San Jose), May 11, 2005.
New York Times, February 15, 2005, p. D1; March 1, 2005, p. D2.
Saint Paul Pioneer Press (St. Paul, MN), February 15, 2005.
St. Petersburg Times, February 20, 2005, p. 2C.
Star Tribune (Minneapolis, MN), August 17, 2004, p. 1C; January 20, 2005, p. 3C; March 24, 2005.

—Carol Brennan

Johnny Gill

1966—

Singer

From 1988 to 1991 Johnny Gill was a regular at the number one slot on the rhythm-and-blues (R&B) music charts. His group New Edition had a number one album, *Heart Break*, in 1988. His 1990 solo release, *Johnny Gill*, produced three number one singles on its way to number one. Another song he duetted on, "Where Do We Go From Here," also landed at number one. The *Indianapolis Recorder* gushed, "Like the great soul singers of the past, Gill has all the right stuff: a natural voice of tremendous force, a soaring falsetto and the gift of impeccable timing. Both patient and urgent, sensitive and sultry, Gill raises romance to new heights." Gill continued to use that voice into the 2000s to put out dozens of more hits—on his own, with super-group New Edition, and as the G in R&B soul-meisters LSG.

Graduated from Gospel to R&B

Johnny Gill Jr. was born on May 22, 1966, in Washington, DC, the fourth son of Johnny and Annie Gill. The senior Gill was a Baptist minister who raised his family according to scripture. While secular music such as R&B was forbidden, gospel was embraced and the family formed the group Wings of Faith and, later, The Gill Special. By the age of eight, Johnny Jr., whose deep, baritone voice was already emerging, became the family's main vocalist. Despite his father's efforts, Gill could not resist the pull of R&B. One of his childhood friends was Stacy Lattisaw, a teen R&B sensation on the Atlantic Records label. She encouraged Gill to record a demo tape. "She always knew I could sing and she told the president of her record company about me and that's how everything took place," Gill told *The Jamaica Observer*.

Gill's voice, mature beyond its years, impressed Atlantic executives and they immediately signed him to the label's imprint, Cotillion. Gill was just 16 at the time. "Recording an album was the hardest thing to do," Gill recalled to *Essence*. "You start to ask yourself, 'What if this fails?' But it never dawned on me in the studio, because the producers were so great to work with." The result, titled *Johnny Gill,* came out in 1983. Despite the modest hit single "Super Love," the album was lackluster. The following year Gill had more success with *Perfect Combination*, a joint effort with Lattisaw. The album's title song reached the top ten and revealed the depth of Gill's vocal abilities to a broad fan base. In 1985 Atlantic released Gill's sophomore effort, *Chemistry*. It spawned the song "Half Crazy," which went to number 26 on *Billboard's* R&B charts.

By 1988 Gill had left Atlantic and signed a new contract with Motown Records. Meanwhile, the boy band New Edition was looking for a new singer. New Edition had rocketed to fame in 1983 with the mega-hit "Candy Girl." After a string of more hits, lead singer Bobby Brown decided to pursue a solo career. Enter Gill. He had been friends with members of the group since their debut and, according to the New Edition Web site, "[the group] would always joke that if Johnny could hit one of their dance steps right, he could be in the group." With the understanding that he would continue to record as a soloist for Motown, Gill joined New Edition, who were then signed to MCA Records.

At a Glance . . .

Born on May 22, 1966, in Washington, DC.

Career: Singer, 1983–. Recorded with Atlantic Records, 1983-86, and Motown Records, 1987–. Member of New Edition, MCA Records, 1988-2002, and Bad Boy Records, 2002–; member of LSG, Motown Records, 1997–.

Addresses: *Record company*—Motown Records, 1755 Broadway, 6th Floor, New York, NY, 10019. *Home*—Los Angeles, CA.

Scored a String of Chart-Topping Hits

When New Edition first hit the airwaves, its five members were between 14 and 16 years old. Their songs were bubblegum-sweet pop: "The Telephone Man," "Popcorn Love," "Cool It Now." They dressed in matching outfits, pumped out in-sync dance steps, and filled pages of teen magazines. They were as well loved for their youth as for their music. However, by 1988 the boys, nearing their twenties, were ready to be considered men. Gill's rich, soulful voice was the perfect vehicle. Most critics consider 1989's *Heart Break* the group's first foray into mature music. The sultry ballad "Can You Stand the Rain," anchored by Gill's riveting voice, sailed straight to number one on the charts. Three other songs from the album made it into the top five. The album went double-platinum, according to the Record Industry Association of America (RIAA), with confirmed sales of over two million copies.

Despite the phenomenal success of *Heart Break,* New Edition decided to disband in 1989. Gill joined old pal Lattisaw on the single "Where Do We Go from Here," which landed him right back at the number one slot on the R&B charts. With the backing of Motown he also recorded his most successful album to date, 1990's *Johnny Gill.* Motown pulled out all stops for the album, hiring the best producers in urban music and sponsoring a massive marketing campaign. It worked. The public sent the album straight to double-platinum status and pushed three singles to number one on the R&B charts: "My, My, My," "Rub You the Right Way," and "Wrap Your Body Tight."

Johnny Gill earned the crooner a Grammy nomination for best R&B male vocal performance, though he lost to Luther Vandross. The album also established Gill as a master of the musical trend known as New Jack. In its early 1990s heyday, New Jack took the classic soul of R&B vocals, added a shot of sexiness, some slick synthesizers, and a hint of rap. With his self-titled album all over the top of the charts, Gill was labeled "the Marvin Gaye of the new-jack soul generation" by *Entertainment Weekly.*

Reunited with New Edition

Provocative, Gill's second album for Motown, came out in 1993. Again Motown went all out with production and marketing. Gill did the same. "I tried to give the best vocal performance on each song," he told *Billboard*. "I think that's what people expect of me." Unfortunately expectations did not translate into sales and the album barely reached RIAA gold status (sales of 500,000 or more). The first single, "The Floor," made it to number 11 on the charts, and three others reached the top fifty. Not a bad showing, but for Gill it was a big disappointment after the incredible success of his previous album.

For the next several years, Gill collaborated with numerous artists, did countless performances, and made several television appearances. Meanwhile, the members of New Edition were thinking about getting back together. It finally happened in 1986 and both Gill and Brown joined the other four members in the studio to record *Home Again.* The album went double-platinum and landed at number one on both *Billboard's* R&B and top 200 charts. The first single, the sexy "Hit Me Off," went to number one on the R&B and dance charts. The album also spawned a mega-tour. Despite much-publicized rumors about clashing egos on the tour, Gill told *The Jamaica Observer*, "We have our ups and downs and all of that stuff but we're family. I couldn't think of any other group that I'd rather be with."

Just months after *Home Again* came out, Gill released *Let's Get the Mood Right*, his fifth solo album, and his third on the Motown label. Featuring styles from New Jack to classic R&B to gospel, the album went to number seven on the R&B charts and produced several Gill classics, including the title track, "Love in an Elevator," and "It's Your Body." The latter was written and produced by Gill. He also played bass on many of the tracks. Though it did not sear across the charts as *Johnny Gill* had, the album pulled in a lot of praise from music critics. The *Indianapolis Recorder* called Gill "the most passionate balladeer of his generation." *The Cincinnati Post* wrote "this disc is the first time in memory that Gill's material rates high enough to take full advantage of his wonderful pipes."

Completed Two Decades of Music Making

In 1997 Gill joined forces with Gerald Levert and Keith Sweat to form LSG. The trio's first album, *Levert-Sweat-Gill*, led by the hit single "My Body," went double-platinum and landed at the number two spot on the R&B charts, number four on the pop. The group's second effort, *LSG2*, released in 2003, took the third and sixth spots respectively. The same year Motown released *The Best of Johnny Gill.*

Gill also turned his talents to the stage, appearing in several gospel-tinged musicals including *Listen to Your Woman, Will a Real Man Please Stand Up*, and *A Fool for Love.* However, New Edition was never far from his heart. When the group began touring again in 2000, Gill was there. During 2002 New Edition appeared at the Black Entertainment Television (BET) music awards, where they met urban music mogul Sean "P. Diddy" Combs. He signed the quintet to his Bad Boy Records label and in 2004 New Edition released *One Love.* Gill was featured prominently on several tracks, prompting a *St. Louis Post-Dispatch* music reviewer to write, "[Gill] remains the group's ace." Fans were thrilled with the band's return to recording and pushed the record to the top of the charts. Reflecting on the album's success, Gill told *Jet*, "I think we were one of the first groups of our generation to do what we've done, be successful and then spin out and do our own thing and then come back. Most groups can't make it that far."

Working full-time as a solo artist and with two popular bands kept Gill busy. "It's tough, very tough but I enjoy it and that's the challenge," Gill told *The Jamaica Observer.* "You get to work with different personalities and when you are around people that are talented it also keeps your creative juices flowing and that inspires me." Yet despite his prolific creativity, real stardom has eluded him. He has never won a Grammy and his name is largely unknown outside of his R&B fan base. Nonetheless, he viewed his career as a success. "This year makes 20 years," he told *The Jamaica Observer* in 2003. "And a lot of people have come and gone and [the fact that I'm still around] for me, that's a blessing within itself and I just look forward to another 20 years of doing what I'm doing and what I enjoy doing the most."

Selected discography

(With Stacy Lattisaw) *Perfect Combination*, Cotillion, 1983.
Johnny Gill, Atlantic, 1983.
Chemistry, Atlantic, 1985.
(With New Edition) *Heart Break*, MCA Records, 1988.
Johnny Gill, Motown, 1990.
Provocative, Motown, 1993.
Let's Get the Mood Right, Motown, 1996.
(With New Edition) *Home Again,* MCA Records, 1996.
(With Gerald Levert and Keith Sweat) *Levert.Sweat. Gill,* East West, 1997.
(With Gerald Levert and Keith Sweat) *LSG2,* Elektra, 2003.
The Best of Johnny Gill, Motown, 2003.
(With New Edition) *One Love,* Bad Boy Records, 2004.

Sources

Periodicals

Billboard, June 5, 1993.
The Cincinnati Post, October 24, 1996.
Entertainment Weekly, July 16, 1993.
Essence, October 1990.
Indianapolis Recorder, November 9, 1996.
Jet, November 15, 2004.
St. Louis Post-Dispatch, November 18, 2004.

On-line

"About.Johnny," *New Edition*, www.newedition20th. com (March 1, 2005).
"Johnny Gill & Music...A Perfect Combination," *The Jamaica Observer*, www.jamaicaobserver.com/life style/html/20030508T200000-0500_43512_OB S_JOHNNY_GILL___MUSIC.asp (March 1, 2005).

—Candace LaBalle

Jean Grae

1976—

Rapper

Grae, Jean, photograph. Getty Images.

From the moment she picked up the microphone in the early 1990s, hip-hop aficionados have proclaimed the genius of Jean Grae. Her in-your-face raps were fueled by literary lyrics and visceral imagery. Her rise to stardom seemed assured, but the limelight elu- ded her. Despite putting out several acclaimed albums and earning the respect of the most-respected of her rapping peers, Grae was still waiting for major success a decade into her career.

Raised from Musical Roots

Jean Grae was born Tsidi Ibrahim in Capetown, South Africa, in 1976 to Abdullah Ibrahim, a world-renowned jazz pianist, and Sathima Bea Benjamin, a jazz singer. Both of her parents traveled worldwide, performing with legends such as bandleader Duke Ellington. Regardless of their musical stature, Ibrahim and Benjamin were blacks during the dawning of apartheid in South Africa, and therefore second-class citizens. In protest, they joined the African National Congress (ANC)—the anti-apartheid party led by Nelson Mandela—but when the ANC was legally banned in 1960, the Ibrahims found themselves facing possible arrest. As oppression

increased, they decided to go into exile.

Grae and her family arrived in New York City in 1977. The Ibrahim household became a destination for both exiled South Africans and world-class musicians. "I grew up in a home full of music," Grae recalled on her Web site. As independent artists, both Ibrahim and Benjamin struggled to stay true to their musical identities while forging careers. "I remember [my mother] doing her press kits and taking me around to the pressing plants to press up her own records and start her own label, to be independent and make the music she wanted to do," Grae told *Jive Magazine*.

Grae's mother taught her to read by the age of three, setting off a life-long love of reading and writing. The cover photo for Grae's 2004 album, *This Week,* featured her surrounded by books, writing. Grae also began dance classes at a very young age. At 13, she became the youngest dancer ever to earn a spot with the Alvin Ailey Repertory Ensemble, the second company of the famed modern dance company, the Alvin Ailey American Dance Theatre. Meanwhile, Grae excelled in school, soaring through an advanced junior

At a Glance . . .

Born Tsidi Ibrahim in 1976, in Capetown, South Africa; took the name Jean Grae, 2000; daughter of Abdullah Ibrahim (jazz musician) and Sathima Bea Benjamim (jazz singer). *Education:* Attended New York University, music business, 1992.

Career: Rapper, producer, 1990s–; Group Zero, rap group member (as What? What?), 1990s; Natural Resource, rap group member, 1996-99; Makin' Records, co-founder and producer, 1996-99(?);

Awards: Plug Independent Music Awards, Female Artist of the Year, 2004.

Addresses: *Publicist*—Biz 3 Publicity, 1573 N. Milwaukee Ave., #452, Chicago, IL, 60622. *Web*—www.jean-grae.com.

high program and landing in the LaGuardia School of the Arts as a vocal major where she learned to read and arrange music. By the age of 16, she felt she had learned enough and, with her mother's support, she dropped out. After earning a GED, she took a six-month music engineering course and then enrolled in New York University as a music business major. After two months, Grae quit, telling herself, "I've lived this all my life…why is my family going to waste the money on this?," she recalled on her Web site.

Forged Career of Cameos

By her early teens, Grae had begun to hang out in New York's West Village, home to musicians, poets, and emcees. Grae recalled on her Web site that there were "beats everywhere," giving rise to some of rap's most respected performers, including Mos Def and Talib Kweli. In the early 1990s, Grae formed rap group Ground Zero and changed her name to What? What?. She left in 1996 to join Natural Resource. The group's self-produced 12-inch single "Negro League Baseball" went to number one on the college radio charts. The group also launched the record label Makin' Records and Grae produced tracks for local artists such as Pumpkinhead.

After Natural Resource broke up in 1999, Grae was determined to pursue a music career. "I wanted to start over and establish myself as a solo artist, and pretty much just as a grown woman," she told *Eye Weekly.* However Grae would not go solo just yet. Instead she earned the nickname "cameo queen." "I threw myself into any studio that I could get into for the next couple

of years, doing appearances whenever asked," she wrote on her Web site. In 2001 she recorded three tracks for the album *Pity the Fool* by Mr. Len. Though a commercial flop, the album was critically acclaimed. It was also a turning point for Grae. "Len's album gave me the push to stop waiting for that perfect song in my mind and just put myself out there," she wrote on her Web site.

During the years of appearing on other people's albums, Grae earned praise for inserting uniquely female perspectives into the gritty realm of testosterone-driven rap. "She was a protective lover on Masta Ace's 'Hold U'; a covert assassin on Immortal Technique's 'The Illest'; a chillingly rendered molestation victim turned psychopathic schoolyard killer in Mr. Len's epic 'Taco Day,'" wrote a reviewer for the *Minneapolis/St. Paul City Pages.* "With these characters, Grae demonstrated her ability to tell stories male MCs couldn't, lending a voice to the heavier elements of the female psyche that hip hop rarely ventured into."

Found Limited Recognition, Maximum Frustration

Early in 2000, Grae adopted the name Jean Grae, based on an X-Man comic book character who possessed telekinetic powers. Grae released her first solo album in 2002, *Attack of the Attacking Things.* Recorded in her tiny New York apartment in just two weeks, the album was rough around the mixes. Nonetheless the lyricism of the songs came through loud and clear. "What it lacks in flam and polish," wrote a *Village Voice* reviewer, "*Attack* makes up for with the determined and singular power of a compelling personal vision." The album struck a chord with those lucky enough to hear it, and despite no promotion, barely any radio play, and scant representation in even the most independent of record shops, *Attack* managed to sell over ten thousand copies.

Grae's way with words continued to impress on her second album, produced in 2003, *The Bootleg of the Bootleg.* "Grae's lyrical skills are deft in every sense of the word, period," wrote a reviewer for *Vibe.* The reviewer continued, "[Grae] employs tongue-twisting, gut-wrenching metaphors and with sheer ferocity declares that she's back on the scene with a vengeance." Grae also showed emotional diversity moving from the fury of "Hater's Anthem" to the soul-searching of "Take Me."

Grae described the album to *Vibe* as "dark." In it she lashed out against the recording industry and rap in particular. In the song "My Crew," she chanted, "Rap's dead, rap sucks, and thanks to y'all for killin' it // Grillin' it down and spillin' its guts and fillin' it back up with trash // Wait, I mean cash." It was a common theme for Grae. She felt immense anger at the recording industry for praising her music while at the same time refusing to represent her.

Poised to Become Future Rap Star

In 2003 Grae's career arced upwards. She did a successful tour with hip-hop heavyweights, The Roots. "It was incredible to get on the road and just be out there with so many talented people," Grae told *Prefix Magazine*. "[Having] a live band and hearing your music replayed. It just gives it a totally different feel, a totally different emotion." The following year Grae appeared on The Roots's hit album *The Tipping Point*.

Grae released *This Week* in 2004. A musical crawl through a week in Grae's life, it gained immediate praise in the urban culture press. In contrast to the hard-hitting venom of *Bootleg*, *This Week* featured danceable raps such as "Going Crazy" and tender tracks like "Supa Luv." However, her characteristic fury was still present in songs like "Whatever." Grae also used the album to apologize for the anger she had spat out for so long. Of the song "P.S." she told *Prefix Magazine*, "[It's about] the difference from the first two albums, which would be sort of holding a grudge and having more of a negative outlook on things and realizing that when you get older it doesn't pay to keep those feelings."

By 2005 Grae was busy touring, both as a headliner and with other artists. The venues were still small, the record sales still limp, and the struggle for recognition still uphill. Yet, there was hope. Her fourth album *Jeanius* received heavy pre-release buzz and Grae was voted Plug Independent Music Award's female artist of the year. After a decade of performing, Grae was still the next-big-thing, waiting to explode into mainstream, MTV consciousness. She was okay with that. "I've come to terms with the fact that no matter how many times I proclaim quitting, get frustrated with measly financial compensation for my work, or just plain hate what I do some days, this is what I was put here to do," she wrote on her Web site. "Music. It's the only thing that can bring the most beautiful or horribly ugly emotions out of me. Anything that can do that has got to be worth loving, worth fighting for and worth living passionately about."

Selected discography

Albums

Attack of the Attacking Things, Third Earth, 2002.
The Bootleg of the Bootleg, Babygrande, 2003.
This Week, Babygrande/Orchestral, 2004.

Sources

On-line

"Amazing Grae," *Eye Weekly,* www.eye.net/eye/issue/issue_05.15.03/thebeat/extended.html (March 11, 2005).
"Biography," *Jean Grae,* www.jean-grae.com (March 11, 2005).
"Grae's Anatomy," *Minneapolis/St. Paul City Pages,* www.citypages.com/databank/24/1194/article11599.asp (March 11, 2005).
"Jean Grae: Going Against the Grain," *Jive Magazine,* www.jivemagazine.com/article.php?pid=2281 (March 11, 2005).
"Jean Grae: Growing Pains," *Vibe,* www.vibe.com/modules.php?op=modload&name=News&file=article&sid=519 (March 11, 2005).
"Jean Grae, She Wants to Move," *Prefix Magazine,* www.prefixmag.com/features.php?t=interview&f=Jean_Grae_%20PartOne (March 11, 2005).
"Jean Grae X-ecutes the Competition," *Vibe,* www.vibe.com/modules.php?op=modload&name=News&file=article&sid=137 (March 11, 2005).
"Not Your Superwoman," *The Village Voice,* www.villagevoice.com/music/0238,allen,38392,22.html (March 11, 2005).

—Candace LaBalle

Frederick D. Gregory

1941—

Astronaut, NASA administrator

Colonel Frederick D. Gregory became the first black to pilot a space shuttle when he led the *Challenger* on a seven-day mission in 1985. As an astronaut he has spent more than 455 hours in outer space, and he commanded three major space missions from 1985 to 1991. Colonel Gregory was a decorated helicopter pilot during the Vietnam War and a jet test pilot prior to working with the National Aeronautics and Space Administration (NASA). From 2002 to 2005, Gregory held the second highest administration position, deputy administrator, with NASA. In 2005 he briefly rose to the top spot as acting administrator, becoming the first African American to lead NASA.

Possessing a relentless work ethic and exceptional versatility, Gregory has piloted a wide range of aircraft. Most unusual about his ascent to astronaut status was that he began his career as a helicopter pilot and only later made the switch to fixed-wing piloting, whereas most astronauts have begun their careers as jet pilots. "He does everything to the max," claimed Curtis M. Graves, the Deputy Director for Civil Affairs at NASA, in *Ebony*. "He flies aggressively [and] even hunts and fishes with unusual dedication."

An only child of two teachers, Fred Gregory grew up in an integrated neighborhood in Washington, D.C., and early learned the importance of education and hard work. He also received a healthy dose of religion from his paternal grandfather, who was a minister at a local Congregational church. Although Gregory's parents tried to protect him against demonstrations of racism, his father was a prime example of its effects. Francis A. Gregory was an electrical engineer who was limited to

teaching professions due to the prejudices of the day. Gregory's uncle, Charles Richard Drew, was a famous surgeon and pioneer in blood plasma production and preservation. Dr. Drew helped prove that there was no difference between white blood and black blood, but couldn't overcome resistance against putting the blood of one race into another.

Pursued Education and Adventure

"Oh, he was adventuresome," Nora Drew Gregory described her son to *Ebony*. The young Gregory developed an obsession with speed, an interest he apparently developed from his father. By age ten he was racing small boats off Columbia Beach in Maryland, near his home. He was also very active in his Boy Scout troop as a youth, an experience that helped stimulate his desire to pursue a military career.

Gregory was bussed across town to attend an all-black school until eighth grade, when schools in his town were integrated. The sacred status of education in the Gregory family was vividly demonstrated one day when students staged a boycott to protest the integration and townspeople said that they would remove black children from the school. The young Gregory attended anyway and was the only student to show up for his class. Despite facing taunts from white students while in high school, Gregory did well and during that time further developed his interest in entering the military service. After becoming a member of the Junior Reserve Officers' Training Corps (ROTC), he was introduced to military aircraft during visits to nearby

Andrews Air Force Base in Maryland and was soon hooked on flying.

In the 1950s Gregory met a member of the Thunderbirds, an Air Force acrobatic flying team, who told him about the new United States Air Force Academy about to open its doors in Colorado Springs, Colorado. Gregory was interested, but decided to stay with family tradition and apply to Amherst College, where his grandfather had attended. Luckily, his father intervened to help the young man do what he loved. Against the odds, the elder Gregory persuaded U.S. Representative Adam Clayton Powell of Harlem to sponsor his son's application. When Fred Gregory enrolled in the U.S. Air Force Academy in the early 1960s, he was the only black in his class. Occasional resistance against his presence on campus did not affect his performance, however, and he excelled as a cadet, student, and athlete. Gregory graduated from the academy in 1964, in a class that produced 25 generals.

Upon graduation, Gregory hoped to become a teacher of military history at the academy or an engineer, but he opted for helicopter flight training at Stead Air Force Base in Nevada because he thought his subsequent assignments would be more pleasing to his wife. He was given his wings in 1965, and after serving as helicopter rescue pilot at Vance Air Force Base in Oklahoma, was shipped to Vietnam to serve as a combat rescue pilot. His primary duties as pilot of an H-43 helicopter in Vietnam were search and rescue and fire suppression. Gregory was awarded a Distinguished Flying Cross in 1967 for rescuing four Marines from a downed helicopter during intense enemy fire.

Tested Cutting-Edge Aircraft

After flying 550 combat missions during a year of distinguished service in Vietnam, Gregory spent the next part of his career learning to fly and test the most advanced aircraft operated by the U.S. armed forces. Gregory flew the UH-1F missile support helicopter in Missouri, and F-4 Phantom Combat jets in Texas, before becoming a U.S. Navy test pilot at the Patuxent River Naval Air Station in Maryland. After his test pilot training, he was assigned to the 4950th Test Wing at Wright Patterson Air Force Base in Ohio as an operational test pilot flying both jet fighters and helicopters. In 1974 he took on a temporary duty assignment as a research test pilot at the NASA Langley Research Center in Virginia. Gregory returned to Vietnam in 1975 during the American evacuation to fly refugees from the American embassy in Saigon to carriers offshore.

By 1977 Gregory had grown tired of being a test pilot and was eager to move on to something else. At this time NASA announced that it was recruiting new astronauts, and he applied without delay. At first the Air Force was reluctant to submit Gregory's application to NASA, since most of his experience was in piloting helicopters rather than high-performance jets. Intent on fulfilling the dream of flying in outer space he had nurtured since he was a teenager, Gregory was prepared to resign his commission in order to be accepted by NASA. In 1978 he was one of 35 candidates accepted and, along with Guy Bluford and Ron McNair, became one of the first American black astronauts to enter the NASA program.

By August of 1979, Gregory had successfully undergone training and evaluation that qualified him to serve as a pilot on space shuttle crews. For the next four years he worked in a variety of capacities for NASA, including a stint in the Shuttle Avionics Integration Laboratory, until he was assigned to pilot the *Challenger* on the Spacelab 3 mission that took off in April of 1985. Gregory led a seven-man crew that performed medical and materials processing experiments during a week of round-the-clock scientific operations. Satellite deployments were also carried out during the flight.

First Black to Pilot American Spacecraft

Although he was the third black to fly into outer space, Gregory was the first to pilot an American spacecraft. He was tremendously moved by his first voyage beyond the earth's atmosphere, and for him it was a highly religious experience. According to *They Had a Dream: The Story of African-American Astronauts*, Gregory said, "when you're in space and you're looking down at earth and you see this perfect globe beneath you and you see the organization and non-chaos, you have to feel, as I did, that there was one great Being—one great force that made this happen." The astronaut was quoted in *Ebony* as saying: "From our vantage in space, we couldn't help but redefine the world, where we all are part of a whole global entity, based on the absence of political and arbitrary boundaries on planet Earth."

Following his maiden flight in outer space, Gregory served as mission control lead spacecraft communicator (CAPCOM) for subsequent flights of the space shuttle. He was communicating with the crew of the shuttle *Challenger* during its tragic flight in January of 1986. In November of 1989, he was appointed spacecraft commander of the orbiter *Discovery* on its five-day flight and both piloted and landed the spacecraft. Gregory directed deployment of the shuttle's classified Department of Defense cargo and other payloads during its 79 orbits of earth. Next, Gregory took the helm for the orbiter *Atlantis* in November of 1991. The *Atlantis* was used to deploy the Defense Support Program (DSP) missile-warning satellite, and it also conducted other military-related operations. Once this mission was completed, Gregory's total time in outer space surpassed 455 hours.

In April of 1992 Gregory became Associate Administrator in the Office of Safety and Mission Quality at NASA Headquarters in Washington, D.C. When he retired as Air Force colonel in 1993, he had logged approximately 7,000 hours of flying time in more than 50 types of aircraft. A highly decorated pilot who has flown everything from helicopters and gliders to jet fighters and spacecraft, Colonel Frederick Gregory has made his mark as a major figure in American space travel during the space shuttle era. In 2002, U.S. President George W. Bush nominated him to be the associate administrator of NASA; the Senate confirmed his posting and he served faithfully until stepping in as acting administrator in 2005. As hearings for the permanent administrator of NASA continued, Gregory managed NASA with characteristic diligence and vision. He returned to his post as deputy administrator on April 14, 2005, when Michael Griffin was confirmed for NASA's top position. Named one of the fifty most important blacks in technology, Gregory remained committed to promoting the U.S. space program.

Sources

Books

Phelps, J. Alfred, *They Had a Dream: The Story of African-American Astronauts*, Presidio Press, 1994.

Periodicals

Ebony, May 1990, pp. 78-82.
Jet, November 20, 1989, p. 23; July 30, 1990, p. 15; July 15, 1991, p. 26; November 29. 2004, p. 46; March 21, 2005, p. 6.
New York Times, November 25, 1991, p. A-7.
Popular Mechanics, April 2003, p. 16.
Washington Post, December 5, 1991, p. A-22; April 29, 1992, p. A-21.

On-line

*NASA,*www.nasa.gov (April 28, 2005).

—Ed Decker and Sara Pendergast

LaShell Griffin

Singer

1967—

LaShell Griffin, a stay-at-home mother of five, devoted wife, and devout Christian who loves to sing in the church choir, once told her children that one day she would appear on *The Oprah Winfrey Show*. She did not know how or why, but she believed it would happen. In the fall of 2003 Griffin's dream came true when she was selected as one of the finalists in Winfrey's Pop Star Challenge. After several performances on the show during February 2004, Griffin was voted the contest's winner, earning her a record deal with Epic Records. Her first album, *Free*, was released in May 2004.

From Housewife to Celebrity

Lashell Griffin was born in 1967 and raised in Detroit, Michigan. Even as a young child she knew that music would be an important part of her life. She learned to sing from her grandmother, who was an influential person in Griffin's life until her death in 2003. At the age of nine Griffin yearned to sing in her church's choir, and when she finally reached the required age of 13, she eagerly joined the choir and regularly performed solos. Despite her obvious vocal talent and the positive response from the congregation, Griffin was frightfully shy about performing in front of people. "I started off holding my head down when I sang," she wrote on her official Web site. "Then I started looking at the ceiling, then the clock on the wall in front of me. Finally, I just started singing with my eyes closed so I could tune out everything and everyone and just deliver."

By her early thirties, Griffin's love of music was sharing the stage in her busy life as a stay-at-home mother to five children. At the age of 18, Griffin had married Lee Griffin, also a talented singer, and set up house in Detroit, where they began raising their children, Levotis, Raphael, LeSahe, Nathan, and Briana. Music is a family affair as all the Griffin children sing, and Levotis, the oldest, began studying music at Michigan State University in 2004. Despite her many family responsibilities, Griffin, encouraged by her husband, continued to sing in the church choir, and her beautiful solos garnered numerous requests for her to perform at weddings. In fact, Griffin became such a popular wedding singer that she was often performing at two or three weddings each weekend, and her pastor had to be enlisted to help manage her scheduling.

In the fall of 2003 Griffin's hectic life was necessarily slowed down after she broke her foot, which required surgery. While watching television during her recovery, Griffin happened to catch *The Oprah Winfrey Show* during which Winfrey called on the audience to send in tapes to enter the first-ever The Oprah Winfrey Pop Star Challenge. Griffin wrote down the information but then waited a couple of weeks before mentioning the idea to her husband. "I had been down for at least four weeks from the surgery and I realized that it was a lot on him with work and taking care of the home," she told the Gospel City Web site. "I said I really, really want to do this and I decided to share it with him and he said 'Go for it.' I was blown away by that response because I would have understood if he said it wasn't the season

At a Glance . . .

Born in 1967 in Detroit, Michigan; married Lee Griffin; children: Levotis, Raphael, LeSahe, Nathan, and Briana.

Career: Homemaker; professional pop, gospel, and R&B singer, 2004–.

Awards: The Oprah Winfrey Pop Star Challenge, winner, 2004.

Addresses: *Record Label*—Epic Records, 550 Madison Ave New York, NY 10022; *Agent*—Covenant Entertainment, (586) 498-9074; *Web*—www.lashellgriffinmusic.com.

for it, just take care of your foot and let's see what happens after that."

The Pop Star Challenge

With her husband's help, Griffin made a recording of a heart-felt rendition of "Amazing Grace" at their church and sent the tape to *The Oprah Winfrey Show*. Eight days later, as Griffin was pulling into the driveway after picking her husband up from work, the telephone was ringing. Much to Griffin's surprise and excitement, it was a producer for *The Oprah Winfrey Show* calling to tell her that she had been selected from over 15,000 entries as one of eight semifinalists. Later she found out that she was not in the original finalist list but producers went back, reviewed the tapes once more, and ended up selecting hers.

In a whirlwind of activity, producers came to Griffin's house, interviewed her and her family, went to church with them, and eventually invited Griffin to perform on the show. On February 9, 2004, after several days of rehearsals, makeovers, and voice coaching, Griffin made her first appearance on the show, singing "Where Do Broken Hearts Go." According to the rules of the contest, celebrity judges comment on the performances but voting is done by the viewing audience via the internete and telephone. Following her opening performance, celebrity judge Brian McKnight told Griffin, "That was one of the sweetest voices I've ever heard," as quoted on the Oprah Web site.

Surviving the cut to the three finalists, Griffin performed again on the show on February 16, this time singing "The Greatest Love of All." Her performance was met with unanimous praise by the panel of expert judges. Simon Cowell of FOX's *American Idol* fame said, "I thought you were absolutely fantastic. What you

have, you feel it all around you, the public already has bought into you. And you are the argument why older singers deserve a chance in a competition like this," according to the Oprah Web site. The audience agreed, and when the votes were tallied, Griffin was announced as the first Pop Star Challenge winner and was awarded a recording contract with Epic Records.

Recorded Her First Album

On the heels of her exciting win, Griffin entered the studio to put together her first album, *Free*, which was released on May 25, 2004. She had exactly nine days to cut the ten songs. "The songs that were chosen were so close to my heart," she told *Christianity Today*. "I fought hard to get those particular songs on the album because one thing I've always wanted to do was to bridge the gaps. There's such segregation between Christian music and gospel music and inspirational music and pop music. I've always wanted to bring that all together."

Free, which debuted at No. 2 on the Billboard Top Gospel Albums charts and earned positive reviews, blends contemporary R&B, pop, and gospel in its offerings. The first cut, "You Are Mine," a soulful R&B mix in the tradition of Patti LaBelle, is followed by the title track, "Free." The Soultracks Web site reviewer noted, "Griffin is at her finest…on the album's title cut, a fairly ordinary ballad that is absolutely lifted up by her explosive performance." She also received praise for her rendition of MercyMe's "I Can Only Imagine" as well as for "Faith," a gospel-styled duet with her husband. The album also included "Learn to Breathe," co-written by Griffin, "This Is Who I Am," "Better Days," "Get Away," "Rise," and "He's Coming Again." Griffin promoted *Free* in a nine-city tour, "Touch a Dream." Some critics, including All Music Guide's Heather Phares, felt the album suffered somewhat from overproduction and weak songwriting that did not allow Griffin the freedom to let her dynamic voice to deliver at its full potential. Despite her reservations, Phares noted in her review, "Griffin clearly has the voice and the 'faith' to make a show-stopping gospel album."

In many ways life has changed significantly for Griffin, who was treated as a celebrity on her return to Detroit after winning the contest. Yet, she continues to focus on her role as a wife and mother and has even maintained her place on the cleaning committee at her church. She told the Music Remedy Web site that, "I always wanted my mission in life to be to spread the messages that are important to me. I knew that I was a good wife and a good mother. But I also knew there would be much more in store for me. I was right. And I hope my music will inspire others to look deeply into their hearts and soul and find out what they are meant to do. Because everyone has their season. And this is mine." Griffin continues to perform in a variety of events and venues as well as remaining active in her church and with her family.

Selected discography

Albums

Free, Epic Records, 2004.

Sources

Periodicals

Billboard, July 31, 2004.
Jet, March 15, 2004, p. 62.
O, The Oprah Magazine, May 2004, p. 70.

On-line

"LaShell Griffin," *All Music Guide,* www.allmusic.com /cg/amg.dll?p=amg&searchlink=LASHELL | GRIF FIN&uid=CAW010502181134&sql=11:8b7tk6ax tkr3~T0 (Feb-ruary 18, 2005).
"LaShell Griffin," *E.O.M.: Evolution of Media,* http: //www.eomentertainment.com/reviews/LaShell_ Griffin/Free.shtml (February 18, 2005).

"LaShell Griffin," *GospelCity,* www.gospelcity.com/ dynamic/artist-articles/interviews/128 (February 18, 2005).
"LaShell Griffin" [radio interview], *HJ's Praise Party,* www.gospel-spotlight.com/lashell_griffin_intvw.htm (February 18, 2005).
"LaShell Griffin," *NewsBeats,* www.newsbeats.com/ lashell (February 18, 2005).
"LaShell Griffin," *Soul Tracks,* www.soultracks.com/ lashell_griffin.htm (February 18, 2005).
"LaShell Griffin: *Free,*" *Christianity Today,* www. christianitytoday.com/music/reviews/2004/free. html (February 18, 2005).
LaShell Griffin Official Web Site, www.lashellgriffin-music.com (February 18, 2005).
"Mom in Pop," *Christianity Today,* www.christianity today.com/music/interviews/2004/lashellgriffin-06 04.html (February 2005).
"Oprah Presents LaShell Griffin," *MusicRemedy,* www.musicremedy.com/articles/index.cfm?FuseAc tion=ShowMessage&Id=693 (February 18, 2005).
"Pop Star Challenge: LaShell Griffin," *Oprah,* www. oprah.com/presents/2004/popstar/contest/pop_ contest_05.jhtml (February 18, 2005).

—Kari Bethel

Calvin Hernton

1932-2001

Social critic, poet, novelist

Though less well known than some of his African-American contemporaries, Calvin Hernton was a writer who stood at the center of several of the cultural developments during the Vietnam War era. Hernton's groundbreaking *Sex and Racism in America* (1965) was a frank look at the role sexual tensions played in the American racial divide, and it helped set the tone for much African-American social criticism over the following decade. His expansive, ambitious poetry was widely read, and he shaped a younger generation of black thinkers after becoming a professor of literature at Oberlin College in 1970s. An original thinker, Calvin Hernton has been underappreciated for his role in stirring the cultural ferment of the 1960s and 1970s.

Calvin Coolidge Hernton was born in Chattanooga, Tennessee, on April 28, 1932. Raised mostly by his grandmother, he attended Talladega College in Alabama, graduating in 1954. He went on for a master's in sociology at Fisk University in Nashville, writing his thesis about letters to the editor and newspaper editorials that had appeared in the wake of the Montgomery, Alabama, bus boycott spearheaded by Rosa Parks two years earlier.

Worked in Welfare Office

After finishing his master's degree, Hernton held a series of one-year teaching appointments at small, historically black Southern colleges and universities: Benedict College in Columbia, South Carolina, in 1957-58, Alabama A&M College (now University) in 1958-59, Edward Waters College in Jacksonville,

Florida, in 1959-60, and Southern University in Baton Rouge, Louisiana, in 1960-61. He married Mildred Webster in 1958, and the couple had one son, Antone. Filled with growing literary ambitions, he headed for New York City in 1961 (he had already lived there briefly in 1956 and 1957) and took a job as a social worker with the New York State welfare department. During this period, Hernton interviewed black and white co-workers in both the South and North, gathering material for what would become *Sex and Racism in America*.

Hernton also wrote poetry, some of which was anthologized in the 1962 collection *Beyond the Blues: New Poems by American Negroes*. In 1963 he was one of the founders of *Umbra,* a New York literary magazine that nurtured the careers of writers such as Alice Walker and Ishmael Reed as well as publishing new works by established writers. Hernton himself was an impressive figure as he read his own poems in the circles that developed around the publication. "He reached zones that we in the *Umbra* Workshop were then only moving towards," poet Joe Johnson told the *Oberlin Review*. "We all wanted to make fierce personal statements. Hernton was there.... We heard Hernton singing what we were talking about." Hernton's "Jitterbugging in the Streets," a long poem on the theme of white indifference to violence against blacks, was widely reprinted and was read by Hernton with a jazz accompaniment on the Folkways-label album *New Jazz Poets*.

In 1965, *Sex and Racism in America* was issued by the major Doubleday publishing house. That book, which was eventually translated into seven languages, had a unique status somewhere between sociological text and crusading polemic. "There is a sexual involvement, at once real and vicarious, connecting white and black people in America that spans the history of this country from the era of slavery to the present," Hernton wrote. With the oppressive system of slavery and its aftermath as a backdrop, Hernton divided his study into four parts, exploring the sexual psychologies of black men, black women, white men, and white women, respectively.

Traced Sexual Tensions to Slavery

"No writer I have come across except Hernton has had the temerity to so frankly tackle that old bugaboo S-E-X as it relates to life, liberty, and the pursuit of integration," black poet Langston Hughes was quoted as saying in the *Chicago Tribune.* Hernton explored the motivations of members of each of his four categories; white women reacted to their own oppressed status, Hernton argued (for example), by simultaneously becoming attracted to black men and taking out their own frustrations upon them. White male slave owners,

Hernton contended, created a myth of perfect Southern white womanhood, with the result that they both stereotyped black men as potential sexual predators and turned to slave women to satisfy their own needs.

Hernton's ideas were controversial. "Many people were outraged by that book," Ishmael Reed told Margalit Fox of the *New York Times.* "He went into a section of the American experience that you were not supposed to talk about." But Hernton's theories were amply buttressed by his numerous interviews, and the book became widely read and discussed. The sexual themes of later books by militant black writers, such as Eldridge Cleaver's *Soul on Ice,* may well have been influenced by Hernton's work. Hernton followed up *Sex and Racism in America* with a collection of sociological essays, *White Papers for White Americans.*

With talk about his ideas in full swing, Hernton made a 90-degree turn that was characteristic of his curiosity and varied interests: he headed for London, England, and studied there for four years with the radical psychologist R.D. Laing. This period of time bore literary fruit in a series of writings that Hernton later penned on the subject of drug use, and also in the novel *Scarecrow,* a violent and surreal tale set in the middle of a transatlantic voyage. Back in the United States in 1970, Hernton spent a year as poet-in-residence at Ohio's Central State University in Wilberforce.

Mentored Avery Brooks

The following year, Hernton was hired as writer-in-residence at Oberlin College in Ohio, and in 1973 he became professor of black studies and creative writing there. The post was beneficial both for Hernton, who found that the position gave him newfound stability, and for his students, who included future *Star Trek: Deep Space Nine* star Avery Brooks. In the 1980s, Hernton carried mentorship to a new level by writing television scripts for another Brooks series, *A Man Called Hawk.*

Hernton also published several books over the course of his teaching career at Oberlin. *Scarecrow* was issued in 1974, as was *The Cannabis Experience: The Study of the Effects of Marijuana and Hashish. Medicine Man,* a collection of his poetry, appeared in 1976. In 1987 Doubleday published Hernton's *Sexual Mountains and Black Women Writers: Adventures in Sex, Literature, and Real Life.* That book was again ahead of the curve; Hernton explored the reactions of African-American women writers to abusive treatment, and his work was praised by members of the growing black feminist movement.

Remaining active at Oberlin until his retirement in 1999, Hernton wrote a new book of poems, *The Red Crab Gang and Black River Poems,* served as illustrator for *Muntu,* a book about African culture, and collaborated in editing a collection of stories by author Chester Himes. In 2000 he participated in a major conference on hip-hop music that was held at Oberlin. He died of cancer at his home on October 1, 2001, survived by his wife Mary, whom he had married after the death of his first wife in 1982. Although *Sex and Race in America* remained his best-known work, he thought of himself as a poet first and foremost.

Selected writings

Fiction

(Contributor) LeRoi Jones and Larry Neal, editors, *Black Fire: An Anthology of Afro-American Writing*, Morrow, 1969.
Scarecrow (novel), Doubleday, 1974.

Nonfiction

Sex and Racism in America, Doubleday, 1965.
White Papers for White Americans, Doubleday, 1966.
Coming Together: Black Power, White Hatred, and Sexual Hangups, Random House, 1971.
(Contributor) D. L. Grummon and A. M. Barclay, eds., *Sexuality: A Search for Perspective*, Van Nostrand, 1971.
(With Joseph Berke) *The Cannabis Experience: The Study of the Effects of Marijuana and Hashish*, Humanities, 1974.

Poetry

(Contributor) Rosey E. Pool, ed., *Beyond the Blues: New Poems by American Negroes*, Hand & Flower Press, 1962.

The Coming of Chronos to the House of Nightsong: An Epical Narrative of the South, Interim, 1963.
Medicine Man, Reed, Cannon, & Johnson, 1976.
The Red Crab Gang and Black River Poems, Reed, Cannon, & Johnson, 1999.

Other

Glad to Be Dead (play), 1958.
Flame (play), 1958.
The Place (play), 1972.
(Illustrator) *Muntu: African Culture and the Western World*, Grove Press, 1991.

Sources

Books

Davis, Thadious M., ed., *Dictionary of Literary Biography, Volume 38: Afro-American Writers After 1955: Dramatists and Prose Writers*, Gale, 1985.

Periodicals

Chicago Tribune, October 17, 2001, p. 9.
New York Times, October 10, 2001, p. D8.
Oberlin Alumni Magazine, Summer 2002.
Oberlin Review, May 7, 1999.
Plain Dealer (Cleveland, OH), April 14, 2000, p. Friday-22; October 4, 2001, p. B7.

On-line

"Calvin Hernton," *Biography Resource Center*, http://galenet.galegroup.com/servlet/BioRC (February 28, 2005).

—James M. Manheim

Jamelia

1981—

Singer

First-name-only diva Jamelia has scored some impressive chart hits in Britain, where the Birmingham native is one of her country's biggest pop stars. Often referred to as "the British Beyoncé"—a nod to her similarly glamorous American soul-diva counterpart—the young singer burst onto the charts in early 2000 with the song "Money," which landed in the top five on the UK pop charts. Jamelia, just 19 at the time, was hailed as "the homegrown, street credible R&B diva that Britain had been waiting for," noted the London *Observer*'s Kitty Empire.

Born Jamelia Niela Davis on January 2, 1981, the future star is of Jamaican heritage and grew up in the Midlands city of Birmingham, one of the most culturally diverse urban centers in England. She was raised by her mother, Paulette, in a single-parent household that also included two younger half-brothers. Though Jamelia loved to sing with her karaoke machine at home, she had little interest in pursuing music as a career and contemplated becoming a child psychologist instead. When she was 15 years old, Jamelia went to a local carnival, where her aunt encouraged her to take the stage for a karaoke event. Her impressive performance was noticed by a record-company scout who was in the crowd. Some time later she sent in a demo tape that she had done at home with the help of her karaoke machine. It landed at the label offices of Parlophone, a division of music-industry giant EMI, which promptly signed her to a development deal.

Scored British Chart Hits

Jamelia spent the next few years honing her vocal talents, and her first single, "So High," was released in 1999. She was also an accomplished songwriter by then, and co-wrote every track on her debut album, *Drama*. The album was a terrific success in Britain, with four songs from it making it into the UK Top 40, but it was the third single, "Money," that made the singer a household name throughout Britain. Co-written with British producer C Swing, who had worked with artists ranging from Mary J. Blige to the Beta Band, the song featured a solo from Jamaican reggae star Beenie Man and was termed "brilliantly histrionic," asserted *Guardian* critic Maxine Kabuubi. That same article also noted the range of tracks on Jamelia's debut, finding "One Day" the singer's "attempt to compete in the overheated American R&B market. Stripped down to just a lilting guitar, the song pushes her vocals to the fore, heightening the quality and purity of her voice," Kabuubi noted.

In October of 2000, Jamelia and the "Money" video won a prestigious Mobo Award, short for "Music of Black Origins," the premier industry event showcasing black music in Britain. Days later, the country's tabloid newspapers reported that the 19-year-old singer was expecting a baby. By then, she was already four months along, and she had been too afraid to tell her Parlophone bosses, fearing they might drop her from the label altogether. In the end, news of her pregnancy was leaked to the media, and the record company

At a Glance . . .

Born Jamelia Niela Davis on January 2, 1981, in Birmingham, England; daughter of Paulette Davis; children: Teja (daughter).

Career: EMI/Parlophone, recording artist, 1996(?)–; model, 2004–.

Awards: Mobo Award (Music of Black Origin), best video, 2000, for "Money"; Mobo Award, 2004, for "See It in a Boy's Eyes"; Mobo Award, for best single, 2004, for "Thank You."

Addresses: *Office*—c/o EMI/Parlophone, 43 Brook Green, London W6 7EF England. *Home*—Wolverhampton, England.

found out about the same way Jamelia's fans did—in a headline. When they called her to ask about it, "I was crying my eyes out," the singer told *Sunday Times* journalist Dan Cairns. "I was literally saying goodbye to them. At the time, I was, like: 'How and why did this possibly happen?' I was taking precautions and everything, but I still got pregnant. Then I got a call from the head of the label, and he said: 'Don't think that we're letting you go. We really want you, and whenever you're ready to come back, just let us know.'"

Jamelia's daughter Teja, named for a combination of Jamelia's name and that of the baby's father, Terry, was born in March of 2001. She virtually disappeared from the public eye for the next two years, returning first as an opening act for Justin Timberlake on his tour of the United Kingdom in May of 2003. Her comeback single, "Bout," was traditional R&B fare and featured a guest appearance from rapper Rah Digga, but failed to do well on the charts. Her next one, however, made up for it: "Superstar" was a disco-glittery tune released in the fall of 2003 that was a hit in both the United Kingdom and Europe. It even migrated across the Atlantic, landing on the official soundtrack to the highly rated A&E television show *Queer Eye for the Straight Guy.*

No Longer a Victim

"Superstar" appeared on *Thank You*, Jamelia's second full-length release. The album peaked at No. 4 on British charts, but it was the title song that surpassed even the success of "Superstar." The torchy ballad, which reached No. 2 on the singles charts, chronicles the end of an abusive relationship, and Jamelia admitted publicly that her longtime romance with Teja's

father had been the source for the song's inspiration. In "Thank You," she expresses gratitude for her bruises, reflecting that they guided her, in the end, to a place of inner strength. "You broke my world [and] made me strong," she sings in it. Cairns, writing in the *Sunday Times*, compared it to disco diva Gloria Gaynor's enduring 1979 female-empowerment hit "I Will Survive," and called the song "one of those (very) rare examples of a lyric shot through with torment being married to an undislodgeable melody—and ripping up the charts."

In interviews Jamelia carefully explained that she had parted ways with her former boyfriend, a music promoter also from Birmingham, when Teja was just a few weeks old. "Because, when it was just me, it was my choice to be there: I could have walked out at any time," she told Marianne Macdonald of the *Evening Standard*. "When it happened when my daughter was there, I was making that choice for her, and what kind of mother was I to make her stay in this household?"

For a young woman who had once feared that her career was over at the age of 20, Jamelia had a stunning year in 2004. She completed her first tour as a headliner, and co-wrote a song with Chris Martin of Coldplay, "See It in a Boy's Eyes," that won her another Mobo that fall; "Thank You" also won for best single of the year. She signed with a modeling agency run by British supermodel Naomi Campbell—to whom the almond-eyed Jamelia has sometimes been compared—and landed a lucrative endorsement deal with athletic-gear maker Reebok. Still hoping to crack the American market, she was spending more time in Los Angeles and working with American songwriter Diane Warren, the hitmaker who boosted the fortunes of Whitney Houston and Aerosmith, and was considering taking some film roles. Certainly Jamelia's career had just begun.

Linked romantically with British soccer player Darren Byfield, Jamelia lives in a house in Wolverhampton, England. Her two half-brothers fared less well in life: one was stabbed to death and the other charged in a case involving the deaths of two Birmingham women in 2002. The singer remained thankful for all that life has given her, as she told Cairns in another interview for the *Sunday Times*: in late 2004, she participated in the new Band Aid charity project, a 20th anniversary reprise of Bob Geldof's original fundraising effort for famine victims in Ethiopia. For the new single, an all-star line-up of pop and rock stars was once more assembled, and Jamelia was among them when Geldof showed the group some film footage before they started to record it. "And there was a little three-year-old girl in this field of dying people, and she could hardly walk," Jamelia told Cairns. "I was thinking, 'This girl is the same age as my daughter, Teja.' Then they brought out the girl who was on that film, and she's now 23, which is the age I am. So many things hit me in the space of a few minutes. Before that day, I would have said I wasn't privileged when I was younger. I was incredibly privileged: I had a house, I had food and water every day, I was getting an education."

Selected discography

Recordings

Drama, EMI/Parlophone, 2000.
Thank You, EMI/Parlophone, 2003.

Sources

Periodicals

Evening Standard (London, England), December 10, 2004, p. 15.
Guardian (London, England), June 23, 2000, p. 11.
Independent Sunday (London, England), August 27, 2000, p. 8.
Observer (London, England), June 13, 2004, p. 12.
Sunday Times (London, England), March 7, 2004, p. 6; December 19, 2004, p. 4.

—Carol Brennan

Donna A. James

1957—

Corporate executive

Plenty of hard work, combined with her superior business and entrepreneurial skills, enabled Donna A. James, once a single, teenage mother, to climb the corporate ladder to become the first black woman executive at Nationwide, one of the country's largest insurance and financial services companies. From her position as vice president of human resources for Nationwide in 1996, through her appointment as president of Nationwide Strategic Investments in 2003, James was the first African American in the company to hold each of her titles, as well as the first African American to sit on the corporation's executive committee. She also was the first to head an operating division of this Fortune 500 company. She reported directly to two successive chief executive officers (CEOs). Her position at Nationwide enabled James to advocate for diversity throughout the corporate world.

Attended College as a Single Mother

Donna Anita Scott was born on June 30, 1957, in Washington, D.C. Although her mother, Bertha (Searles) Scott, had a high school education, her father, Herbert Scott, was illiterate, having only attended school through the third grade. Bertha Scott taught her husband to write his name. After a long career as a driver for a bus company, Herbert Scott opened his own successful car wash and reconditioning business.

When she was six years old, Donna Scott's parents divorced. Donna, her three siblings, and her mother moved to Greensboro, North Carolina. Although she remained close to her father—who remarried and had another child—Donna lived in Greensboro with her mother and grandmother through her college years. Bertha Scott married Paul Hawkins, with whom she had two more children. In all Donna Scott has five brothers and one sister. Bertha Hawkins worked as a lab assistant in a textile factory until her retirement.

As a child, Donna loved the chemistry set that she received for Christmas and was fairly certain that she wanted to become a chemist. But her interests were wide-ranging. She liked to make things, she loved math, and she loved to read. She also loved being in charge and organizing people. Throughout her school years she was a leader in sports and student government.

As a single mother of a young son, Christopher Michael, Scott attended North Carolina A&T State University in Greensboro. Although she considered becoming an engineer, the accounting department offered her more scholarship money than the engineering school. With her bachelor's degree in accounting and as a certified public accountant (CPA), James procured an auditing position with the large accounting firm of Coopers & Lybrand in Columbus, Ohio.

Joined Nationwide Insurance

In 1981 Scott was recruited as an accounting specialist by Nationwide, based in Columbus. She became a one-woman accounting and finance office for Nationwide's first heath maintenance organization (HMO). Over the following decade she moved rapidly up the corporate ladder, holding various management positions in accounting operations and compliance and in annuities, pensions, and mutual-fund operations for Nationwide's tax-shelter-products division.

In 1989 Donna Scott married Larry James, an attorney and later a full partner with Crabbe, Brown, & James in Columbus. Larry James's son, Justin Michael, was the same age as Christopher Michael, and they formed a close-knit family of four.

Donna James was named director of operations and treasury services in 1990. In 1993 she became executive assistant to Nationwide's chairman and CEO, Dimon R. McFerson. In this position she was exposed to the management of all of Nationwide's business divisions. Three years later she was named vice president of the human resources (HR) division.

Headed Human Resources

James was promoted to senior vice president and chief human resources officer in 1998, with responsibility for 290 employees and a $35-million budget. The following year she spoke with Dawn M. Baskerville of *Essence* magazine about her work: "My division oversees compensation, training and development, recruiting and staffing, benefits, executive development, EEOC compliance, and organizational management for the corporation's more than 27,000 employees. Understanding how a company works as well as the people who drive it are essential skills for effective HR management."

In 1998 James announced that Nationwide Insurance Enterprise would make a four-year $600,000 investment in the College Fund/UNCF (United Negro College Fund), a nonprofit consortium that raised money for historically-black colleges and universities. The Nationwide-funded scholars program provided scholarships, internships, and mentorships for undergraduate students in business management, financial services, and administrative sciences. James was quoted in the *PR Newswire*: "We are pleased about the opportunity to bring students into our company where they can learn first hand and help us build long-term partnerships with UNCF schools across the country.... This program will help to fulfill our mutual goal of preparing students for the changing workforce of the next century."

The Nationwide board of directors appointed James executive vice president and chief administrative officer in July of 2000. A consolidation put her in charge of corporate communications, human resources, information technology, and the Nationwide Services Company that included corporate real estate and philanthropy.

In 2001 James represented American business leaders in joining with National Urban League President Hugh Price to call on colleges and universities to de-emphasize standardized tests—such as the Scholastic Aptitude Test (SAT)—in college admissions. Such tests had proved to be a barrier to college admissions for talented black and other minority students. The Urban League commissioned a survey of top business executives to evaluate the importance of such tests in identifying future corporate leaders. James was quoted in *Black Issues in Higher Education*: "Long-term success is determined by an individual's ability to solve problems creatively," rather than by the results of standardized tests.

Elected President of Nationwide Strategic Investments

James became president of Nationwide Strategic Investments in 2003, overseeing several of Nationwide's businesses including GatesMcDonald, Nationwide Advantage Mortgage Company, Nationwide Health Plans, Nationwide Global Holdings—the corporation's international arm—and Nationwide Mutual Capital. The latter business was Nationwide's $150-million venture capital division. James told *Contemporary Black Biography* that the purpose of Nationwide Mutual Capital was to develop and incubate new ideas, innovations, and businesses involved in financial services. The division developed innovative ideas and started new businesses, as well as investing in existing businesses. As examples, James cited "real life" problems that Mutual Capital was trying to address: individual healthcare costs, planning for healthcare in retirement, and innovative means of turning a home into a realizable asset, given that most people's major asset is their home.

James served on numerous corporate and nonprofit boards. In 2001 she joined the board of directors and the audit committee of Intimate Brands, Inc. (IBI). She served as chair of the special committee on recombining IBI with Limited Brands, the Columbus-based retailer and parent company of IBI. In 2003 she joined the Limited Brands board of directors and the audit committee. James also served as a board member of the Ohio College Access Network and was a member of the Columbus chapter of Links, Inc. From 1995 until 2000, James was a member of the board of trustees of the Wexner Foundation. In 2001 she was awarded the DeVry Spirit of Advocacy award for her work as an advocate for high-school women in science and technology.

James told Baskerville of *Essence* magazine in 1999: "Being a teenage mother without much money placed a lot of odds against me from the start. It was hard clearing those hurdles, as well as those inherent for all Black businesswomen, so I'm proud of where I am and how I got here."

Sources

Periodicals

Black Enterprise, November 2004, p. 78.
Black Issues in Higher Education, May 10, 2001, p. 9.
Ebony, October 2003, p. 10.
Essence, July 1999, p. 60.
PR Newswire, December 23, 1998, p. 9191; July 11, 2003.

Other

Additional information for this profile was obtained through an interview with Donna A. James on January 10, 2005.

—Margaret Alic

Clara Stanton Jones

1913—

Library administrator, educator, civic leader

Jones, Clara Stanton, photograph. Courtesy Clara Stanton Jones.

Clara Stanton Jones' contributions as the first African-American president of the American Library Association (ALA) have advanced the education of blacks and helped all throughout the country who value and use libraries. She helped develop branch libraries in Detroit, created outreach programs to give access to citizens who never used libraries previously, and showed many what the library can do to enhance learning and by extension, their lives. Jones has stood tall in the face of adversity, earning the admiration of her peers. Known as an important and skilled speaker on behalf of issues facing librarians, she has spoken around the country and is considered to be one of the foremost women in communications.

Jones was born on May 14, 1913, to Ralph Herbert Stanton, a supervisor with the Atlanta Life Insurance Company, and Etta J. Stanton, a schoolteacher. Her father's family traces their ancestry back to a slave owner by the name of Stanton, Jones' great-grandfather. The slave owner must have acknowledged his black progeny for he passed on some of his land to Jones' grandfather. Stanton Mansion and Stanton College in Natchez, Mississippi, are both named after the family. Jones' maternal grandparents were born during the last decade of slavery on a farm in Saint Geneve, Missouri, later moving to St. Louis. They were hard-working farmers who bartered with neighbors for what they needed.

Jones graduated from Summer High School in Atlanta in 1929 at the age of 15. After a year at the Milwaukee State Teachers College, Jones began studying at Spelman College in Atlanta where she completed a bachelor's degree in 1934. Clara went on to earn another bachelor's degree in library science from the University of Michigan in 1938. One week later Clara married Albert Jones, a social worker from New Orleans and began work as a reference librarian at Dillard University library in New Orleans at the invitation of the head librarian. Albert had met Jones during a visit to Atlanta. "I made it my business to try to meet her again and show her some 'courtesies,'" Albert Jones said in an interview with *Contemporary Black Biography* (*CBB*). "We ended up courting through the mail and once by telephone each year. Can you imagine lovers planning to get married and we only

At a Glance . . .

Born Clara Stanton on May 14, 1913, St. Louis, MO; married Albert Jones, 1938; children: Stanton William, Vinetta Claire, Kenneth Albert. *Education:* Milwaukee State Teachers College, 1930; Spelman College, AB, 1934; University of Michigan, AB, library science, 1938. *Religion:* Presbyterian.

Career: Dillard University, New Orleans, LA, reference librarian 1938-40; Southern University, Baton Rouge, LA, associate librarian, 1940-41; Detroit Public Library, Detroit, MI, director, 1944-78.

Selected memberships: American Library Association; ALA Black Caucus; Advisory Committee for SLIS.

Selected awards: ALA Black Caucus Distinguished Service to Librarianship Award, 1970; University of Michigan School of Library Science Distinguished Alumnus Award for Outstanding Service to the Library Profession, 1971; University of Michigan Athena Award for Humanitarian Service as an Alumna, 1975; Wayne County Community College Distinguished Service to the Community Award, 1978; ALA Honorary Life Membership Award, 1983.

Addresses: *Office*—American Library Association, 50 E. Huron, Chicago, IL 60611.

spoke once a year? We made great preparation for that one phone call! For a while we didn't know what to talk about, but we finally got it together."

In 1940 Jones became associate librarian at Southern University in Baton Rouge. In 1944 the family relocated to Detroit where she worked fort the Detroit Public Library earning several promotions over the next 26 years. She became the first African American and the first woman director in the Detroit Public Library System in 1970, but it was not without controversy.

Jones' appointment to director raised the ire of several board members and the controversy played itself out in the press. One local journalist wrote several articles against Jones' appointment. During the 1970s the automotive industry in Detroit employed large numbers of blacks, many of who were United Auto Workers (UAW) union members. Because of the auto industry's importance to the local economy, heads of automakers like Chrysler and Ford and union leaders like Walter

Reuther of the (UAW) could and often did influence community politics and could sway the rank and file. Sometimes it was simply a matter of a phone call from the right office. Members of a coalition of progressive businessmen, community leaders, and educators working for advancement in race relations, threw their support behind Jones' appointment, as did Reuther and the UAW. With help from her many supporters, Jones won appointment and was told by one library board member to "Go on up there to your office and run the library system," her husband Albert recalled. To show their dissatisfaction two other board members and the acting director quit immediately.

Jones recognized that many blacks were not accustomed to visiting libraries. Many had come from the segregated South and subconsciously associated institutions like the library system with "whites only" policies. Prior to emancipation, few blacks had learned to read; many blacks simply did not relate to visiting a library. Jones understood the problem and instituted outreach programs urging inner-city participation in order to solve it. She visited neighborhood churches, schools, and community centers. She visited radio stations and spread the message on television, any place that would allow her to get the word out that the library was there for their use.

Not unlike most large library systems Detroit had its share of funding issues. Jones proved to be skillful with these matters as well. Understanding the politics of funding for a system like Detroit, she urged the state to provide money for the library system's operation, making a convincing argument about its importance to the state as well as the city. Her success earned her speaking engagements at several state library associations around the country. She spoke on many related subjects over the years. One landmark speech she gave at the American Library Association's (ALA) Annual Conference was "Reflections on Library Service to the Disadvantaged," which was published in an ALA pamphlet.

In 1974 Jones ran for the presidency of the ALA but was defeated. But in 1976 the winner, Allie Beth Martin of the Tulsa Public Library, fell ill and died before the end of her term. Jones was nominated by petition the previous year but was reluctant to pursue the position. Her supporters within the organization urged her on, and on July 22, 1976, she was seated as the first black president of the ALA.

In 1977 Jones' "Issues & Answers" Program at the Annual ALA conference highlighted major concerns of its members. Fifteen hundred members participated in a discussion of the social, economic, and technological changes facing libraries. The success of her work like this ALA conference and her abilities as a speaker showcased her as a skillful leader of the organization. The high profile position and her work through the years placed her along side many noted blacks of the twentieth century, counting many as friends and peers, including the poet James Weldon Johnson, the civil rights activist W.E.B. Du Bois, the theologian Howard Thurman, the poet Langston Hughes, and the librarian Dorothy Porter Wesley, to name only a few.

Jones has done much in her lifetime to make learning and books more accessible to the public. She was instrumental in dispelling misconceptions about library access, and her determination has endeared her to many as she fought her battles. Recalling her fortitude in response to the obstacles she faced during her early career Albert Jones told *CBB,* "She has always had a strong personality and I knew she could handle herself in any situation. I knew she could do it and did do it. After her appointment to director of the Detroit Public Library System people started calling her from all over the country because they wanted to see who this person was. Before she was appointed some people tried to beat her down but she never let it bother her. It was like it wasn't even happening."

Sources

Books

McCook, Kathleen de la Pena, ed. *Women of Color in Librarianship: An Oral History,* ALA, 1998.

Periodicals

Rocky Mountain News, February 13, 1996.

On-line

"Clara Stanton Jones," *Notable Black American Women,* www.galenet.gale.group.com/servlet/Bio RC (January 16, 2005).

Other

Additional information for this profile was obtained through an interview with Albert Jones on January 20, 2005.

—Sharon Melson Fletcher

Leleti Khumalo

1970—

Actress

A few times every generation, an actor or actress emerges whose performances can change the way the public thinks about an issue. Leleti Khumalo is such an artist. Her powerful star turn in both the stage and screen versions of *Sarafina!* changed the way people viewed apartheid at a time when it was still official policy in South Africa. Her portrayal more than a decade later of the title character in *Yesterday* swayed public perceptions about the AIDS epidemic in Africa.

Leleti Khumalo was born in 1970 in Kwa Mahu, a small black township north of Durban, South Africa. Like most black families there, Khumalo's lived in dire poverty. Her father died when she was three years old. Her mother supported the family by working as a domestic laborer. Khumalo and her three siblings lived in a home whose sole piece of furniture was a bed. In spite of these harsh circumstances, Khumalo found happiness in music and dance. She was a born performer. At an early age, she participated in Amajika, a backyard dance troupe organized by entertainer Tu Nokwe, a member of one of South Africa's most celebrated musical families.

Khumalo, Leleti, photograph. Matthew Simmons/Getty Images.

At age 15, Khumalo was swept out of obscurity in almost fairy-tale fashion. When South African musician, actor, and playwright Mbogena Ngema was looking for new talent for a musical he was developing, he came to the garage in which her youth group was rehearsing to scout for performers. After seeing what Khumalo could do, Ngema simply asked if she wanted to do a play. She said yes. The musical eventually evolved into the international blockbuster *Sarafina!* Ngema cast Khumalo in the title role, and neither her career nor her personal life has slowed down since. She became a star and, eventually, married Ngema.

Sarafina! tells the story of a 1976 student uprising in Soweto against apartheid, and includes moving and horrible accounts of youth being tortured and "disappeared" by the white South African regime. Until she auditioned for the play, Khumalo rarely considered the injustice of apartheid—it was just the way things were. "When I was a little girl, I just thought it was natural for all black people to be so very poor," she was quoted as saying in a 1992 *Premiere* magazine story. "In South Africa, you don't think you're oppressed. You don't

At a Glance . . .

Born Leleti Khumalo in 1970 in Kwa Mahu Township, South Africa; married Mbogena Ngema, 1992.

Career: Actress and dancer, 1985— ; landed first professional stage role in *Sarafina!*, 1985; made film debut in the movie version of *Sarafina!*, 1991.

Awards: NAACP Image Award, 1987; Tony Award nomination, Best Actress, for *Sarafina!*, 1988.

Address: *Home*—Johannesburg, South Africa.

know until you get out of the country. They don't show what's happening on TV."

Sarafina! delighted audiences in South Africa. The show also enjoyed a two-year run on Broadway, for which Khumalo was nominated for a Best Actress Tony Award in 1988. Following that Broadway stint, the show embarked on a worldwide tour that met with raves all over the globe. In 1987 Khumalo was honored by the NAACP with an Image Award for Best Stage Actress.

Sarafina! came to Hollywood in 1991, with Khumalo reprising her title role alongside costar Whoopi Goldberg in a production directed by Darrell James Roodt. The movie was distributed all over the world, and become the biggest movie ever released in Africa. Goldberg, who plays a revolutionary teacher in the movie, gave Khumalo high marks for her budding acting skills. "She's extraordinary," Goldberg was quoted as saying in *Premiere.* "The camera loves her. I loved her, too."

Throughout the 1990s, Khumalo appeared in a number of Ngema's productions, including *Magic at 4 A.M.* in 1993, *Mama* in 1996, and the 1997 sequel *Sarafina 2.* Her movie and television roles started coming in rapid succession as well. She was featured in, among other things, Roodt's 1995 film adaptation of the Alan Paton novel *Cry, the Beloved County* along with Richard Harris and James Earl Jones, and she appeared in the television series *The African Skies.* Meanwhile, she was also discovering new outlets for her powerful singing voice. In 1993 she release her first album of music, *Leleti and Sarafina.*

Khumalo also remained very active on the South African stage. She received favorable notice for her performance in the Ngema-directed *The Zulu,* a 1999 show about the Anglo-Zulu War. In 2003 she stared in *Stimela SasaZola,* a musical extravaganza that enjoyed a successful run at Johannesburg's African Bank Market Theatre.

Khumalo's international profile rose to new heights in the mid-2000s with roles in a several widely seen films and television shows. In 2004 she starred in *Yesterday,* a powerful movie about the social aspects of the AIDS crisis in Africa. Khumalo's character, named Yesterday (because her father believed everything was better yesterday), is a South African woman who is ostracized by her community after being diagnosed with AIDS. *Yesterday* is thought to be the first move to be made in the Zulu language for wide release. "I hope it can be an eye-opener about the effects of AIDS, especially on women," Khumalo was quoted as saying in an interview with the *Toronto Star.*

Yesterday was received enthusiastically by audiences in several countries. It became the first South African film ever to be nominated for an Oscar in the Best Foreign Language Film category. Khumalo followed up that success with a role in the movie *Hotel Rwanda,* a true story about a hotel manager, Paul Rusesabagina (Don Cheadle), who harbors more than 1,000 people during the 1994 genocide in Rwanda, which saw the slaughter of nearly one million members of the Tutsi minority by the Hutus. In *Hotel Rwanda,* which was shot primarily in Johannesburg and also features actor Nick Nolte, Khumalo plays Cheadle's sister. It was not a huge role, but the film received numerous honors and awards, including the People's Choice Award at the Toronto International Film Festival and Best Feature Film at the AFI (American Film Institute) Festival in Los Angeles. It was nominated for three Oscars, but came up empty when the envelopes were opened.

In 2005 Khumalo announced that she was taking on the small screen. That year, she joined the cast of *Generations,* a popular South African soap opera. She signed on to play the role of Busiswe Dlomo, the sister of a power-hungry businessman. While television presented an intriguing new challenge for Khumalo, she indicated that she did not intend to make TV acting a long-term habit.

Soap opera acting is a big change indeed for an actress whose career has focused mainly on big issues like AIDS and apartheid. But this is the kind of versatility that allows young actresses to successfully navigate the transition to not-so-young actress. Watching Leleti Khumalo grow into new kinds of roles is an exciting prospect indeed for her many fans all over the world.

Selected works

Films

Sarafina!, 1991.
Cry, the Beloved Country, 1995.

Yesterday, 2004.
Hotel Rwanda, 2004.

Plays

Sarafina, 1985.
Mama, 1996.
Sarafina 2, 1997.
The Zulu, 1999.
Stimela SaseZola, 2003.

Television

African Skies, 1991.
Generations, 2005.

Sources

Periodicals

Africa News, March 2, 2005 *Cleveland Plain Dealer,*
    September 20, 1992.
Premiere, November 1992, pp. 75-76.
Sunday Times (South Africa), January 9, 2005, p. 9.
Toronto Star, September 16, 2004, p. E2.
USA Today, October 2, 1992, p. 4D.

On-line

"Leleti Khumalo," *Yesterday,* www.yesterdaythemovie
    .co.za/leleti.asp (March 1, 2005).

—Bob Jacobson

Rick Kittles

1976 (?)—

Geneticist, educator

Geneticist Rick Kittles, a professor at Ohio State University, became one of the hottest young scientific researchers in the country in the early 2000s. When he was hired by Ohio State in 2004, the *Columbus Dispatch* reported that he would bring to the university more than $1 million in research grants in addition to his teaching expertise. He was a nationally recognized investigator whose specialties encompassed such vital topics as prostate cancer and the role of genetics in disease.

Yet it was outside of the academic world that Kittles made headlines. His company, African Ancestry, Inc., used his expertise in genetic testing to put African Americans, from celebrities to ordinary genealogy buffs, in touch with their roots in a way that Americans of European descent took for granted but that a displaced and enslaved people had mostly only dreamed of. Kittles offered his customers a glimpse into their specific African ancestries, pinpointing an actual African ethnic group to which one or two of the customer's ancestors had belonged. The path that led to the founding of African Ancestry was complicated and not without controversy, but Kittles found that his research often fed into the deep interest in African-American genealogy that had been awakened by the publication of Alex Haley's book *Roots* in the 1970s.

Rick Antonius Kittles was born in 1976(?) in Sylvania, Georgia, in an area his family had inhabited for several generations, but he grew up in Central Islip, New York, on Long Island outside of New York City. When he was young he hoped to become a rap musician, but he was curious from the start about human origins and differ-ences. "I used to always wonder in school why everybody looks different," Kittles told Alice Thomas of the *Columbus Dispatch*. "I was always the only black kid in the class."

Concocted African Ancestry

By the time he reached his teenage years, Kittles found his curiosity intensifying as his white classmates began to identify more strongly with European ethnic groups. "I would say, 'Africa'" when other students asked him about his own roots, Kittles was quoted as saying in the *Seattle Times*. "Other times I would make stuff up and say, 'I'm a Mandingo.' That bothered me, not knowing more about where in Africa."

Kittles attended the Rochester Institute of Technology in upstate New York as an undergraduate, earning a biology degree there in 1989. He taught biology at the high school level in the New York and Washington areas for several years, winning admission to the graduate biology program at George Washington University in Washington, D.C. As a graduate student, Kittles did research on melanin, the pigment that darkens human skin and protects it from solar radiation; Africans and other equatorial peoples frequently exposed to the sun have higher levels of melanin than do humans of European descent. Giving occasional public lectures about melanin, Kittles speculated that high levels of the chemical in the inner ear might account for what some considered a heightened sensitivity to music and rhythm among humans of African descent.

At a Glance . . .

Born 1976(?) in Sylvania, GA; raised in Central Islip, NY. *Education:* Rochester Institute of Technology, Rochester, NY, BS, biology, 1989; George Washington University, PhD, biological sciences, 1998.

Career: Various New York and Washington, DC, area high schools, teacher, early 1990s; Howard University, Washington, DC, assistant professor and director of National Human Genome Center African American Hereditary Prostate Cancer Study Network, 1998-2004; African Burial Ground Project, New York City, researcher; African Ancestry, Inc., founding partner (with Gina Paige) and scientific director, 2002–; Ohio State University, Columbus, OH, associate professor, 2004–.

Addresses: *Office*—Department of Molecular Virology, Immunology & Medical Genetics, 690C Tzagournis Medical Research Facility, 420 W. 12th Ave., Columbus, OH 43210. *Web*—www.africanancestry.com.

He also investigated interactions between melanin and prescription drugs, and between melanin and illicit drugs such as cocaine. Interest in public-health implications would be typical of Kittles's scholarly research. His published papers, most of them (as is typical in the hard sciences) done in collaboration with other investigators, bore lengthy titles like "High Incidence of Microsatellite Instability in Colorectal Cancer from African Americans." But he gravitated toward subjects with broad social importance, and his eventual scholarly specialties were all hot topics: prostate cancer and its underlying causes, the relationship between genetics and disease prevalence more generally, and the validity (or lack of validity) of the concept of race.

Directed Prostate Cancer Study

As he was completing his doctoral degree at George Washington University in 1998, Kittles was hired as an assistant professor of microbiology at Washington's Howard University and was named director of the African American Hereditary Prostate Cancer (AAHPC) Study Network at the university's National Human Genome Center. This project involved setting up national network of mostly African-American medical scientists who would enroll 100 families with at least four members who were afflicted with prostate cancer; blood samples were subjected to genetic research, with the intent of finding a genetic marker that might explain the high incidence of the disease among African-American men.

Kittles faced a public-relations problem of long standing in his new post, for the AAHPC Study Network was a government-funded project. "There is very strong resistance in the African-American community to participate in government-sponsored research," Kittles pointed out to the *Chicago Sun-Times*. "The first thing they say is 'Tuskegee,'" referring to the infamous 40-year United States Public Health Service study in which hundreds of black men were unknowingly denied proper treatment for syphilis infections. Kittles and his associates hoped that a project carried out mostly by African American researchers might break down these walls of mistrust.

Another research enterprise in which Kittles became involved at the beginning of his career was the African Burial Ground Project in New York City, where Howard researchers led by anthropologist Michael Blakey exhumed the remains of 408 African Americans from an eighteenth-century graveyard. Some of the research followed traditional anthropological models: caskets were examined in search of links to traditional African practices, and the scientists learned what they could from dry bones about how these enslaved African Americans had spent their working life. But Kittles was able to merge anthropology and biology, gathering DNA samples from the remains and comparing them against a growing database of DNA obtained from modern Africans in order to find out where the eighteenth-century African Americans had originally come from.

It was while doing this work that Kittles and his associates had a brainstorm. If they could trace the origins of buried African Americans, they could do the same thing with living individuals. As a pilot project, they began to gather genetic material from Boston-area school children. The idea gained support from a group of Boston ministers who helped organize the program. Boston was selected because its African-American population was relatively self-contained; many black Boston families could trace their roots to the American Revolution or even earlier.

Callers Jammed Howard Switchboard

As he began to work toward realizing his ideas, Kittles encountered both excitement and controversy. When word of his efforts leaked out, Howard found its switchboard jammed with calls from reporters and from ordinary African Americans who wanted to know how they could sign up to be tested. Investors sensed something big in the making, and *Washington Business Forward* estimated that if just one-tenth of one percent of the 33 million Americans of African descent took Kittles's ancestry test each year, his potential annual gross would be in the $10 million range.

The obstacles in his way were just as sizable as the potential. Scientific observers questioned whether Kittles could generate useful results in view of the fact that DNA testing could illuminate only a small sliver of a person's ancestry, and questions were raised about the size of the African DNA database on which he planned to rely. Kittles ran into trouble with the government funders who had underwritten the African Burial Ground research as he moved toward profit-making enterprises, and he parted ways with his former associate Michael Blakey in a disagreement over the new project's aims. Kittles had a few fierce critics within the African-American community as well; charging African Americans a fee to learn about their African origins was "like charging Holocaust victims a fee to confirm their relatives were in fact gassed," University of Maryland anthropologist Fatima Jackson told the on-line magazine *Salon*.

Though he hoped to launch African Ancestry, Inc. by 2001, Kittles faced months of delays as he patiently worked to answer the objections of critics and deal with the complexities of running a business while working in the academic world. He took on a partner, Washington businesswoman Gina Paige, to handle the financial side of African Ancestry, taking the title of Scientific Director for himself. Compiling data gathered by other researchers, he amassed a large enough sample of African DNA to pass muster with other scientists. His collection of 10,000 samples "to me sounds pretty good," University of Chicago professor Chung-I Wu told the *Chicago Tribune* (as quoted by the Knight Ridder Tribune News Service). And he was careful to inform potential customers of the method's limitations, pointing out that a person's ancestors over several centuries numbered in the hundreds or thousands, only two of which (one on the father's side, one on the mother's) could be identified by African Ancestry's DNA tests.

Attracted Celebrity Customers

Any genealogy researcher, however, knows that filling in one piece of an ancestry puzzle can shed light on many other parts of the puzzle. Any criticism Kittles encountered was overshadowed by the enthusiastic response he immediately received from African Americans interested in learning more about their backgrounds. Filmmaker Spike Lee, former United Nations ambassador Andrew Young, and actors LeVar Burton and Vanessa Williams were three of African Ancestry's celebrity clients, while over 2,000 others paid about $300 or $350 for the company's DNA tests in its first year in business. Customers could choose to have either the paternal line (though the Y chromosome, the genetic marker responsible for the development of male characteristics) or the maternal line (through mitochondrial DNA) investigated; a discount was available for the pair. The test was simple and painless—the customer took a cell sample from the inside of the cheek with a swab—and could be handled entirely by mail, with a guarantee of confidentiality.

Customers, who were often able to put Kittles's results together with bits of family oral history to fill in blanks in their family trees, had strong emotional responses to what they learned from African Ancestry's tests. James Jacobs, who knew of a Louisiana ancestor called Jacko Congo, told the *Houston Chronicle* that "the feeling is hard to describe, like having a long-lost parent and you found them." Many customers made plans to visit African countries after receiving their test results. Kittles's tests also confirmed what researchers had long suspected; around 30 percent of African Americans had European ancestors, primarily due to the rape of slave women by white slaveholders. Kittles himself found German ancestry on his father's side and identified a Portuguese forbear in Paige's background, and he observed that his own research, as well as other work showing the frequency of African ancestry among Europeans and European Americans, further weakened the idea of race as a scientific category.

African Ancestry continued to grow and to gain national attention; an article on the company appeared in *People* in the fall of 2004. By that time, Kittles had been hired as an associate professor at the Ohio State University medical school, in the department of molecular virology, immunology, and medical genetics. Controversy continued to dog him—an anonymous letter was submitted to Ohio State's search committee, accusing him of blurring scientific and for-profit work—but it was his strong record as a prostate cancer researcher, not his work with African Ancestry, that interested his new employer. By 2005 Rick Kittles was on his way to prominence in both academic and public spheres.

Sources

Periodicals

Boston Globe, August 13, 2000, p. B3.
Chicago Sun-Times, May 14, 1998, p. 8.
Columbus Dispatch, March 18, 2004, p. B1.
Houston Chronicle, February 24, 2005, p. Star-1.
Human Biology, August 2003, p. 449.
Knight-Ridder Tribune News Service, September 9, 2003, p. 1.
Los Angeles Times, May 29, 2000, p. 12.
People, September 27, 2004, p. 97.
Richmond Times-Dispatch, January 31, 1994, p. C1.
Seattle Times, May 30, 2000, p. A1; April 25, 2003, p. A7.
Times (London, England), April 26, 2000.
Washington Business Forward, August 2001.

On-line

"About Us," *African Ancestry, Inc.,* www.africanancestry.com (March 1, 2005).

"Flesh and Blood and DNA," *Salon,* http://archive.sa
lon.com/health/feature/2000/05/12/roots/print.
html (March 1, 2005).

"Milestones Leading to the NHGC," *National Human
Genome Center,* www.genomecenter.howard.edu/
milestones.htm (March 1, 2005).

"Rick A. Kittles," *Ohio State University Medical
School,* http://cancergenetics.med.ohio-state.edu/
2749.cfm (March 1, 2005).

—James M. Manheim

Jewel Stradford LaFontant

1922-1997

Lawyer, government official

Jewel Stradford LaFontant became a key player in the fields of law and politics long before the women's movement gained momentum in the 1960s. Her father, renowned U.S. Supreme Court attorney C. Francis Stradford, carefully groomed her to become a pioneer in the male-dominated arena of law. LaFontant achieved many firsts for women in the field, becoming in 1946 the first woman to graduate from University of Chicago Law School, in 1955 the first black woman to be name Assistant U.S. Attorney, and in 1973 the first woman Deputy Solicitor General of the United States.

LaFontant's first political experience came at the age of 12 when her father ran for precinct captain and encouraged her to distribute campaign leaflets in the community where they lived. But the exuberance she derived from visiting courtrooms with her father was the real catalyst in LaFontant's decision to follow in his footsteps. In fact, LaFontant credits him with helping her develop the ability to successfully compete in a milieu controlled by men. "My father always taught me there is room at the top regardless of sex," LaFontant told Andrew Malcolm in the *New York Times*, "and if you worked hard enough, recognition would come."

LaFontant took her father's advice and in 1943 became a third-generation graduate of Ohio's Oberlin College where, like her father and her grandfather before her, she earned a bachelor of arts degree in political science. Interestingly enough, Oberlin, Ohio, was once a stop on the Underground Railroad that is said to have helped one of LaFontant's distant ancestors, a runaway slave, to freedom.

In 1946 LaFontant became the first woman to earn a law degree from the University of Chicago. She was admitted to the Illinois Bar in 1947. That same year she plunged into handling more than three thousand cases as a trial lawyer the Legal Aid Bureau of Chicago, which provided free legal representation for the poor. LaFontant embraced her job with a passion, believing this a cause worthy of her training. Because of her deep commitment, she later became chairperson of the agency. In addition to this work and various positions with the NAACP and the American Civil Liberties Union, LaFontant, as Jewel S. Rogers (her first married name), formed a Chicago law firm in 1949 with her first husband, John W. Rogers.

In 1955, President Dwight D. Eisenhower appointed LaFontant to the post of Assistant U.S. Attorney for the Northern District of Illinois. As the first African-American woman assigned to this position, she began a personal tradition of preparing the way for minorities and continued to hold her own in a forum dominated by men. In an *Ebony* interview, LaFontant admitted, "Men usually stereotype me or underestimate my ability because I'm female." So to prove that women are not any less qualified than their male counterparts, LaFontant not only joined the Cook County Bar Association and became its treasurer and a board member but was also elected secretary of the National Bar Association—a post she held from 1956 until 1964. During this time, LaFontant continued to lend her legal expertise to civic organizations and became involved with the Congress of Racial Equality. She was also instrumental in integrating several Chicago restaurants and the

At a Glance . . .

Born Jewel Carter Stradford on April 28, 1922, in Chicago, IL; died of breast cancer on May 31, 1997, in Chicago; daughter of Cornelius Francis (an attorney) and Aida Arabella (maiden name, Carter; an artist) Stradford; married John W. Rogers, 1946 (an attorney, divorced 1961); married H. Ernest LaFontant, 1961(an attorney; died October 1976); married Naguib Soby MANkarious, 1989; children: (first marriage) John Rogers. *Education*: Oberlin College, BA, 1943; University of Chicago Law School, JD, 1946.

Career: Lawyer and government official. Legal Aid Bureau of United Charities of Chicago, trial lawyer, 1947-54; Rogers, Rogers, and Strayhorn (law firm), Chicago, partner, 1949-55(?); U.S. Attorney's Office, Northern District of Illinois Assistant U.S. Attorney, Chicago, 1955-58; Stradford, LaFontant, and LaFontant (law firm), partner, 1961-(76?); Illinois State Treasurer's Office, Inheritance Tax Division, advisor, 1962-64; United Nations, representative, 1972; U.S. Department of Justice, Washington, DC, Deputy Solicitor General, 1973-75; Stradford, LaFontant, Fisher, and Malkin (law firm later called Stradford, LaFontant, Wilkins, Jones, and Ware), Chicago, president and partner, 1976-83; Vedder, Price, Kaufman, and Kammholz, partner, 1983-89; U.S. Department of State, Washington, DC, ambassador at large and U.S. coordinator for refugee affairs, 1989-93; Holleb and Coff (law firm), partner, 1993-97.

Selected memberships: NAACP, Chicago branch secretary, 1948-52; American Civil Liberties Union, board of directors, 1948-54; National Bar Association, secretary, 1956-64; Chicago Bar Association, member of board of managers, 1962-64; board member for Jewel Companies, Inc., Continental Bank, Transworld Corporation, Mobil Corporation, Revlon, Inc., and Ariel Capital Management.

Selected awards: Cook County Bar Association Achievement Award, 1956; International Academy of Trial Lawyers, fellow, 1984; University of Chicago citation for public service, 1990; CARE Foundation, International Humanitarian Award, 1994; honorary degrees from numerous colleges and universities.

Stateville Prison in Joliet, Illinois. After divorcing her first husband in 1961, she remarried and started the Chicago law firm Stradford, LaFontant, and LaFontant, with her father and new husband, H. Ernest LaFontant.

A true highlight in LaFontant's career came in 1963, when she argued and won her first case before the United States Supreme Court. The case, *State of Illinois vs. Beatrice Lynum,* later served as a case law for the 1966 constitutional law case *Miranda vs. the State of Arizona,* which helped establish the Miranda warning police must read upon placing a person under arrest.

A third generation Republican, LaFontant began to expand her political ties in the 1960s. Having been a supporter of then-U.S. senator Richard M. Nixon for more than a decade, she took an active role in the Republican National Convention of 1960, which yielded him as the party's presidential candidate. LaFontant was honored by being asked to travel with Nixon's running mate, Henry Cabot Lodge, as his civil rights advisor for the length of the campaign. Nixon lost the election in 1960, but when he finally did become president of the United States in 1968, he did not forget LaFontant.

Throughout the 1960s, LaFontant honed her managerial skills as a member of the board of managers of the Chicago Bar Association, and she was chosen to serve as advisor to Inheritance Tax Division of the Illinois State Treasurer's Office from 1962 to 1966. She also tried to become a judge. In 1962 LaFontant was the first woman nominated for Superior Court judge in Illinois. Her campaign was unsuccessful, as was her 1970 campaign for Appellate Court judge. Though she did not win the elections, she did put up a good fight. Her opponent, Robert L. Hunter, presiding judge of Chicago's Divorce Division, admitted in *Ebony* that when LaFontant was running for the Superior Court position, "She scared the hell out of me." Commenting on the unsuccessful election and a later bid for a spot on the Illinois Appellate Court in Cook County, LaFontant revealed in a *New York Times* interview, "I felt I owed it to my sex to run, but never again. I've paid my dues. I hate to lose. But I have matured and realize losing makes you a bigger person after all. It sure knocks any conceit out of you."

LaFontant certainly did become "bigger." In 1969, U.S. President Nixon turned to LaFontant to serve as vice-chairman of the U.S. Advisory Commission on International Educational and Cultural Affairs. Nixon also appointed her to be a representative to the United Nations in 1972. And in 1973 Nixon appointed LaFontant to be the first woman to hold the post of Deputy Solicitor General in the Justice Department. She excelled at the position until 1975, when she returned to Chicago to practice law.

In 1976, after the death of her second husband, LaFontant continued to practice law and acted as president of Stradford, LaFontant, Fisher, and Malkin law firm (the name later changed to LaFontant, Wilkins, Jones, and Ware). In 1983, she joined the prestigious 114-lawyer firm of Vedder, Price, Kaufman and Kammholz, where she practiced corporate law until March of 1989. In 1985 she was admitted to the Washington, D.C. Court of Appeals. In 1989—the year she married her third husband, Naguib Soby MANkarious—she returned to government service when President George Bush appointed her as Ambassador-at-Large and U.S. Coordinator for Refugee Affairs of the State Department. LaFontant was the first African-American woman appointed to serve in these positions. When she left these positions in 1993, she returned to practicing law at the Chicago firm of Holleb and Coff. LaFontant lost her life to breast cancer on May 31, 1997.

Her success in the American legal and political arenas helped erode the barrier of discrimination that has undermined the ascent of blacks and women in these fields in the past. She also served on the board of directors, often as the first woman, for several of America's largest corporations, including her son's Ariel Capital Management. Throughout her career LaFontant told women to concentrate on their work and not on their sex in order to find success. When asked by a *New York Times* interviewer to offer advice to women in business, she said: "You can't see yourself first as a woman or a black and then trade in on it.

You've got to get the job done. Then recognition will come." Her life was proof of that. Her legacy papers are collected in the archives of Oberlin College.

Sources

Books

Swiger, Elinor Porter, *Women Lawyers at Work,* Julian Messner, 1978.

Periodicals

Barrister, Winter 1985.
Ebony, February 1974.
Jet, October 3, 1983; August 7,1989; August 3, 1992; July 5, 1993; June 23, 1997.
New York Times, March 16, 1972; September 10, 1972; June 3, 1997.
Sepia, November 1976.
Washington Post, February 2, 1974; June 3, 1997.
Working Woman, February 1980; February 1981.

On-line

"Jewel LaFontant-MANkarious," *Oberlin College Archives,* www.oberlin.edu/archive/holdings/finding/ RG30/SG310/adminhist.html (April 26, 2005).

—Barbara L. Baker and Sara Pendergast

Aylwin Lewis

1954(?)—

Retail executive

When Texas native Aylwin Lewis became president and chief executive officer of the Kmart Holding Corporation in the fall of 2004, the job carried the distinction of making Lewis the highest ranking African-American executive in the U.S. retail industry. His authority increased immeasurably just a month later, when Kmart announced an $11 billion merger with another leading American retailer, Sears, Roebuck, which made him head of the third-largest retail chain in the United States. Lewis, noted *Detroit News* writer Tenisha Mercer, arrived at Kmart headquarters in Michigan "with a reputation as a high-energy team builder with a flair for marketing. He now faces the daunting challenge of reshaping a company on a long losing streak."

Lewis was 50 years old when he took the Kmart job in 2004. A native of Houston, Texas, he grew up in a Southern Baptist household headed by a father who held a number of jobs at a pipe-bending company over the years. Lewis recalled in one interview that his father was usually out the door by daybreak. "My mother and father were very hard working, believed in education, being honest and not taking shortcuts—always doing

Lewis, Aylwin, photograph. AP/Wide World Photos Reproduced by permission.

your best work," he said in a Knight Ridder/Tribune Business News article.

Guided by his parents' positive attitude, Lewis went on to captain his high school football team, and entered the University of Houston after graduation. He had earned dual bachelor's degrees in business management and English literature by 1976, and planned on a career in academia. In order to defray graduate school costs, he took a job with the fast-food chain Jack in the Box while pursuing his doctorate in English literature. The job prompted a change in career plans, Lewis said in a *Chicago Tribune* interview with Barbara Rose and Michael Oneal that appeared in the Knight Ridder/Tribune Business News. "I fell in love with the notion of serving customers," he recalled. "Even as an assistant manager, I liked doing the hiring, the ordering, overseeing the food quality. I loved being a leader."

Lewis earned his M.B.A. from the University of Houston, and went on to 25-year career as a fast-food industry executive. After moving up through the Jack in the Box ranks, he joined the restaurant division of Pepsico, which was later spun off into a corporate entity called Yum Brands. Based in Louisville, Kentucky, Yum was the world's largest restaurant company, with holdings that included Taco Bell, Pizza Hut, KFC, Long John Silver's and A&W All-American Food restaurants. Lewis headed various management posts within the company, including supervision of franchise operations. In the early 1990s, he oversaw KFC's area operations for Chicago and the Great Lakes region, and in 1996 was promoted to the post of chief operating officer of the KFC and Pizza Hut divisions.

Long known for a strong work ethic, Lewis was usually in the office at 6:30 a.m. He was also a skilled people person with a knack for putting others at ease while motivating them to improve sales numbers, which prompted co-workers to tag him with the nickname "Coach." He was also fair-minded and committed to leveling the playing field, once issuing a decree that forbid his company executives from discussing business while playing golf, on the premise that those who didn't play the sport were left out. By 2003 he had been made president and chief multibranding and operating officer of Yum's 33,000-restaurant empire.

On Labor Day weekend of 2004, however, he visited financier Edward Lampert at Lampert's Greenwich, Connecticut home. Two years earlier, Lampert had emerged as the largest shareholder of Kmart, the ailing Michigan-based retailer, and then managed to pull it out of bankruptcy. A string of retail veterans installed in the top slot had failed to improve the company's fortunes

in the retail sector, however, and Lampert was looking for someone with a fresh vision. Lewis's track record in rebranding KFC and the other Yum entities certainly made up for what some industry analysts described as his lack of retail experience, and the announcement that he would take over the reins of one of America's leading retailers was greeted with some surprise in the business press in October of 2004.

Lewis embarked upon a four-month trip to 120 Kmart stores to meet with employees and take the pulse of the company from its most important nerve center: the sales floor. "My mission…is to come here and build a great company," the *Detroit News* report from Mercer quoted him as saying. "Kmart is a great brand in America. The hallmark again is to make the stores the essence of what we do. You can only make customers one place and make money one place. Customers are essential to what we do." Yet others noted that Kmart's situation was dire. Badly trounced by competitors Wal-Mart and Target in the past decade, Kmart's fortunes had declined so considerably that some analysts believed that the real estate holdings on which its stores and company headquarters in suburban Detroit sat were likely worth more than the company itself.

Predictions of Kmart's demise were shelved, however, when just a month after Lewis took over, Lampert announced that the company was merging with Sears to create a retail empire of nearly 3,500 stores and $55 billion in potential sales. Lewis only learned of the top-secret deal during his usual daily call with Lampert, and at the eleventh hour. Lampert asked him if he was ready for the challenge of running what would become the nation's third-largest retail chain, and as Lewis admitted to Rose and Oneal, "it was a little overwhelming. [But] immediately I thought, 'Well, why not?'…I'm a realist, so I understand the difficulties ahead, but the upside is tremendous."

Lewis is married, inherited his bookworm habit from his mother, and travels the world for pleasure when not in the office. He downplayed the significance of becoming one of the highest-ranking African Americans in corporate America in interviews, preferring to talk about the company and its attributes. "I have a positive and a negative reaction to it," he said in the Knight Ridder/Tribune Business News interview about his feelings about joining a small club that included Richard Parsons, chairman and chief executive of Time Warner, and Merrill Lynch president Stan O'Neal. Reflecting that much had changed since his own early youth in Texas in the 1950s, he conceded, "the notion that I could have a job like this shows us how far we have come in America. The fact that you had to ask the question shows us how far we have to go."

Sources

Periodicals

Chain Store Age, December 2004, p. 39.

Detroit News, October 19, 2004.
Houston Chronicle, October 19, 2004, p. 11.
International Herald Tribune, November 19, 2004,
p. 19.
Knight Ridder/Tribune Business News, October 19,
2004; November 21, 2004.
Seattle Times, November 18, 2004, p. E1.

—Carol Brennan

Marvin Lewis

1958—

Professional football coach

When he was named head coach of the Cincinnati Bengals on January 14, 2003, Marvin Lewis became the seventh African American to hold the position of head coach in the modern National Football League (NFL). The promise shown by his distinguished career as an assistant coach was fulfilled when he reversed the fortunes of a team that had been a perennial basement dweller in league rankings. Part of Lewis's success as a coach rested on his genuinely inspirational qualities; he was a living example of the power of hard work, and his life was an all-American success story.

Marvin Lewis was born in McDonald, Pennsylvania, in the state's steelmaking region outside Pittsburgh, on September 23, 1958. Lewis remembered that his father, who worked in a steel mill and often spent his days swinging a sledgehammer at iron ore, would come home and rest his sore elbows on pillows. Lewis's mother was a registered nurse and later a nurse practitioner. His family instilled in him a strong work ethic. One uncle became a Pulitzer Prize-winning newspaper photographer. As a high school student, Lewis worked summers on a garbage truck and spent plenty of time at church as the first youth Sunday school superintendent in the history of the First Baptist Church.

Became Senior Class President

Local youths could dream of a way out of the steel industry; McDonald's Fort Cherry High School had an impressive football program that also produced future San Diego Chargers head coach Marty Schottenhe-imer and several other NFL players and coaches. A quarterback in midget football, Lewis took to sports immediately, joining the football, baseball, and wrestling teams, and often changing out of his garbage collecting clothes and into his team uniform on his way to practices or games. He excelled as a safety and quarterback on the football field and became president of his senior class.

Lewis planned to attend Purdue University in West Lafayette, Indiana, but he changed his mind when he heard about an open football scholarship at faraway Idaho State University, in Boise, and applied, hoping to save his parents his tuition bills. He was admitted and began studying engineering, his determination to succeed strengthened after spending a summer working at a steel mill's coke ovens back in Pennsylvania and sweating in the blast of their 2,800-degree temperatures. Too small to dream of a professional career himself, he continued to pursue football with a passion and began to dream of becoming an NFL coach.

His father Marvin, Sr., who had hoped for a stable career in the engineering profession for his son, did not take this news well. But Lewis—according to Chick Ludwig of the *Dayton Daily News*—convinced his father by telling him to think back on his 31 years in the mills: "Daddy, you go into that mill every day and you hate that job. I want to do what I love to do," Lewis said. Fresh out of Idaho State, where he three times won All-Big Sky Conference honors as a linebacker, quarterback, and safety (in 1978, 1979, and 1980), Lewis was hired as a graduate assistant in 1981 by his alma mater at an annual salary of $10,000.

At a Glance . . .

Born on September 23, 1958, in McDonald, PA; son of Marvin Lewis, Sr. (a steelworker and foreman), and Vanetta Lewis (a nurse); married Peggy; children: Whitney, Marcus. *Education:* Idaho State University, BS, physical education, 1981; Idaho State University, MS, athletic administration, 1982.

Career: Idaho State University, linebackers coach, 1981-84; Long Beach State University, assistant coach, 1985-86; University of New Mexico, assistant coach, 1987-89; University of Pittsburgh, assistant coach, 1990-91; Pittsburgh Steelers, linebackers coach, 1992-95; Baltimore Ravens, defensive coordinator, 1996-2001; Washington Redskins, assistant head coach and defensive coordinator, 2002; Cincinnati Bengals, head coach, 2003–.

Awards: Inductee, Idaho State Hall of Fame, 2001.

Addresses: *Office*–Cincinnati Bengals, One Paul Brown Stadium, Cincinnati, OH 45202.

Hired as Assistant Coach

Coaching Idaho State's linebackers in his first year, Lewis got a taste of the satisfaction the profession could bring when the Idaho State Bengals notched a 12-1 record and won the National Collegiate Athletic Association's Division 1-AA championship. He stayed on as an assistant coach at Idaho State through 1984 (having earned a master's degree in athletic administration in 1982) and then moved on to assistant coach posts at Long Beach State University in California (1985-86), the University of New Mexico (1987-89), and the University of Pittsburgh (1990-91).

That powerhouse coaching job in his home area put Lewis within reach of a pro coaching slot, and in 1992 he was hired as a linebackers coach by the Pittsburgh Steelers. His Steelers squads from 1992 to 1995 spawned several NFL defensive stars, and in 1996 he was hired by the Baltimore Ravens as defensive coordinator even though head coach Brian Billick originally wanted someone else for the position. Once again Lewis proved himself; the Ravens' defense steadily improved, and the defensive team on the 2000 squad, which won the Super Bowl, set a record for fewest points allowed (165) in a 16-game season and is considered one of the best in NFL history. In 2002 Lewis became defensive coordinator and assistant head coach with the Washington Redskins.

Although NFL teams had interviewed Lewis for head coaching jobs several times, he had been passed over. The biggest heartbreaker came in 2002, when Tampa Bay Buccaneers general manager Rich McKay offered the team's head coach slot to Lewis but was overruled by the team's owners. Discouraged, Lewis nevertheless turned down a $7.5 million offer to coach football at Michigan State University in order to keep pursuing his goal. Finally he was hired in 2003 for $1.5 million a year to coach the Cincinnati Bengals, which in 2002 had amassed a dismal record of 2 wins and 14 losses, worst in the history of the franchise. The team's last winning record had come in 1990.

Took Visible Role in Cincinnati

In Cincinnati, Lewis became a popular and charismatic figure; some even credited him as a calming force in a city torn by deep-rooted racial unrest. Appearing at a ribbon-cutting ceremony for a new downtown public library shortly after his arrival, he became a fixture at civic functions and was an energetic speechmaker who drew on his small-town roots and experiences. He often spoke out against the crudeness that was endemic to the game of football, on one occasion urging league officials to take action against players who intimidated others by spitting on them. Married and the father of one daughter and one son, Lewis was the voice and face of the Bengals to an unusual degree. Bengals president Mike Brown, previously notorious for his detailed management style, turned not only football decisions but also day-to-day management chores such as staff hires and even the choice of training-camp location over to Lewis.

Shaking up the Bengals squad and recruiting a mixture of veteran free agents and talented young players, Lewis delivered impressive results in his first year as Bengals coach. Although the team lost its first three games, the Bengals bounced back to finish with an 8-8 record. They had a chance to make the NFL playoffs for the first time since 1990, but lost their final game. In the words of the *Washington Post,* "Marvin Lewis restored the dignity of the Cincinnati Bengals" in his debut campaign.

The Bengals went 8-8 once again in 2004 as Lewis took a chance on rookie quarterback Carson Palmer. The offense jelled toward the end of the year, but, ironically in view of Lewis's wealth of defensive experience, it was the Bengals defense that struggled. Still, Lewis had clearly built the nucleus of a potential playoff contender, and his position as Bengals coach seemed secure. "You can't worry about the bad days getting in the way of the good days that are coming," Lewis told the *Columbus Dispatch.* "You keep your eyes focused on what you're trying to get done. You work at it and work at it, and if things aren't to your liking, you work at changing them."

Sources

Periodicals

Buffalo News, December 17, 2004, p. B1.

Columbus Dispatch, January 15, 2003, p. E1; February 4, 2003, p. E1; September 12, 2004, p. F5; November 10, 2004, p. D4; November 14, 2004, p. E13; December 12, 2004, p. E1; January 9, 2005, p. E11.

Dayton (OH) *Daily News,* April 20, 2003, p. C1.

Denver Post, August 31, 2003, p. CC7.

Pittsburgh Post-Gazette, February 12, 2002; November 21, 2004, p. D4.

St. Louis Post-Dispatch, December 21, 2003, p. E1.

USA Today, December 29, 2003, p. C7.

Washington Post, November 10, 2004, p. D4.

On-line

"Coaching Staff: Head Coach Marvin Lewis," *NFL. com,* www.nfl.com/teams/coaching/CIN (March 3, 2005).

"Marvin Lewis," *Cincinnati Bengals*, www.bengals. com (March 3, 2005).

—James M. Manheim

Tommie Lindsey

1951—

Teacher, forensics coach

Considered one of the country's top forensics coaches, Tommie Lindsey has taught countless public high school students to achieve success as public speakers and to use these skills to help build satisfying college and professional careers. While debate teams have traditionally attracted students from elite schools, Lindsey has made his inner city public school team with a diverse student membership and limited budget—a force to reckon with. As of 2004, his students had won six consecutive National Forensics League School of Excellence awards and four California High School Speech Association championships. In 2004 Lindsey received a prestigious MacArthur fellowship in recognition of creativity in his field.

Inspired by Caring Teacher

One of nine children of an ironworker and a homemaker, Lindsey grew up in Oakland, California, and was raised by his grandmother after his parents died. From her he learned about the importance of family bonds, a value which he considers central to his decision to enter the teaching profession. Indeed, he was particularly inspired by the generosity of his sixth grade teacher who, noticing his torn shirt and jeans, bought him new clothes. "That made me want to be a teacher," he told *Parade* writer Tom Seligson. "I wanted to care for other people the way she cared for me."

Lindsey's first experience with public speaking occurred when he was in ninth grade and was asked to participate in graduation events for his class. Not only

did his English teacher doubt his ability to prepare and deliver a successful speech; his topic, he told NPR interviewer Dick Gordon on an episode of *The Connection*, was a difficult one: "investing in learning to cultivate the intellect." He didn't know where to start at first, but his landlord, Josephine Dukes, helped him to break the topic down into smaller parts and organize his thoughts. He received a standing ovation for his performance, and the experience gave him the confidence to continue in the field. "I knew that I was destined to do something with speech," Lindsey told *Bay Area Parent* writer Lisa Lewis.

Though he lacked formal training in public speaking, Lindsey had grown up listening to the powerful rhetoric of Baptist ministers and civil rights leaders. Church sermons, he told Gordon, helped him to develop a feeling for the power of words. The stirring speeches of such leaders as Martin Luther King, Jr., and Malcolm X were also central influences.

Lindsey went on to compete in Rotary and Lion's Club contests during high school, and then enrolled at the University of San Francisco. He earned a degree in Communications Arts and Social Science in 1973, becoming the first African-American valedictorian at the university.

Drew Diverse Students to Debate

Lindsey has taught in the California public school system since 1975, when he took a job at the Alameda County Court Schools, setting up speech contests for students who had been incarcerated for serious crimes.

At a Glance . . .

Born in 1951 in Oakland, California; divorced; children: Erica and Terence. *Education:* University of San Francisco, BA, 1973, BS and secondary teaching certificate, 1976.

Career: Alameda County Court Schools, California, teacher, 1975-80; El Rancho Verde High School, Moreno Valley, CA, teacher, 1980-88; James Logan High School, Union City, CA, teacher and forensics coach, 1988–.

Memberships: KEY Coach Society, National Forensics League.

Awards: National Forensics League School of Excellence Award, 1999 and 2000; National Forensics Coach of the Year, 2000; Use Your Life Award, Oprah Winfrey's Angel Network, 2003; MacArthur Fellowship, 2004.

Addresses: *Office*—c/o James Logan High School, 1800 H. St., Union City, CA 94587.

"These kids were murderers," he said in *Bay Area Parent,* "and I was only about nine years older than them." Seeing the tragic waste of potential among his students in juvenile detention, he determined that he would find a way to reach kids before they turned to crime. In 1980 he moved on to El Rancho Verde High School, an alternative school, and in 1988 began teaching at James Logan High School in Union City.

When Lindsey arrived at Logan, there was no program in forensics, which comprises a range of public speaking activities including debate, extemporary speaking, and dramatic interpretation. So he created one. To draw students in, he told Gordon, he focused on "crossover" students like athletes, who did not fit the image of the typical "preppy" debater. In some cases, Lindsey said, he would challenge athletes by suggesting that public speaking was something at which they could not succeed. Their competitiveness made them want to prove their ability to him. Lindsey also told prospective team members that public speaking is an invaluable skill, and that experience on the forensics team would improve their chances of getting into college. In its first year, the Logan forensics program had 13 students. By 2004, enrollment was about 200, making it the largest program in the country.

Lindsey is proud of the diversity on his team. Though forensics is usually associated with elite students, his program appeals to students of all abilities, from those in honors and advanced placement classes to those with special needs. These differences, he told Gordon, are actually a good thing for the program, because "it's great for honors or AP kids to know that they have to work with others" while it is also beneficial for less advanced students to know that their teammates will help them. The program also reflects the ethnic diversity of the school, comprised of African-American, Asian, Filipino, Hispanic, Caucasian, and Pacific Islander students. "They all help each other," Lindsey told Tom Seligson in *Parade.* "They find refuge here. I've tried to create an environment where it's safe for them to stand up and speak in public."

Indeed, Lindsey has emphasized how important it is for his students to honor their particular backgrounds. As he commented to Gordon, he never assigns passages for dramatic interpretation that perpetuate negative stereotypes. He encourages his students to bring their own unique perspectives to their public speaking projects; they have won championships with pieces on such topics as racism and street life. "People are amazed" by the success of his students, he told television host Oprah Winfrey, "because these kinds of kids aren't supposed to be in forensics. [But] I expect them to be champions and to conduct themselves that way, and they respond."

Lindsey's results have been impressive. While only about 38 percent of Logan High's graduating class typically attend college, the acceptance rate among forensics team members is 90 percent. Much of this success has been attributed to Lindsey's careful mentoring, both in and outside of the classroom. He requires every team member to take a forensics class (he teaches five of these each school year), and also encourages them to attend the six-week, full-day summer forensics academy he offers as a sort of "boot camp" to help disadvantaged students catch up to competitive levels. During the regular school year he makes his classroom available for students who want a place to do homework. He has helped students navigate the college application process and apply for financial aid. In one case, he arranged for an aspiring architecture student to get a summer internship at an architecture firm in nearby San Francisco. Lindsey has also bought suits for needy students so that they could be properly dressed for competitions. According to a *Bay State Parent* article, students "note that Lindsey is always willing to take the extra step, whether it's sitting down one-on-one to find out what's going on, or offering a kid a ride home when the team is returning from a tournament because he know the student doesn't have transportation."

Remained Dedicated

Such dedication, Lindsey has noted, can be exhausting. He often works from about 8 o'clock in the morning to 10:30 or later at night. With a limited budget for his program, he must take on secretarial tasks on top of his already heavy load of teaching, coaching, and school bureaucratic work. Dealing with his students' personal issues also consumes significant time, as does fundraising—a constant necessity for a program whose budget is constantly at risk of cuts. The demands of his job, Lindsey told Gordon, frequently kept him away from his family; his wife, from whom he was recently divorced, was often left to deal alone with the day-to-day challenges of raising their children, Erika and Terence.

Yet Lindsey's devotion to his program has also reaped invaluable rewards. Many of his students consider him a father figure, and remain in touch with him after graduation. One former student who phoned in to Gordon's program explained that "we never wanted to disappoint Mr. Lindsey" and that forensics is truly "the love of his life." Lindsey's students, many of whom have attended top colleges and universities, have achieved success in a wide range of fields, including business, medicine, law, and education. Whatever they choose to pursue, Lindsey commented to Seligson, "I want them to go back and be a voice in their communities."

Lindsey has recently received national recognition for his professional achievements. He received the National Forensics League School of Excellence Award in 1999 and in 2000; also in 2000, he was also named National Forensics Coach of the Year. In 2003 he received a Use Your Life Award from Oprah Winfrey's Angel Network. In 2004 he was granted a prestigious MacArthur fellowship: he was the only high school teacher among 23 recipients that year. Noting that Lindsey's students surmount many obstacles—including poverty, broken homes, and the stresses of inner city environments—to achieve success in a field domi-

nated by elite schools, the MacArthur Foundation cited Lindsey's devotion and example. "Through his tireless efforts to support, inspire, and lead his students," the Foundation noted in a press release, "Lindsey serves as a role model...for all who seek to shape the future of young people."

Sources

Periodicals

Bay Area Parent, January, 2005.
Parade, February 20, 2005, p. 13.
People Weekly, December 20, 2004, p. 130.
San Jose Mercury News, September 28, 2004.

On-line

"Accidental Hero, Room 408: Meet Tommie Lindsey," *Public Broadcasting Service,* www.pbs.org/accidentalhero/Tommie/ (February 4, 2005).
"Tommie Lindsey," *The MacArthur Fellows Program,* www.macfdn.org (February 4, 2005).
"Use Your Life Awards," *Oprah,* www.oprah.com (February 28, 2005).

Other

Accidental Hero, Room 408, television documentary, PBS, 2002.
"Interview with Tommie Lindsey," *The Connection*, National Public Radio, December 30, 2004, available online at www.theconnection.org (February 4, 2005).

—E. M. Shostak

Karl Malone

1963—

Professional basketball player, entrepreneur

Karl Malone made a 19-season career as professional basketball's premier power forward, scoring points on and off the court as an NBA superstar with the Utah Jazz in all but one season, which he played for the Los Angeles Lakers. Malone is the only player in the history of the National Basketball Association (NBA) to score 2,000 points or more in ten consecutive seasons. At 34 Malone, it seemed, had reached the pinnacle of his career when he won the 1996-97 MVP Award, averaging 27.6 points, 10.1 rebounds, and 4.5 assists. He was the oldest MVP in league history, having had a better and more complete year than Michael Jordan, according to some. Remarkably, two years later he won a second MVP after the 1998-99 season. And at age 38 he had a career high of 152 steals. He completed his career with the NBA's second highest scoring list with a career total of 36,928 points, less than 1,500 points behind basketball great Kareem Abdul-Jabbar.

In childhood, Malone was an unlikely superstar. His path to Salt Lake City started in Summerfield, Louisiana, where he was born in 1963. The young Malone grew up scrawny and wild in another town called Mount Sinai. Only a regular "whupping" from his mom kept the little terrorist in line. "I didn't get enough whuppings," Malone laughingly said in *Playboy*. "If I had gotten more, I probably would have changed sooner than I did," he continued.

When he got his life turned around, Karl built himself up from a scrawny kid and town trouble-maker to become a standout high school basketball player. He led his high school team to three consecutive state titles. But poor grades nearly ruined his chances to play college ball, so at his mother's urging he attended Louisiana Tech and sat out his first year to improve his grades.

Selected by Utah Jazz

Once academically eligible, Malone become a star. He led the school to two NCAA tournament invitations and, according to *Playboy*, earned his famous nickname from a sportswriter who drove through rough weather to watch Malone play and penned words to this effect: "Neither rain, nor snow, nor sleet, nor hail, nor double-teaming stopped 'The Mailman' that night." In 1985, The Mailman dropped out of college a year early to turn pro. He's still a year shy of a degree in Elementary Education, but vowed to get his diploma some day. Passed over by a dozen other teams, the Jazz selected him as the 13th pick. Malone quickly showed how wrong the other teams were when he averaged 14.9 points and 8.9 rebounds and made the NBA All-Rookie team. In 1997, he joined Kareem Abdul-Jabbar, Wilt Chamberlain, Elvin Hayes, and Moses Malone in the 25,000-point, 10,000-rebound club.

Who is the greatest power forward of all time? Images of past greatness at that position included Bob Pettit, who averaged 26 points and 16 rebounds per game and made the All-Star team in each of his 11 years in the NBA. Dave DeBusschere and Gus Johnson were prototype power forwards who won games with "dirty work"—rebound, bang bodies, set picks, block shots, fight, scratch, claw but let others do the scoring. Elvin

At a Glance . . .

Born Karl A. Malone on July 24, 1963, in Summer-field, LA; eighth of eight children to Shirley (sawmill worker) and J.P. Malone (divorced 1967, died of cancer 1977); stepson of Ed Turner (grocer, plumber); married Kay Kinsey, 1991; children: Kadee, Kylee, and Karl, Jr. *Education*: Louisiana Tech University, 1981-85.

Career: NBA basketball player, Utah Jazz, 1985-2003; Los Angeles Lakers, NBA basketball player, 2004.

Awards: Member NBA All-Rookie team, 1986; member NBA All-Defensive team, 1988, 1997-1998, 1999; named to NBA All-Star first team, 1989-94 and 1996-98, second team, 1988; recipient NBA All-Star team MVP award 1989, co-recipient, 1993; named to US Olympic Basketball Team, gold medal, 1992 and 1996; voted NBA MVP, 1997; selected by *Salt Lake Tribune* as its inaugural "Utahan of the Year," 1998; Henry P. Iba Citizen Athlete Award, 1998; voted NBA MVP, 1999.

Addresses: *Home*—Newport Beach, CA.

Hayes, who averaged 24 points and 15 rebounds per game in his first 11 years in the NBA and Spencer Haywood, who also averaged 26 points and 16 boards in his first three years in the NBA showed that a big man could score, not just do the dirty work. But as their game fell off, the scoring power forward became extinct—that is, until Karl Malone, Charles Barkley, and Kevin McHale came along to resurrect and redefine what coaches call the #4 position.

Malone, who displayed exceptional staying power, in 1996 joined Barkley, Pettit, and Hayes as the only power forwards to post 10 or more 20-point, 10-rebound NBA seasons. Having won an Olympic gold medal as a member of the United States Dream Team at the Barcelona Olympics in 1992, Malone picked up a second gold medal in Atlanta at the 1996 Olympics. Three years later, when he renewed his contract for the third time in 1999, he signed for an impressive $66.5 million over four years, to join the most highly paid echelon of players in the NBA. He continued to prove his worth, becoming the NBA's second all-time scorer in 2000 when he surpassed Wilt Chamberlain's career record by collecting 31,443 points; Malone then set an all-time NBA career free throw record of 8,534 successful shots in 2001.

Prepared Himself Physically and Mentally

Malone has been compared to a "raging bull" and a "runaway truck." But that unfairly overlooks the physical preparation and mental discipline that Malone brought to each game. For years, he has punished and polished his 6-foot-9, 256-pound frame into a well-sculpted mass of muscle that tapers to a 31-inch waist with less than 5 percent body fat. His deeply private, year-round training sessions include arduous running drills, high-intensity weight lifting, and brutal StairMaster workouts. His off-season regimen also includes bailing hay on his 50-acre ranch in the steamy heat of an Arkansas summer, just down the road from where he grew up as a kid.

Never good enough to get by on talent alone, Malone was considered the "strongest and best-conditioned basketball player on the planet" according to *The Sporting News*. He missed just one game in the last eight seasons. Until receiving a one-game suspension in April of 1998, Malone had started 543 consecutive games, the longest consecutive starts streak in the NBA. The secret, Malone said, was mental. "If you find something to give you motivation—whether it's negative or positive—ride it. Mine happened to be negative, when people said I wouldn't be a good basketball player," he told *Sport*.

"My workouts are important to me," Malone told a *Sporting News* reporter. "I don't do it for fun, and I don't do it for glory. I do it because it's necessary. I feel my strength and endurance give me an advantage, and I want to keep that advantage," he added.

The eighth of eight children to Shirley and J.P. Malone, Karl was raised mostly by his mom. Shirley worked at three jobs, after his dad abandoned the family when Karl was four. He died of bone cancer in 1977. His mother remarried and had another child, his sister Tiffany. Shirley has always been Malone's confidante, his "fishing and hunting buddy," and his moral example. Malone credited his mom with instilling in him "bedrock religion" including the value of hard work and forgiving his father for abandoning him. Karl talks to Shirley before every game. Always and lovingly, he told *Playboy*, that his mother tells him how many points to get, how many rebounds, how many assists. He'll tell her, "OK, you got 'em!" Then he'd go out and get even more.

One blemish on the Mailman's superstar status and fan appeal was that one flagrant foul—some would say intentionally vicious sledge-hammer elbow—on Isaiah Thomas in December of 1991. The hit caused Isaiah to get 40 stitches near his eye and Malone a $10,000 fine and one-game suspension. Malone claimed it was an accident and did not mean to hurt Thomas. Right after the incident, he and Isaiah talked it out (no apology given, but a denial that it was deliberate).

In April of 1998, Malone was suspended yet again for a flagrant elbow. The injured victim was David Robinson of the San Antonio Spurs. He was fined $5,000 and suspended for one game. It ended his starts streak of 543. Malone apologized to Robinson after the game.

Still, the media perpetuated the image of Malone as a villain on the baseline. After a game in which Malone sent Atlanta Hawk Sidney Moncrief sprawling, according to *Sports Illustrated*, fellow Hawk, Dominique Wilkins stung the Mailman with a rebuke, to this effect: "You're a cheap-shot artist. You're not a man. You always go out there to hurt somebody smaller than you." Not everyone buys the Mailman-as-Villain image. Chicago Bulls coach Phil Jackson differed in *Sports Illustrated,* "There's no way I consider him a dirty player. He's physical, throws his body around and does play the enforcer role on that team. But that's not the same thing as being dirty. The main thing a coach asks from his players is to be competitive *every* minute. And Karl Malone is." According to an informal poll cited by *Sports Illustrated*, "50% of NBA players consider Malone physical but entirely within the rules, 40% say that he tests the upper limit of physicality too frequently, and 10% believe that he's outright dirty."

Those who believed the worst about Malone usually did not know him away from the game. "People think I'm the meanest guy in the world when I'm on the court, and maybe I am," Malone told *Sport* magazine. "But off the court I'm a nice guy. When I go home, I'm just Karl, I'm just Daddy," he continued. And not just to his own kids. In the summer of 1995, he befriended 13-year-old cancer victim Danny Ewing. The friendship went both ways, and Karl learned there's more to life than basketball.

Balanced Basketball and Family

An eligible bachelor until 1991, in that year Malone married Kay Kinsey, a former Miss Idaho USA. The couple formed a strong family that Malone relished. "Everybody is a kid to some degree. My father passed away when I was young, and I could never be the kid I wanted to be. Now I have kids [Kadee and Kylee] and I want to be a kid with them. My wife is like the husband and the father. I'm the son my wife and I don't have right now" he commented in *Sport*. That son, Karl Jr., came along in 1996.

Karl shared many child-like passions in common with his wife Kay. Both are nuts about pro wrestling, tractor pulls and trucking. While better known for delivering big buckets and handling beefy opponents, Malone is also a beefmaster cattle breeder on 52-acre ranch in El Dorado, Arkansas, where a prized purebred animal can be sold for as much as $200,000. "Eight years from now when they say, 'Where is he now?' this is where I'll be," Malone once told *Ebony*.

When Malone was a little boy, he never mentioned the possibility of playing pro basketball, but always dreamed of owning a big truck. In March of 1993, Karl turned his dream into a business, his own trucking company—a six-rig fleet called Malone Enterprises. However two years later, he shut down his trucking business due to industry competition and Malone's limited involvement with the business. "Basketball is my job," Malone said in *Sports Illustrated*, "but this is my love.... I'd be lying if I said I didn't like the feeling of being the most powerful thing on the road, yet under control, too." Malone still drives his favorite 18-wheel tractor-trailer, an $190,000 rig that is painted with a rambling, breath-taking panorama of the Old West, with a familiar-looking cowboy riding the range.

Malone announced his retirement from professional basketball in 2005. Still physically fit, Malone admitted that he just wasn't mentally up for more of the game. "I look at basketball as 100 percent physically and 100 percent mentally. And if I can't bring you 200 percent, from me, I can't bring you anything," Malone said during his retirement press conference, according to *Jet*. Although he retired with the most respected playing statistics, some point out that Malone will not be considered truly "great" because he did not win the big one—an NBA championship for his team. "I wanted a championship. I'm not going to lie to you. That was my ultimate goal, but that was a team goal. That wasn't an individual goal," Malone admitted to *Jet*. Even without an NBA championship sports analysts predicted Malone, whose work ethic helped redefine how the game is played and how all-time greatness is measured, would be inducted into the Basketball Hall of Fame.

Sources

Periodicals

America's Intelligence Wire, February 14, 2005.
Buffalo News, February 20, 2005, p C8.
Ebony, Feb 1991, p.67; Nov 1991, p. 96.
Jet, April 13, 1992, p. 50; Jan 19, 1998, p. 46; March 7, 2005.
Knight-Ridder/Tribune Business News, July 8, 1996, p. 7080233.
Playboy, April 1989, p. 80.
Sport, May 1992, p. 48; Dec 1994, p. 86; March 1996, p. 20; Feb 1998, p. 76.
The Sporting News, Nov 8, 1993, p. 10; Feb 21, 1994, p. 38; April 21, 1997, p. 38; February 25, 2005, p. 67.
Sports Illustrated, Jan 14, 1985, p. 88; Nov 7, 1988, p. 72; March 25, 1991, p. 68; April 27, 1992, p. 62; March 17, 1997, p. 101; February 21, 2005, p. 17.
Sports Illustrated for Kids, July 1994, p. 14; Dec 1995, p. 25; Nov, 1997, p. 40.
Wisconsin State Journal, April 11, 1998, sec D, p. 2, col 1.

Westina Matthews Shatteen

1948—

Corporate executive

Westina Matthews Shatteen's rise to the upper echelons of corporate leadership was unusual. "It has been a surprising journey because I started out as a classroom teacher," she told *The Network Journal*. Yet, that is not to say she has not fulfilled her early career aspirations. From a deeply spiritual background, Matthews was drawn to teaching as a way to give back to society. When she made the leap to big business, she only changed job titles, not her personal goals. As a key player in the philanthropic wing of financial powerhouse Merrill Lynch, Dr. Matthews, as she is professionally known, has helped hundreds of children go to college, sponsored countless community initiatives, and created mentoring programs for young women of color. As she told *The Network Journal*, "The one common thread throughout my career has been my commitment to helping others."

Developed Early Desire to Teach

Westina Matthews was born on November 8, 1948, and raised in Yellow Springs, Ohio, where her father, Wesley Matthews, served as an African Methodist Episcopalian minister and her mother, Pat Matthews, worked as a journalist. Even as a child, Matthews showed a desire to lead. In the third grade she ran for class president. Unfortunately she lost by one vote. "I didn't vote for myself, because I thought to be a nice person I had to vote for the other guy," Matthews recalled to *Essence*. "Since then I've always believed in and voted for me first."

Reverend Matthews had a deep influence over his daughter. "My father gave me spirituality, kindness, open-mindedness, and integrity," Matthews said in an article on the *Working Women 2000 and Beyond* Web site. The result was a life infused with faith. "Under my picture in the yearbook at Yellow Springs high school, a friend wrote the scripture verse, 'Go ye therefore and teach all nations,'" Matthews told the *Catholic Expert* Web site. "Early on, people identified within me a strong faith and a sense of service and community and giving back."

Matthews earned a bachelor's degree and a master's degree in education from the University of Dayton, a private Catholic school. Though she was only one of 19 African-American students when she arrived in 1967, Matthews quickly established herself as a campus leader. She was elected the first black homecoming queen in the university's history. "I remember on the float as we went through Dayton we went through the black community, there were people on the street crying," Matthews recalled in a press release on the University of Dayton's Web site. "It finally hit me that they were crying because they were so proud." Before graduating, Matthews would also be named Outstanding Elementary Education Senior and one of Dayton's Top Twenty Students.

Learned Leadership and Faith from Strong Mentors

Though Matthews was able to take advantage of the best that college life had to offer her, she was not

Springs, OH, 1970-76; Stanford Research Institute (SRI), administrative assistant, Menlo Park, CA, 1976-77; The Chicago Community Trust, senior program officer, Chicago, IL, 1982-85; Merrill Lynch, director, philanthropic programs, 1985-97; Merrill Lynch, first vice president, global diversity, 1997-2000; Merrill Lynch Bank, senior vice president, community development services, 2000-01; Merrill Lynch, first vice president, community leadership, global private client group, 2001-03; Merrill Lynch, first vice president, community leadership, chief financial office, 2003–.

Memberships: New York City Board of Education, member, 1990-93; University of Dayton, trustee, 2002–; Executive Leadership Council, board member; Bank Street College of Education, trustee; Merrill Lynch Foundation, trustee.

Awards: Black Women Hall of Fame Foundation, Kizzy Award, 1985; New Urban League, New York, Donald H. McGannon Award, 1994; Girl Scout Council of Greater New York, Woman of Distinction Award, 1998; Brooklyn Center for the Performing Arts, Corporate Leadership Award, 2001; New York Theological Seminary, Urban Angel Award, 2004.

Addresses: *Office*—Merrill Lynch, Community Leadership, 4 World Financial Center, 31st Floor, New York, NY, 10080.

immune to the ongoing struggle for equal rights. She was a sophomore when Martin Luther King, Jr., was shot. "Being a student in the civil rights movement gave me a commitment and passion to education and to equality," she told the University of Dayton. She began fulfilling that commitment as an elementary teacher in her hometown, a position she held for six years.

Berry, a prominent civil rights activist in Chicago. As a child she had tagged along to civil rights meetings with her father and Berry. In Chicago he became her mentor. "My great uncle gave me my people skills. He taught me to convene meetings, to be a conciliator, to be honest, to say what needs to be said and to say it in a way that folks can receive it," she told *Working Women 2000 and Beyond*.

Built Scholarship Program for Underprivileged Children

Matthews began her professional career in 1982 with the Chicago Community Trust, a grant-making foundation. Three years later Merrill Lynch tapped her to be a manager in its philanthropic programs. Matthews moved to the firm's New York offices and through the positions of assistant vice-president and vice-president to become a director by 1997. She also became the first woman, as well as the first minority, to be elected a trustee for the Merrill Lynch foundation.

One of the most ambitious programs that Matthews helped launch during that time was ScholarshipBuilder. Through the innovative program 250 first graders from across the country were guaranteed tuition to the college of their choice if they graduated. Getting Merrill Lynch to sponsor the program was easy. The hard part was getting it up and running. "It all seemed to rest on me," Matthews recalled to *Essence*.

With the help of the National Urban League, ScholarshipBuilder launched in 1988. Over the years, Merrill Lynch and its employees donated $16 million to the program. The pay-off was a 90 percent graduation rate among the participating students—a considerable achievement given that these kids came from backgrounds where less than 50 percent usually graduated. Matthews attributed this success to the timing of the program. "No one started as early as we did," she told CBS News. "We started at the first grade. Everything we found out was that you had to start early." For a woman long dedicated to the education of children, ScholarshipBuilder was a fitting legacy.

Rose to Corporate Prominence in Diversity

When Merrill Lynch wanted to expand its diversity programs in the mid-1990s, it turned to Matthews. By this point, she had developed a stellar reputation. The mayor of New York had appointed her to the New York City Board of Education. She had earned several prestigious national awards and served on the boards of several prominent organizations. Still she was surprised at the job offer. "I was invited to a meeting with some senior executives and lawyers. It turned out they wanted to talk about diversity. I don't know what I had to do with diversity, so I just walked in there and said what I thought," Matthews recalled in *Cracking the Corporate Code*.

Within three months, Matthews was installed as Merrill Lynch's first head of global diversity. She oversaw corporate-wide diversity initiatives. The new position gave her power to effect change at the firm. One policy she took particular pride in was diversity reporting. "We've created diversity scorecards that keep track of the work force three times a year for every business group around the world," she told *Cracking the Corporate Code*. "When they have to turn in these qualitative and quantitative reports, you start seeing a difference."

In 2000 Matthews moved to Merrill Lynch Bank where she became senior vice president of community development. Her role was to oversee the bank's charitable and community relations efforts. The following year she became first vice president of community leadership for the firm's global private client group. She held that position until 2003 when was promoted to first vice president of community leadership for the firm's global human resources. In that position Matthews was responsible for developing strategic alliances to support new business development and community relations throughout the corporation.

Shared the Gift of Faith with the Public

In 2002 Matthews launched the "Black Women on Wall Street" symposium. Her goal was two-fold—to provide a forum for sharing experience and strategies, and to create a mentoring environment between seasoned Wall Streeters and eager newcomers ready to make it in the traditionally white, male world of finance. The success of the program has touched Matthews. "To be able to look into the faces of over 200 young, bright, smart and talented women who are eager to climb the corporate ladder on Wall Street is certainly a very proud moment," she told *CBB*.

Matthews desire to help reached well beyond the moneyed boardrooms of Wall Street. Through a venture called *Have a Little Faith*, she began publicly sharing the lesson she learned from her mother—with just the faith of a mustard seed you can overcome anything. Matthews self published *Have a Little Faith: The Faith of a Mustard Seed* in 2003. She bought five pounds of mustard seeds and hand filled thousands of packets of seeds to include with each book. The sequel, *Have a Little Faith: For Women Fully Grown*, came out in 2004. Through the internet, speaking engagements, and word of mouth the books have sold over 7,000 copies. "This has become a labor of love for me," she told *CBB*. "The response has been overwhelming. I receive notes from perfect strangers, and people are passing the books along to others. They're comforting people during an illness, a loss, a broken relationship, a lost job. That was the intent, and it's been very rewarding to watch that."

Matthews's third book *Have a Little Faith: In the Midst of Relationships* was released early in 2005. Meanwhile she continued to spearhead innovative community programs in her role with Merrill Lynch. The woman, who long ago planned on a teaching career in small-town Ohio, had very successfully found a way to touch thousands around the world through both her corporate work and her spiritual convictions.

Sources

Books

Cracking the Corporate Code, From Survival to Mastery: Real Stories of African-American Success, Executive Leadership Council, 2000.

Periodicals

Business Wire, June 27, 2002.
Essence, August 1989.

On-line

"Chosen Children Go Off To College," *CBS News*, http://cbsnews.cbs.com/stories/2000/06/27/national/main209844.shtml (February 15, 2005).

"Faith of a Mustard Seed," *Catholic Experts*, www.catholicexperts.org/MustardSeed.html (February 15, 2005).

"Say What Needs to Be Said," *Women Working 2000 and Beyond*, www.womenworking2000.com/success/index.php?id=47(February 15, 2005).

"University of Dayton Alumna Remains Faithful to King's Dream," *University of Dayton*, www.udayton.edu/news/nr/011102.html (February 15, 2005).

"Westina Matthews Shatteen, Twenty Five Influential Women in Business," *The Network Journal*, www.tnj.com/march_03_issue/20.html (February 15, 2005).

Michelle McKinney Hammond

1957—

Author, motivational speaker

A successful advertising executive up to the mid-1990s, Michelle McKinney Hammond then invented a new career providing insights into how to be a single Christian woman in pursuit of a healthy, fulfilling life, with or without a husband. McKinney Hammond published her first book, *What to Do until Love Finds You: Getting Ready for Mr. Right,* in 1997 and has since authored some twenty self-help books and become a sought-after relationship expert.

West Indian and African Roots

McKinney Hammond was born in London, England, in 1957. When she was two years old her parents divorced, and McKinney Hammond, whose mother is of West Indian descent, was sent to Barbados to live with her grandmother and aunt and uncle. McKinney Hammond's mother remained in London to complete her studies, and during this time she met and married William McKinney. When McKinney Hammond was seven years old, her mother came to Barbados with her new husband to reclaim her daughter. The family then moved to Muskegon, Michigan, in the United States, where McKinney Hammond spent the remainder of her childhood.

As a child, McKinney Hammond struggled with the changes in culture and with her own insecurities. She told *Today's Christian Woman,* "Each place left me with a heavy accent that made me different from all the other children in our next home. Besides that, I was an ugly duckling—with a gap between my front teeth, glasses, and an extremely thin body. I was an easy target for neighborhood bullies!" During high school she developed an interest in music and theater and earned leading parts in both community and school stage and musical productions.

McKinney Hammond's father, George Hammond, returned to his native home of Ghana, West Africa, after he divorced McKinney Hammond's mother, and thereafter McKinney Hammond lost touch with him. When she was 14 years old, an aunt accidentally encountered her birth father while on a trip to Africa. As a result her father then flew to Michigan to be reunited with his daughter, rekindling the father-daughter relationship; the two have been close ever since. McKinney Hammond has never lived in Africa but visits her extended family once or twice a year, and she began using the last names of both her fathers.

Moved to Chicago

After completing high school McKinney Hammond moved to Chicago, where she attended and graduated from the Ray-Vogue College of Design (now known as the Illinois Institute of Art). Following her graduation she flew to Ghana to meet her father's family for the first time. During the trip McKinney Hammond, who was raised in the Episcopalian church but was not a practicing Christian at the time, was deeply influenced by her paternal grandmother, a devoutly religious woman who spend several hours every day in prayer at a local church.

Five months after McKinney Hammond returned from her trip to Africa, she was devastated when her boy-

Selected Awards: U.S. Television ~~Award~~ ~~(~~
producer); multiple Creative Excellence in Black Advertising awards; Windy Award; International Television Association PHILO Awards.

Addresses: *Office*—HeartWing Ministries, P.O. Box 11052, Chicago, IL 60611. *Web*—http://www.michellehammond.com.

friend was shot and killed. Her life in shambles, she searched for validation in a series of relationships and friendships that did not stick. Having emerged from her self-professed ugly-duckling stage, she sought the excitement of a glamorous life and interviewed to become a Playboy bunny. But she continued to feel unfulfilled and without purpose.

McKinney Hammond's life was impacted by two life-altering events. First, searching desperately for the peace she witnessed in her grandmother's life, McKinney Hammond was moved by her reading of Hal Lindsey's *Late Great Planet Earth*, which lays out a particular vision of what God intended for Christians. Second, a woman who shared a bus ride with on her way to work each morning constantly pestered McKinney Hammond to attend church with her. Finally McKinney Hammond acquiesced, and during the service the minister prayed for McKinney Hammond, telling her that God loved her very much. McKinney Hammond, who was very moved by the experience, claimed to finally begin to feel at peace with herself.

From Advertising Executive to Author

Having become a committed Christian, McKinney Hammond decided to forego becoming a Playboy bunny and landed a job with the nation's largest minority-owned advertising firm, the Chicago-based Burrell Advertising, where she eventually became an associate creative director. During her tenure at Burrell,

ended, McKinney Hammond was once again feeling devastated and alone. Searching for some help, she went the bookstore to purchase a book about being single. Dissatisfied with what she found, McKinney Hammond decided she should write her own book. Although she began writing the book in 1991, she did not actually finish it until 1995, when a bad accident in which she was struck by a car laid her up for a year and a half. The result was *What to Do until Love Finds You: Getting Ready for Mr. Right,* published in 1997.

The gist of McKinney Hammond's message is that single women must first find enjoyment and fulfillment in their singleness. Writing from her own often painful experience, McKinney Hammond told *Today's Christian Woman,* "I've found that when we single women stop asking, 'Why am I alone?' and start asking God 'Why am I here?' our whole world changes. We start rediscovering old dreams and discover creative ideas on how to use our gifts to bless other people. Finding a mate becomes less important when we find joy and meaning, because that hole in our heart isn't about a person. It's about fulfilling our God-given purpose—what we were created to do and be. Only then will you find true peace and satisfaction—whether you're married or not."

Became Relationship Expert

Following on the success of *What to Do until Love Finds You,* over the next ten years McKinney Hammond penned twenty books dealing with a Christian understanding of singleness. Although she affirms that single women must "get a life," she does not negate the value of the marriage relationship or leave finding the right man to pure happenstance. Many of her titles—including *Secrets of an Irresistible Woman* (1998), *The Power of Femininity* (1999), *If Men Are Like Buses, Then How Do I Catch One?* (2000), *101 Ways to Get and Keep His Attention* (2003), *The Power of Being a Woman: Embracing the Triumph of the Feminine Spirit* (2004), and *Ending the Search for Mr. Right: How to Be Found by the Man You've Been*

....es, McKinney Hammond has many faithful readers who find her down-to-earth, girlfriend-in-your-living-room writing style refreshing and inspiring.

With the success of her books, McKinney Hammond became a sought-after relationship expert, and as a result she created HeartWing Ministries to promote and coordinate her writing and speaking obligations. She travels the country teaching at women's conferences, seminars, churches, and universities, co-hosts the Emmy-nominated Christian television talk show *Aspiring Women*, and regularly appears on other Christian television shows. She also does voice-overs for television and radio commercials. In early 2005, McKinney Hammond, who once aspired to a professional music career, was finishing up her first CD, *It's Amazing,* produced by Inner Light Records.

Selected works

Books

What to Do Until Love Finds You: Getting Ready for Mr. Right, Harvest House Publishers, 1997.
Secrets of an Irresistible Woman, Harvest House, 1998.
The Power of Femininity, Harvest House, 1999.
If Men Are Like Buses, Then How Do I Catch One?, Multnomah Publishers, 2000.
How to Be Blessed and Highly Favored: Living Richly under the Smile of God, WaterBrook Press, 2001.
Where Are You, God?, Harvest House, 2002.
Why Do I Say "Yes" When I Need to Say "No"?, Harvest House, 2002.

Albums

It's Amazing, Inner Light Records, 2005.

Sources

Periodicals

Black Enterprise, November 2004, p. 188.
Black Issue Book Review, July 2001, p. 64; January-February 2003, p. 72-73.
Library Journal, January 1, 2005, p. 134.
Publishers Weekly, April 10, 2000, p. 95; July 23, 2001, p. 71.
Today's Christian Woman, March-April 1999; September-October 2001; March-April 2003, p. 11.

On-line

"Michell McKinney Hammond," *Biography Resource Center,* www.galenet.com/servlet/BioRC (February 18, 2005).
"Michelle McKinney Hammond," *Harvest House Publishers,* http://www.harvesthousepublishers.com/mediaauthor.cfm?EDID=100463 (February 18, 2005).
"Michelle McKinney Hammond: Her Life, Ministry, and Career," *Kregel Christian Books and Resources,* http://www.parable.com/1539167/spotlight.asp?sid=41&ct=Biography (February 18, 2005).
"Michelle McKinney Hammond Official Web Site," http://www.michellehammond.com (February 18, 2005).

—Kari Bethel

Joseph C. Mills

1946—

Nuclear engineer

In a career spanning more than three decades, Dr. Joseph C. Mills contributed significantly to our understanding of nuclear reactor safety and the development of a new generation of nuclear reactors for use in space. He played pivotal roles in the design, construction, launch, and assembly of the International Space Station (ISS). Dr. Mills also headed The Boeing Company's effort to design and build the Jupiter Icy Moons Orbiter (JIMO) for the National Aeronautics and Space Administration's (NASA's) Jet Propulsion Laboratory (JPL).

Remained Focused on Education

Born on February 26, 1946, in Los Angeles, California, Joseph C. Mills, Jr., grew up in the tough neighborhoods of South Central L.A. His mother, Mildred Craddock Mills (subsequently Lehman), a clerk for the Los Angeles County Marshall's Office, stressed the importance of education for her children's success. Joe's father, Joseph C. Mills, Sr., worked for the U.S. Postal Service for a few years, but was often unemployed. The Mills divorced when Joe was eleven and he and his younger brother and sister were raised by their mother. She kept Joe focused on his education at a time when athletics and friends pulled him in other directions.

In addition to his mother, Joe Mills was strongly influenced by his fourth-grade teacher who recognized his abilities and challenged him in mathematics. He also looked to Dr. Martin Luther King, Jr., as his role model—a man from a humble background who accomplished great feats.

However, for the most part, it was negative experiences that challenged Mills. He attended Los Angeles High School, which was about 70 percent white, and shared his accelerated classes with only one or two other black students. He told *Contemporary Black Biography* (*CBB*) that during his junior year a school counselor told him: "Sometimes you can keep up with the other students just by working harder." The counselor was implying that, despite being a superior math and science student, Mills lacked innate ability. When he entered the University of California at Los Angeles (UCLA), a counselor said to him: "Are you really this good?" as he related to *CBB*. Mills took such negative comments as challenges to succeed.

Became a Reactor Safety Expert

Despite having grown up near the heart of the aerospace industry, when he entered U.C.L.A. in 1963, on a four-year California State Scholarship, Mills had only the vaguest notion of what an engineer did. In the end he chose engineering because it lacked a foreign-language requirement. However Mills soon found that he loved engineering and its applications. He told *CBB*: "Engineers take science and turn it into practical things…. God put me in the right place for my skill set." Mills earned his Bachelor of Science degree in engineering in 1967.

Fellowships and traineeships from the Atomic Energy Commission enabled Mills to complete his graduate

project and program manage... ...p... ... ...development of new nuclear power systems, 1972-87, Rockwell International, program director for development of nuclear power systems for military and exploratory space missions, 1987-94, Rockwell and the Boeing Company, director of the Power Module/Cargo Element Team for the International Space Station, 1994-97; Boeing, Canoga Park Site Director, 1997-98; Boeing, Huntington Beach Site Director, 1998-99; Boeing, Houston, TX, vice president and deputy program manager for ISS contract, 1999-01; Boeing, vice president and program manager for ISS contract, 2001-03; Boeing Integrated Defense Systems, Pasedena, CA, vice president and program manager for JIMO Phase A Trade and Concept Design Study, 2003-04; Boeing, Canoga Park, CA, vice president and executive focal of space science initiative, 2004-05.

Memberships: American Nuclear Society; American Institute of Aeronautics and Astronautics.

Awards: LA-San Fernando Engineers' Council, Distinguished Engineering Project Achievement Award for the ISS Electric Power System, 1998; *Aviation Week*, Laureate of the Year for Space, 2002; Boeing 30-Year Service Award, 2002; *Black Engineer*, Black Engineer of the Year Pioneer Award, 2004; Rotary National Award for Space Achievement (RNASA) Stellar Award, 2004.

Addresses: *Office*—c/o The Boeing Company-NASA Systems, 13100 Space Center Blvd, Houston, TX 77059-3556.

..., Mills published ... ...nuclear power systems and safety a... ... ...n internationally-known expert on safety systems for liquid-metal fast-breeder nuclear reactors (LMFBRs). During the early 1980s he served on numerous task forces and committees that studied the development of LMFBRs, both domestically and internationally.

Designed Power Systems for Spacecraft

Between 1987 and 1994 Mills was a Rockwell program director in charge of developing nuclear power systems for military applications and civilian exploratory missions in space. Among his projects were the NASA Space Exploration Initiative and the Dynamic Isotope Power System for the U.S. Department of Energy (DOE) and the U.S. Air Force. Mills also was program manager for Rockwell's space nuclear power systems component of the "Star Wars" missile defense—the Strategic Defense Initiative Organization (SDIO)—initiated by President Ronald Reagan. Mills worked on both a multimegawatt nuclear power system for the DOE/SDIO and a 40-kilowatts-electric (kWe) Thermionic Space Nuclear Power System for the DOE/Air Force/SDIO.

However by the early 1990s the world had changed dramatically. When the predicted energy crisis failed to materialize, plans for a new generation of nuclear-powered electrical-generating systems were put on hold. With the end of the Cold War in the early 1990s, interest in the military applications dwindled. In 1994 Mills went to work on the International Space Station (ISS). It was to be the high point of his career.

Initially Mills worked on Rockwell's solar power systems for the ISS, as director of the Power Module/Cargo Element Team at Canoga Park. When Rockwell merged with The Boeing Company in 1996, followed by Boeing's acquisition of McDonnell Douglas, the companies' ISS contracts came under Boeing's administration. In 1997 Mills became the site director at Canoga Park and in 1998 he became site director at the Huntington Beach, California, facility. In these positions Mills oversaw the design, development, testing and evaluation, production, and flight preparation of the hardware and software used for the assembly of ISS components in space. These out-board and in-board trusses and their associated electrical power systems, produced under McDonnell Douglas and Rockwell contracts, were launched from the space shuttle for the construction and instrumentation of the ISS.

Spent Nine Years on the ISS

In 1999 Mills spent three months as the ISS site director in Huntsville, Alabama, correcting problems and overseeing the production of pressurized element hardware and associated software for the ISS. From there he moved to the central ISS headquarters in Houston, Texas. As vice president and program manager in Houston, Mills was in charge of the entire Boeing role as prime integrating contractor for the ISS. To service this multibillion-dollar contract that saw the orbiting laboratory through its design, development, testing, launch, and operation, Mills coordinated several thousand Boeing engineers at five major locations around the country, as well as subcontractors and suppliers in 23 states. Additionally Mills was responsible for integrating the contributions of the ISS's 16 partner countries. Dr. Mills told CBB that his work on the ISS was, by far, the most satisfying project of his career. "In the early part of my career, working at the leading edge of nuclear science—Star Wars and nuclear energy—nothing was ever built. The ISS was my first opportunity to see the fruits of my labor—from design all the way to launch, utilization, and discoveries. I was leading the thousands of folks who were doing it and nurturing young careers."

Because of his background in nuclear power systems, in 2003 Boeing asked Mills to try to secure NASA's JPL JIMO contract. JIMO was a major component of NASA's ambitious Prometheus Program to develop nuclear-fission-powered propulsion systems for the exploration of deep space. The Prometheus Jupiter Icy Moons spacecraft would be designed to orbit three planet-sized moons of Jupiter—Callisto, Ganymede, and Europa—which may contain huge oceans beneath their icy surfaces. Plans for JIMO included the use of nuclear-electric power, a technology that uses converters to transform reactor heat into electricity to power the spacecraft thrusters more directly than conventional reactors that heat steam to turn turbines. Mills believed that such a system would enable JIMO to orbit the Jovian moons for years, conducting detailed scientific observations and experiments.

Failed to Win JIMO Contract

From the fall of 2003 to the spring of 2004, Mills was in charge of Boeing's JIMO Phase A Trade and Concept Design Study, working in Pasadena, California, for Boeing Integrated Defense Systems, one of the world's largest defense and space businesses. Boeing hoped to win the JPL contract to co-design, develop, build, launch, and operate JIMO. However in the fall of 2004, Northrop Grumman Space Technology was awarded the contract.

Mills stayed on at Canoga Park as vice president and executive focal of Boeing's space science initiative, one of four NASA initiatives to which a Boeing executive was assigned as the focal contact between the company and NASA. In this position Mills helped plan Boeing's future undertakings in space.

In 2003 Mills was named Aviation Week's Laureate of the Year for Space in recognition of his contributions to the ISS. In 2004 he was awarded the Rotary National Award for Space Achievement (RNASA) Stellar Award—also known as the NASA Rotary Stellar Award for Late Career Achievement—for his nine years of leading the Boeing ISS program and his contributions to the development and delivery of every major ISS component and system. Mills also was recognized with Black Engineer's 2004 Pioneer Award for his work on the ISS. The Pioneer Award is reserved for engineers who have made contributions to areas in which very few black Americans have worked. Dr. Joseph C. Mills retired from the Boeing Company in March of 2005, devoting more time to his family, to volunteering in the community, and to playing golf.

Selected writings

"An Axial Kinetics Model for Fast Reactor Disassembly Accidents," Proceedings of the Conference on New Developments in Reactor Mathematics and Applications (Idaho Falls, Idaho), March 1971.

"An Industry-University Cooperative Program: AAP," Blacks in Science and Engineering Manpower Symposium (Cleveland, Ohio), October 1974.

"Inherent Safety in Liquid Metal-Cooled Breeder Reactors," Los Angeles Energy Symposium, October 1980.

"Development of Scaling Requirements for Natural Convection LMFBR Shutdown Heat Removal Test Facilities," Specialists Meeting on the Safety Aspects of Natural Circulation Decay Heat Removal in LMFBRs (Grenoble, France), May 1981.

"Phenomenological Sodium Tests to Investigate Intank Natural Circulation Behavior under LMFBR Design Heat Removal Conditions," ANS/ENS Reactor Safety Meeting (Lyon, France), July 1982.

"An Analytical Study of Stratification in Horizontal Pipes with Fluid Temperature Transient Imposed at Inlet," ASME Winter Meeting (New Orleans), December 1984.

"COMMIX Code Validation Studies with Phenomenological Sodium Natural Convection Experiments,"

BNL Specialists Meeting on Decay Heat Removal and Natural Convection in LMFBRs (New York), April 1985

Sources

On-line

"Black Engineer of the Year Award Winners, 2004," *Black Engineer.com*, www.blackengineer.com/art man/publish/printer_204.shtml (February 4, 2005).

"Four Boeing Engineers Receive National Black Engineer Awards," *Boeing News Release*, www.boeing com/news/releases/2004/q1/nr_040218s.html (February 4, 2005).

"Jupiter Icy Moons Orbiter, *Jet Propulsion Laboratory, California Institute of Technology*, www.jpl nasa.gov/jimo/ (February 8, 2005).

Other

Additional information for this profile was obtained through an interview with Dr. Joseph C. Mills on February 16, 2005, and through materials provided by Boeing Company-NASA Systems.

—Margaret Alic

Marc H. Morial

1958—

Executive, civil rights activist

Morial, Marc H., photograph. AP/Wide World Photos Reproduced by permission.

As both politician and leader of the National Urban League, Marc H. Morial has dedicated himself to helping others. Morial served two terms as mayor of New Orleans. His tenure marked the third time in the city's history that an African-American held the top post. When he first won the election in 1994 few, it seemed, expected this politically inexperienced son of Ernest "Dutch" Morial—the city's first African-American mayor—to accomplish what he did during his first term. By putting in place a series of anti-crime measures, reforming the police department, and capturing federal funding for other programs, Morial and his administration set in motion a precipitous drop in violent crime in the city. Enjoying near-unprecedented support and popularity—among both black and white residents of New Orleans—he easily won a second term in 1998. "Morial," noted New York Times reporter Rick Bragg, "has always been one of the crown princes of this city," and remarked that the younger politician's popularity had now surpassed that enjoyed by his late father. So popular did Morial remain that he petitioned to revise his post's term limits in order to run for an unprecedented third term as New Orleans' mayor. Unable to lift the law, Morial moved on in 2003 to become president and CEO of the National Urban League. He has brought the same enthusiasm and skill to the Urban League, and in his first years of leadership has initiated new, revitalizing programs aimed at addressing the most pressing problems for black Americans.

Born on January 3, 1958, in New Orleans, Louisiana, Morial was the second of five children in the family of lawyer Dutch Morial and his schoolteacher wife, Sybil. Both parents were politically active in local issues and the wider civil-rights struggles of the 1960s. Dutch Morial eventually became a judge and was elected New Orleans's first African-American mayor in 1978. Marc Morial, then a college student at the University of Pennsylvania, served as a campaign coordinator for his father. After earning a degree in economics in 1980, Morial attended Georgetown Law School and received his degree in 1983. After two years with a New Orleans firm, he opened his own firm in 1985.

Morial soon became actively involved in the Democratic Party both on the local and national levels. During the Rev. Jesse Jackson's bid for the 1988

At a Glance . . .

Born Marc H. Morial on January 3, 1958, in New Orleans, LA; son of Ernest "Dutch" (a lawyer, judge, and politician) and Sybil (a teacher) Morial; married Michelle Miller. children: Kemah and Mason. *Education*: University of Pennsylvania, BA, 1980; Georgetown University, JD, 1983. *Politics*: Democrat.

Career: Barham & Churchill, New Orleans, LA, associate, 1983-85; Marc H. Morial Professional Law Corp., New Orleans, LA, managing partner, 1985-94; Xavier University, adjunct professor of political science, 1987-90; Louisiana State Senator, District Four, 1992-94; City of New Orleans, mayor, 1994-2002; Adams and Reese (law firm), New Orleans, attorney, 2002; National Urban League, president and CEO, 2003–.

Memberships: American Bar Association, National Bar Association, Louisiana Trial Lawyers Association, National Conference of Black Lawyers, Louisiana State Bar Association, Harare, chair, 1983-86, Louisiana Association of Minority and Women-Owned Businesses, Louisiana Special Olympics, board of directors, 1991–.

Awards: Sargent Shriver National Center on Poverty Law, Shriver Award for Equal Justice, 2004.

Addresses: *Office—* The National Urban League, 120 Wall Street, 8th Floor, New York, NY, 10005.

Democratic Party presidential nomination, Morial was a key player in Jackson's New Orleans support organization. That summer, he also served as a delegate to the Democratic National Convention. In 1991, he ran for and won a seat in the Louisiana State Senate in Baton Rouge. During his first few years, he earned accolades as a "rookie" legislator for his voting record and sponsorship of bills. Strongly liberal in his politics, Morial supported reproductive rights for women and opposed the death penalty.

Entered Mayoral Race

By the early 1990s, Morial's hometown of New Orleans was in trouble. The city's skyrocketing crime and murder rates attracted national media attention and began to undermine the financial health of a city heavily dependent on tourism. In addition, there were several highly publicized incidents of police brutality and allegations of widespread corruption within the police department. Believing he could turn New Orleans around, Morial decided to enter the mayoral race.

Morial announced his candidacy for mayor in late 1993 at a press conference in which he exhorted, "We need to clean up City Hall with a shovel and not a broom!" according to his biography on his personal Web site. Although still relatively inexperienced politically, Morial was an enthusiastic campaigner who quickly gathered popular support. Most African-American adults still held his father, Dutch Morial, in high regard and were willing to throw their support behind his son. The mayoral race intensified dramatically when Morial's top opponent, Donald Mintz, a Jewish lawyer long active in New Orleans politics, tried to divide the city's electorate along racial lines. During the campaign anonymous, racially-charged fliers began appearing across the city. Many of these fliers denounced Mintz with slogans such as "Stop the Colored/Jew Coalition," and one depicting Mintz with a man resembling Nelson Mandela.

Morial and his campaign team accused the Mintz camp of creating the offensive fliers themselves, and were partially vindicated. The New Orleans Human Relations Commission launched an inquiry, and found that at least two fliers originated from within the Mintz organization. More damaging to Mintz, however, was the fact that his campaign staff had used the fliers in a national fundraising effort to evoke sympathy for victims of anti-Semitism. These fundraising efforts helped generate $200,000 in donations for the Mintz campaign. The National Jewish Relations Advisory Council in New York "had concluded that they [the fliers] were probably not the work of hate groups," according to Ronald Smothers in the *New York Times*.

Until the hate literature debacle, Mintz had been slightly ahead of Morial in the polls. On election day, Mintz received more votes than Morial, but was unable to win a clear majority. As a result, a runoff election was scheduled to determine a winner. In the weeks heading up to the runoff election, the campaign grew increasingly bitter. There were allegations that Morial had once been admitted to a hospital for an erratic heartbeat. Allegedly, Morial had told medical personnel that he had snorted cocaine earlier that evening, a claim that Morial strongly denied. Voters, however, were not swayed by the negative attacks on Morial. "Morial, despite his relative youth and perceived inexperience, has basked somewhat in the aura of his father's reputation for assertiveness and savvy," declared Smothers. His *New York Times* article went on to describe the toll that rampant crime and financial mismanagement had taken on New Orleans residents and how Morial's presence in the race had "evoked a time when a Morial was in City Hall and things were better," wrote Smothers.

Curbed Crime in New Orleans

In the runoff election of March 5, 1994, Morial emerged victorious with 54 percent of the vote. In his victory speech, Morial urged city residents of all ethnicities to come together to work toward the future, declaring, "tomorrow we will start rebuilding the city in the physical sense and the spiritual sense. We don't plan to take a vacation," *Jet* reported him as saying. Morial also broke with tradition by choosing not to hold the inauguration during the day at City Hall. Instead, he was sworn in during the evening at the Ernest N. Morial Convention Center, a change that allowed more residents to attend the inauguration. During his first 100 days in office, Morial worked to improve and expand youth programs sponsored by the city's recreation department in order to reduce the high rates of juvenile crime in New Orleans. He recalled that becoming involved as a youth in many city-sponsored recreational programs had kept him out of trouble.

In an attempt to bring the crime rate in New Orleans under control, Morial implemented a controversial "community policing" program and instituted a curfew for all juveniles. Anyone under the age of 17 had to be off the streets after 8 p.m. on weekdays, and by 11 p.m. on weekends. Juveniles who broke the curfew and their parents were required to attend a counseling session and repeat offenders were subject to fines. Two months after the program went into effect, crime during curfew hours decreased by 38 percent, and in the span of three months, the city's overall crime rate dropped over 14 percent.

To address problems within the New Orleans police department, Morial hired a new police chief, put more officers on the street, gave the force pay increases, and moved the citizen-complaint department out of a police precinct building. By the end of 1995, reported Mary-Margaret Larmouth in *Nation's Cities Weekly*, New Orleans' murder rate had dropped 18 percent, and civil-rights complaints against police officers also dropped by 30 percent. During Morial's first term in office, the crime statistics continued to plummet: the murder rate fell from a high of 424 in 1994 to 266 in 1997. At the city's housing projects, people began using the picnic tables and playgrounds again. *New York Times* reporter Bragg also wrote that young residents of one the city's most crime-plagued housing projects no longer slept on the floor because of stray bullets.

Earned Respect as Mayor and Organization Leader

Some of Morial's detractors pointed out that the overall violent crime rate had dropped nationwide, and that the mayor and his policies did not deserve full credit for the drop in crime in New Orleans. However, Morial remained extremely popular within the city's African American community and he easily won a re-election bid in 1998. Poll results showed that Morial had received 93 percent of the city's African American vote and 43 percent of the white vote.

In his second term, Morial continued his efforts to clean up and improve New Orleans. He focused on maintaining and re-opening many of the city's parks and recreation facilities, rebuilding and repairing historic Canal Street, and expanding the city's convention center and airport. As his second term came near its end, speculation had begun regarding Morial's plans. Morial so enjoyed his position as mayor that in 2001 he gathered enough signatures to vote on rescinding the mayoral term limit requirements, so that he could run for a third term in office. His effort did not work, however, and he soon sought other work. *Ebony* writer Muriel L. Whetstone asked Morial what he hoped his legacy would be. "We want to leave a mark that we took a city that was dying and we reinvigorated it, we revitalized it," Morial told the magazine. "Also that we, in a very real way, created an opportunity for the African-American community to participate in the economics of this community, and that's a tough challenge."

After leaving the mayor's office, Morial accepted a new challenge; this time one with national impact. He became president and CEO of the National Urban League in 2003. A community-based civil rights group formed in 1910, the National Urban League Morial took over had a budget of $40 million and over 100 affiliates. Great things were expected from Morial, the man who turned around the "murder capital" as New Orleans was often referred before his tenure. "Anyone who can successfully manage a city like New Orleans and turn it around like he has done demonstrates he has a capacity to lead," the National Urban League's search committee chairman, Charles Hamilton Jr., told *Jet*. For his part, Morial knew exactly how he wanted to lead the organization. "We are in [the] post-Civil Rights Era where the work of so many organizations is respected in history and not understood in a contemporary context, and that is going to be one of our challenges, so that people understand what our role is," he explained to *Jet*. From the outset, Morial set a new course for the organization, embarking on a plan he called an "Empowerment Agenda." Citing the inequality that plagued the lives of black Americans, Morial focused his agenda on educating youth, connecting blacks with meaningful employment, addressing healthcare issues in the black community, taking positive steps toward civil and racial justice, and promoting civic engagement.

Sources

Periodicals

Black Collegian, October 2003, p. 106.
Ebony, November 1994, p. 80; August 2003, p. 28; April 12, 2004, p. 4; August 2004, p. 18.

Jet, February 21, 1994, p. 8; March 21, 1994, p. 4; June 2, 2003, p. 4; August 25, 2003, p. 4; August 23, 2004, p. 6.

Nation's Cities Weekly, November 6, 1995, p. 3.

New York Times, February 27, 1994, p. 20; March 27, 1994, p. 24; February 17, 1998, p. A10.

PR Newswire, May 10, 2002.

Washington Post, January 6, 1995, p. A21.

On-line

Marc H. Morial, www.marchmorial.com (April 27, 2005).

National Urban League, www.nul.org (April 27, 2005).

—Carol Brennan and Sara Pendergast

Sir William "Bill" Morris

1938—

British trade union leader

Arguably the most influential black Briton in history, labor leader Bill Morris moved to England in 1954 from Jamaica. He joined the Transport and General Workers' Union in 1958 and became one of the union's full-time officials in 1973, rising through the ranks to become its leader in 1991. A moderate and a supporter of Tony Blair at a time when the Labour Party and the British trade union movement were battling with their radical tendencies, Morris was not popular at first. But he was re-elected in 1995 and served a total of 12 years as general secretary. As the leader of Britain's biggest and most powerful trade union, Morris had great influence over the Labour Party and indirectly, from 1997, government policy. He later became a critic of the Blair administration.

Morris's quiet but authoritative leadership helped rein in the more militant elements of the union during the 1980s and 1990s and ushered in a period of modernization. It was also significant in regaining respect for trade unionism in British public life after decades of conflict and decline. His ability as a leader has also been recognized outside trade unionism and he has been an adviser for various public bodies, including universities and the BBC. In 1998 he became a non-executive

Morris, Bill, photograph. Julian Herbert/Getty Images

director of the Bank of England, a remarkable achievement for a first-generation immigrant with almost no formal education beyond the age of 16. He received a knighthood, Britain's highest civil honor, in 2003.

Morris was born in Bombay, Jamaica, on October 19, 1938, the son of William Morris, a part-time policeman, and Una Morris, a domestic science teacher. He grew up in Manchester, Jamaica, and attended Mizpah school, where he excelled at cricket and hoped one day to play for the West Indies. He was also intending to go to agricultural college, but when his father died he moved to Birmingham, England, in 1954 to live with his mother. Like many immigrants from the Caribbean, Morris found it difficult to adjust to life in Britain at first, not least because the cold, wet weather was unlike anything he had ever experienced. But he found a job at Hardy Spicers, an engineering company based in Birmingham, and began studying at Handsworth Technical College, near to his home. He married Minetta in 1957 and they had two sons, Garry, and Clyde; Minetta died in 1990.

In 1958 Morris joined the Transport and General Workers' Union. Now known simply as the T&G, the

At a Glance . . .

Born William Morris on October 19, 1938, in Bombay, Jamaica; married Minetta (died 1990); children: Garry, Clyde. *Education:* Handsworth Technical College.

Career: Joined Hardy Spicers, a Birmingham engineering firm, 1958; Transport and General Workers Union (T&G), became shop steward, 1963; T&G, Nottingham and Derby District, full-time union official, 1973-76; T&G, Northampton District Secretary, 1976-79; T&G, National Secretary for the Passenger Services Trade Group, 1979; T&G, Deputy General Secretary, 1986; T&G, General Secretary (elected), 1991-2003; University of Technology, Jamaica, Chancellor, 1999–.

Memberships: T&G General Executive Council member, 1972-73; Trade Union Congress (TUC) General Council and Executive Committee, 1988-03; Bank of England, non-executive director, 1998–; Royal Commission on Reform of the House of Lords, 1999-2000; The Prince's Youth Business Trust, advisory committee; Open University Foundation, trustee board member; City and Guilds of London Institute, fellow.

Awards: Order of Jamaica, 2003; Knighthood, November 2003; many honorary degrees.

union dates back to 1922, the date that fourteen unions representing workers from heavy industry, transport, and general trades merged. At its founding the T&G became one of the largest and most powerful unions; its first general secretary was Ernest Bevin, one of the founders of the British welfare state after World War II. Morris joined at a time when union membership was rising quickly and when the political climate in Britain was favorable to union lobbying. He quickly became involved with the day-to-day running of the union branch at Hardy Spicers and in 1963 was elected shop steward, representing a group of employees to the company's management.

Morris became a full-time union official in 1973, when he took the post of organizer for the Nottingham and Derby District; he later became the Northampton District secretary. His first national role came in 1979, when he was appointed national secretary for the Passenger Services Trade Group, negotiating pay and conditions in the bus industry. In 1986 he became deputy general secretary of the union at a time when the Thatcher government was introducing legislation to

limit union power. Under new laws union leaders had to be elected and in 1990 his appointment was confirmed by a postal ballot. As deputy general secretary he held responsibility for managing union activities in four transport sectors, in the energy sector, in engineering, as well as representing many white collar workers. Morris had benefited personally from the T&G's educational services and he used his position to champion worker education and training as a factor in promoting equal opportunities.

Morris took over the leadership of the union when he was elected to the position of General Secretary in 1991. At the time of his election he insisted that he did not see himself as the black candidate, saying: "I am not the black candidate, rather the candidate who is black." As a moderate in the British trade union movement, Morris was an ally of the Labour Party, then struggling to regain credibility as a political force. Part of that struggle was its desire to control the extreme left wing of the party, known as the "militant tendency," and Morris himself took steps to control militants in his union. Despite becoming unpopular with many members as a result, he was re-elected in 1995.

When the Blair government came to power in 1997 Morris became a powerful friend to the new prime minister, but the relationship soured over policies introduced following the destruction of the World Trade Center on September 11, 2001. When the first plane flew into the towers Morris was chairing the annual conference of the Trade Union Congress in Brighton, on the south coast of England, and was looking forward to introducing Tony Blair as a keynote speaker that afternoon. As the news emerged, Blair returned to London immediately and in the days that followed Morris declared his support for the government in the war against terror. But it wasn't long before Morris's relationship with the Blair government turned sour. He told *The Guardian* newspaper in 2002: "When we said on September 11 that we support our prime minister, we didn't say we would support the government undermining our liberty, our freedom, and our democracy. And we didn't say that we should declare war on Islam as we have seen."

Perhaps Morris's most bitterly fought dispute, however, was not with the government or with hard-nosed employers, but with his own members. In 1995 the Liverpool-based Mersey Docks and Harbour Company sacked 500 workers for refusing to cross a picket line, an act that triggered an unofficial dispute that lasted 28 months and led to Liverpool-registered ships being turned away by dock workers at ports around the world. Because no ballot was held the T&G could not publicly support the strike and as its leader Morris became a target for vitriolic attacks, including being portrayed as an enemy of the dockers in a 1999 British TV drama, *Dockers.* It is believed that the T&G gave over £700,000 to support the strikers' families.

During his twelve-year term of office, Morris was involved in many campaigns to improve workers' rights and establish greater equality in the workplace. In the 1980s and 1990s he was a prominent campaigner for a minimum wage in Britain and in fact one of the Blair government's first achievements after the landslide election victory of 1997 was to implement a minimum wage. Morris also fought throughout his career with the union to secure the right of British workers to organize and to have their unions recognized, a right that was fiercely denied by employers' organizations such as the Confederation of British Industry (CBI). After Blair's 1997 victory the debate raged fiercely, but Morris and others stood firm and eventually prevailed.

Alongside his work for the T&G, Morris worked as an adviser to several important national British organizations, including sitting on the advisory councils of the British Broadcasting Corporation (BBC) and the Independent Broadcasting Authority (IBA). His reputation as a high-level negotiator with an ability to grasp complex issues and address them in a fair and balanced way also saw him appointed to the Economic and Social Affairs Committee of the European Union. In 1998 he became a non-executive director of the Bank of England and in 1999 he was part of the Royal Commission for Reform of the House of Lords. He was listed for a knighthood, Britain's highest civil honor, in 2003. On hearing of the award Morris said: "I hope that in this recognition today's young black Britons will find some inspiration. I have always held the view that race can be an inspiration, not a barrier."

Sources

Periodicals

The Guardian (London), September 9, 2002; December 16, 2002; February 5, 2003; April 19, 2004.
New African, June, 2002.
New Statesman, February 27, 1998; September 10, 2001; March 10, 2003.

On-line

"Biography of Sir Bill Morris," *Transport and General Workers Union*, http://www.tgwu.org.uk/Templates/Internal.asp?NodeID=89667&L1=-1&L2=89 667 (February 3, 2005).
"Black British Citizens: Sir Bill Morris," *The Black Presence in Britain*, http://www.blackpresence.co.uk/pages/citizens/morris.htm (February 3, 2005).
"Sir Bill Morris," *100 Great Black Britons*, http://www.100greatblackbritons.com/bios/bill_morris.html (February 3, 2005).

—Chris Routledge

Lester C. Newman

1952—

College president, political scientist

Dr. Lester C. Newman, president of Mississippi Valley State University (MVSU) in Itta Bena, Mississippi, has become nationally-known for his achievements in improving the funding and administration of historically black colleges and universities (HBCUs). Newman turned MVSU—located in the rural, poverty-stricken Mississippi Delta—into the fastest-growing institution in the state. Between 1998, when Dr. Newman became president, and 2004, MVSU's enrollment grew from 2,200 to 4,400. Under Newman's leadership, MVSU became one of the best-respected, as well as one of the fastest-growing universities in the Southeast. Newman began calling MVSU "The Valley of Scholars" and gave his innovations the theme of "Moving from Excellence to Preeminence." Newman's major goals have been to promote MVSU as a center of academic excellence and as a catalyst for economic development in the Delta.

Newman, Lester C., photograph. AP/Wide World Photos Reproduced by permission.

Raised with High Expectations

Born on February 18, 1952, in Shreveport, Louisiana, Lester C. Newman and his brother and five sisters were raised by their grandparents. The family lived in the Cooper Road Community, a close-knit, active, predominately black, and economically diverse community on the north side of Shreveport. Newman told Eric Stringfellow of Mississippi's state newspaper, the *Clarion-Ledger*, in September of 2004, that the Cooper Road Community was a comfortable, fun, and exciting place to grow up.

Newman's grandfather served as his role model. With only a third-grade education, he had become a successful contractor and owned his own community water business. Above all else, Newman's grandparents stressed the importance of a good education, of sharing, and of helping others. During their daily family time, the grandparents read to the children from newspapers and magazines, turning reading into an adventure.

Newman's family, teachers, and, indeed, the entire community assumed that he would earn a college degree. In high school Newman spent two weeks at Bayou Boys' State at Southern University in Baton Rouge, Louisiana. The experience convinced him that he wanted to become a college professor and, eventu-

At a Glance . . .

Born Lester C. Newman on February 18, 1952, in Shreveport, LA; son of Earlee Newman; married Gloria; children: Russell, Eddreaka. *Education:* Southern University, BA, *cum laude*, 1973; Atlanta University, MA, 1976; Atlanta University, PhD, 1987.

Career: University of South Florida, assistant professor of Afro-American Studies, 1976-78; Southern University, assistant professor, 1978-86, assistant to the dean of the Junior Division, 1986-88, associate director of Institutional Self-Study, 1987-88; Kentucky State University, associate professor, dean of the College of Arts and Sciences, 1989-93; Shelby State Community College, professor, vice president for academic affairs, 1993-95; Johnson C. Smith University, vice president for academic affairs, 1995-98; Mississippi Valley State University, president, 1998–.

Selected memberships: National Association for Equal Opportunity, board of directors; Southern Association of Institutional Researchers; Southern Political Science Association; U.S. Department of Education, Historically Black College and University Capital Financing Advisory Board, 2003–; American Council on Education, board of directors, 2004–.

Selected awards: Governor Brereton Jones, "Kentucky Colonel" commission, 1993; Shelby State Community College, award for outstanding leadership and service, 1995; Greenwood-Leflore Retired Teacher's Association, Educator of the Year; Miller Brewing Company, Gallery of Greats, 2003; *Delta Business Journal*, Profiles in Leadership Award.

Addresses: *Office*—Mississippi Valley State University, 14000 Highway 82 West, #7272, Itta Bena, MS, 38941-1400.

ally, a college president. He planned to major in political science and Southern University had one of the best political science programs in the country. He earned his Bachelor of Arts degree in political science at Southern in 1973. As an undergraduate Newman was active in the civil rights and antiwar movements. He told the *Clarion-Ledger*: "I do believe that people from my generation need to do a better job at helping students become more civically engaged." During

1972 Newman worked as a staff assistant intern in Washington, D.C., in the office of U.S. Congresswoman Shirley Chisholm.

Remained in Academia

Newman loved campus life and enjoyed interacting with students. With the help of fellowships and faculty development grants he earned his Master of Arts in 1976 and his Ph.D. in political science in 1987 from Atlanta University in Atlanta, Georgia. His Ph.D. dissertation was entitled "The Political Orientation of Black Students from All-Black Towns: The Cases of Boley, Oklahoma; Grambling, Louisiana; and Mound Bayou, Mississippi."

Newman's first academic position, in 1976, was as assistant professor of Afro-American Studies at the University of South Florida in Tampa. Two years later he returned to Southern University as an assistant professor of political science. There, in addition to his research and teaching, Newman began to take on various administrative functions. As seminar director of "The Family as an Agent of Socialization," funded by the Louisiana Board of Regents, Newman conducted workshops throughout South Louisiana in 1980. During that summer he served as assistant director of the Robert A. Taft Seminar for Teachers, funded by the Robert A. Taft Institute for Government at the university. That same year Newman served as assistant director of the Youth Leadership Program at Southern. Between 1980 and 1981, he was coordinator and consultant for the political science component of Southern's Rural Intern Program.

In 1986 Newman became assistant to the dean of the Junior Division at Southern University. The following year he was named associate director of Institutional Self-Study, the university's first accreditation review program.

Left Alma Mater

In 1989 Newman moved to Kentucky State University in Frankfurt as an associate professor and dean of the College of Arts and Sciences. In 1993 he left for Shelby State Community College in Memphis, Tennessee, to become Vice President for Academic Affairs and professor of political science. Two years later he became Vice President for Academic Affairs at Johnson C. Smith University in Charlotte, North Carolina. There, in addition to his other accomplishments, Newman was instrumental in securing the university a $750,000 "genius grant" from the MacArthur Foundation, the first such award to an HBCU.

Newman designed his career to ready himself for becoming a university president. He read biographies of university presidents, particularly those of HBCUs. However Newman told the *Clarion-Ledger* in 2004,

"Being a university president is so unique that few things can truly prepare you for what you actually face on a day-to-day basis."

As soon as he took over as MVSU's fifth president in July of 1998, Newman began to reorganize academic programs and initiate innovative programs for improving the overall quality of the university. Founded in 1950 as Mississippi Vocational College for teacher and vocational training in the Delta, during the 1960s the college expanded into nursing, business administration, and the liberal arts. MVSU opened its first graduate program in 1976; however beginning in the 1980s enrollment declined. MVSU lost some degree programs and twice was threatened with closure.

Guided MVSU into the Twenty-First Century

In 1999 Newman launched a five-year, $25-million fundraising campaign—the largest in MVSU's history—with actor Morgan Freeman as chairman and national spokesman and blues legend B.B. King as honorary chair. In addition to facility improvements, the campaign's goal was to fund academic programs, faculty and departmental chairs, and student scholarships. Funds also were earmarked for helping local school districts improve their accreditation ratings and for university outreach to public school students. Newman told the *Clarion-Ledger*: "A good education should not be reserved only for those who can afford to pay for it or for those who live in wealthy school districts." He was quoted in the December 23, 1999, *Black Issues in Higher Education*: "The campaign signifies a new era in MVSU's history as the university establishes new relationships and forms partnerships that will ultimately improve the entire Delta region."

At a time of budget cuts and funding crises, Newman pursued new external grants and contracts for MVSU. Between 1998 and 2004, donations increased by 400 percent and federal funding increased by more than 100 percent. In addition, the average faculty salary increased by $10,000. Already one of the largest employers in the community, MVSU embarked on major landscaping and construction projects.

Newman initiated internal reviews of academic programs and an external review by outside consultants. An outside consultant was hired to review the school's athletic program, an important factor for the community, as well as for attracting new students. Newman told Karen Bryant of the *Delta Business Journal* in May of 2000 that he wanted MVSU "to be considered the premier regional institution in Mississippi and, ultimately, one of the top regional institutions in the nation."

Introduced New Academic Programs

Well aware of the "digital divide" that separated blacks and whites in terms of access to technology, Newman upgraded MVSU's technological infrastructure. He instituted Mississippi's first academic program in bioinformatics, the application of computer sciences to biology, as well as an automatic identification technology program. Newman told Jack Criss of the *Delta Business Journal* in July of 2003: "Because of such programs, we have entered into partnerships and negotiations with several major private companies who need this technology for their own business purposes. We can then not only benefit this campus and our students, but also impact economic development in our community."

In addition to automated information technology, Newman established an international program, a service learning program, and a master's in business administration program with evening and weekend classes. Student and faculty recruitment improved. MVSU's graduate programs increased from 50 students in 1998 to almost 400 in 2004. However teacher training remained MVSU's largest component.

In line with his long history of community service, Newman established an annual Family and Community Day at MVSU, as well as a science and technology summer academy for middle- and high-school students. MVSU freshman were required to perform 60 hours of community service.

Reached Out to the Community

By offering evening classes, Newman tried to make MVSU as convenient as possible for nontraditional students of all races, including older students, and single and working parents. The university's second off-campus site opened in 2001.

MVSU's Delta Research and Culture Institute, devoted to research on the Delta's educational and economic priorities, opened in 2001 under the direction of former Mississippi governor William Winters. Newman told the *Clarion-Ledger* that "improving the quality of education and attracting and retaining viable industry are two of the most difficult challenges facing the Mississippi Delta." The region's poorly performing public schools were under-funded and had difficulty attracting and retaining good teachers. Newman told the *Clarion-Ledger* that the Delta desperately needed industry that paid decent wages and that "oftentimes luring business and industry to an area is directly tied to the quality of the educational system."

Although administrative functions and fundraising took up the preponderance of Newman's time, he told the *Clarion-Ledger* that his favorite aspect of his career remained "seeing students who first come to the university with a lot of anxiety and apprehension later graduate with a level of excitement that they didn't initially think was possible.... This is what makes higher education exciting, watching people at difference levels discover and explore a whole new world of possibilities."

Throughout his career Newman has been very active in both professional and community service organizations including the Leflore County Industrial Board, the Greenwood Leflore Chamber of Commerce, and the Boys and Girls Clubs of America. He has served as a board member of the Delta Health Alliance, the Delta Council, and Big Brothers Big Sisters of Mississippi. Newman has received numerous fellowships and professional and community service citations and awards.

Maintained Research Interests

In addition to his many successful proposals to private, state, and national agencies throughout his career in higher education, Newman has delivered countless professional presentations, as well as written reports. His teaching and research interests have included American government and institutions, rural politics, urban policies and governments, public policy in the areas of housing, education, and transportation, political behavior, and African politics.

Newman and his wife Gloria had a grown son and daughter and had been married for more than 30 years when they became the legal guardians of a young son of an MVSU graduate. As of 2005 Newman's demanding career had kept him from his dream of owning his own business. He told *Contemporary Black Biography* in a written statement that "I'm a frustrated entrepreneur."

Newman told *CBB* that the most important lesson learned during his career "is that you have to always be prepared for the unexpected, and when the unexpected happens, you must handle matters appropriately. Also, you should always have a contingency plan and be ready to execute it if necessary."

Selected writings

(With others) *The Freshmen Survey: Values, Attitudes, Goals, Perceptions*, Southern University, 1986.

Southern University Self-Study Manual, Southern University, 1988.

"The African-American Vote and The Crisis in Voting Rights: Views From the Inside," *Proceedings from the 5th Symposium on African-American Voting Rights*, Norfolk State University, 1996.

Sources

Periodicals

Clarion-Ledger (Jackson, MS), September 5, 2004, p. 2G.

Delta Business Journal (Cleveland, MS), July 2003.

Black Issues in Higher Education, December 23, 1999, p. 41.

On-line

"Ayres Case 32 Years Later," *WTOK-TV News*. www.wtok.com/news/headlines/781067.html (December 30, 2004).

"Mississippi Valley State Has an Eye on the Future," *Delta Business Journal Online*, www.deltabusinessjournal.com/HTML/archives/5-00/valley.html (December 30, 2004).

Other

Additional information for this profile was provided by Dr. Lester C. Newman and his executive assistant/chief of staff Tonjanita L. Johnson.

—Margaret Alic

Robert N.C. Nix, Jr.

1928-2003

Pennsylvania Supreme Court Chief Justice

Nix, Robert N.C., Jr., photograph. AP/Wide World Photos Reproduced by permission

As the first African American to head any state supreme court, Robert N.C. Nix Jr. holds an historic place in the United States legal system. He was born into a family of high achievers. His grandfather was born a slave but earned a doctorate in mathematics and became a college dean; his father was Pennsylvania's first black congressman. Nix Jr. made rapid progress through the Pennsylvania courts, rising to the position of Supreme Court Justice in 1972, just sixteen years from his bar qualification, at the age of 44. He won his election by a landslide to become the highest ranking black official in Pennsylvania's history and began a 24-year career in the state's supreme court. He became the state's chief justice in 1984, a position he held until 1996. Nix Jr. is remembered as a man of high ideals, and fairness; as a judge he had a reputation for fighting discrimination wherever he saw it and for supporting individual rights in the face of government authority.

The only child of Robert N.C. Nix Sr. and Ethel Lanier Nix, Nix Jr. grew up heavily influenced by the law and lawyers. His father was Pennsylvania's first black congressman, serving from 1958 to 1980 and becoming well known for his aphorisms and witty speeches; he gave the eulogy in Congress for President John F. Kennedy. Nix Jr. was educated at Central High School in his home city of Philadelphia where he graduated with highest honors. He attended Villanova University, where he majored in philosophy, graduating at the top of his class with an A.B. in 1952 before serving in the United States Army, 1953-55. He graduated with a J.D. from the University of Pennsylvania in 1955 then attended Temple University graduate school to study business administration and economics.

Nix qualified for the Pennsylvania bar in 1956 and became a deputy attorney general, but in 1958 he joined his father in private legal practice with the firm Nix, Rhodes, and Nix, where he became an important lawyer in civil rights trials. Nix resigned from the firm when he became a judge in Philadelphia County's common pleas court in 1968, a post he held until 1971. He was a lifelong advocate of equality, using his position as a judge to challenge the morality and legality of racial segregation and discrimination. Judge Arlin Adams, formerly of the U.S. Court of Appeals Third Circuit, told the *Penn Law Journal*: "The legacy of decisions during Justice Nix's term encompass great

At a Glance . . .

Born Robert Nelson Cornelius Nix Jr., on July 13, 1928, in Philadelphia, PA; died on August 23, 2003; married Dorothy Lewis (deceased); married Renate E Beckert-Bryant; children (first marriage): Robert Nelson Cornelius III, Michael, Anthony, Jude Stephen; children (step): Timothy Bryant, Kimberley Bryant. *Education:* Villanova University, AB, philosophy, 1952; University of Pennsylvania, JD, 1955; Temple University, postgraduate business administration and economics. *Military Service:* US Army, 1953-55.

Career: State of Pennsylvania, deputy attorney general, 1956-58; Nix, Rhodes and Nix, partner, 1958-68; Common Pleas Court Philadelphia County, judge, 1968-71; State of Pennsylvania, Justice of the Supreme Court, 1972-84, Chief Justice, 1984-96.

Memberships: NAACP; Board of directors, Germantown Boys Club, 1968; member, council president's association La Salle College, 1971; advisory board La Salle College High School; board of consultors Villanova University School of Law, 1973; member, Pennsylvania Electoral College; member, President's Committee on Civil Rights; member, Omega Psi Phi; president-elect, Conference of Chief Justices, 1990-92, president, 1991-92.

Awards: Guardian Civic League Achievement Award (first Pennsylvanian to be so awarded); honorary degrees from Villanova University, Delaware Law School of Widener College, and Chestnut Hill College.

empathy for those suffering the excesses of government authority.... What is remarkable is the grace and dignity with which he conducted himself over the years when he encountered the distasteful actions of those who continued that type of discrimination."

Nix began his career as a supreme court judge when he was elected by a landslide in 1972 to become the first African American to hold such a high position in the state of Pennsylvania. But he was not without opponents. In 1981 fellow justice Rolf Larson is alleged to have tried to force Nix off the court, triggering a bitter struggle that lasted almost up to Nix's retirement; Larson was later removed from the court himself following a Grand Jury investigation in 1994. Nix's career as a Pennsylvania supreme court justice lasted 12 years, in which time he became a role model for many black Americans who saw him as an example of what could be achieved with determination, hard work, and dignity.

His record as a judge was one that marked him out as an original and courageous thinker capable of making new law. The *Penn Law Journal* records a 1975 judgment in which Nix decided that the influence of drugs or alcohol could mitigate specific intent in the case of homicide. In that case a burglar who had been convicted of first degree murder was awarded a new trial by the high court. He became Chief Justice in 1984 and served until his retirement in 1996, presiding over a court that left a legacy of judgments that protected the individual from longstanding inequalities. Pennsylvania Governor Edward G. Rendell said of Nix: "during the course of his entire career as lawyer and judge, Chief Justice Nix dedicated his considerable intellect and energy to breaking down barriers that have no place standing in any system of Democracy."

Nix was also involved in many community projects, serving on school and college committees, as a member of the electoral college, and as a member of the President's Committee on Civil Rights. Besides his work as a judge and in community service Nix was dedicated to his family of four sons, Robert N.C. Nix III, Michael, Jude, Steven, and Anthony, two stepchildren, Timothy and Kimberly Bryant, and nine grandchildren. He was survived by his second wife, Renate E Beckert Bryant.

Sources

Periodicals

Jet, January 12, 2004, p19.

On-line

"Governor Rendell Orders Flags Flown at Half-Staff," *PAPower*, www.state.pa.us/papower/cwp/view.asp ?A=11&Q=435459 (January 10, 2005).
"In Memoriam: Robert N.C. Nix, Jr.," *Penn Law Journal*, Spring 2004, www.law.upenn.edu/alumni /alumnijournal/Spring2004/in_memoriam/nix. html (January 10, 2005).
"Robert N.C. Nix Jr.," *Biography Resource Center*, www.galenet.com/servlet/BioRC (January 10, 2005).

—Chris Routledge

Russ Parr

196(?)—

Radio disc jockey

Parr, Russ, photograph. Lenny Furman/Getty Images.

Russ Parr became a leading radio talk show host in the twenty-first century, with the *Russ Parr Morning Show* syndicated in 45 cities and reaching an estimated 3.2 million listeners. "Parr's outspokenness, mixed with his banter with the many black listeners who call," noted Krissah Williams in the *Washington Post*, "has made his program the top-ranked morning show among 18-to-34-year-olds in the Washington market...." His success is the culmination of 20 years of experience garnered as a stand-up comic, record label owner, and television actor. Parr's talent for satire and gift for celebrity mimicry (including Magic Johnson, Michael Jackson, Jesse Jackson, and Mickey Mouse) add a freewheeling quality to his radio program. Although first known for his comic gifts, Parr has shown a willingness to examine socially sensitive subjects including domestic abuse, voting, and breast cancer. The success of Parr's weekly radio program also led to *On the Air with Russ Parr*, a weekend program that reached two million listeners in 40 cities.

Parr attended Cal State University-Northbridge, where he attained a Bachelor of Arts degree in Radio, TV, and Film. Initially, he launched his career in television,

working as a production services supervisor for ABC. He also worked as a stand-up comic for eight years, performing his first show as an opening act for Joan Rivers in Santa Monica, California. Parr also found parts on a number of television shows including, *Martin*, *Jenny Jones*, and *Turnstyle*, and appeared in television commercials for Kodak, Thrifty's, and McDonald's. Despite Parr's success, he left Hollywood in 1989 and found his niche working as a disc jockey on KJMZ in Dallas, Texas. The popularity of his radio program quickly bolstered KJMZ rating from 15th to 9th in the Dallas-Fort Worth area. "Listeners are drawn to his assortment of impressions—from Little Richard to Mike Tyson," noted Ken Parish Perkins in the *Dallas Morning News*, adding that listeners "seem to have a love-to-hate affair with his mostly improvised, sometimes dark humor."

Parr also found success when he wrote the lyrics to "We Like Ugly Women," a comic rap song that sold 50,000 copies. "When I got that big, fat check," Parr told Perkins, "I said, 'Hey, we might have something here.'" The hit led to the founding of his own record label, Rapsur Records, in the mid-1980s, though he

At a Glance . . .

Born Russ Parr in 196(?), in San Antonio, TX.
Education: California State University-
Northridge, BA, radio, television, and film, 1981.

Career: KDAY, Los Angeles, CA, radio disc jockey,
1980s; KRBV, Dallas, TX, radio disc jockey, 1989-
1996; WKYS, Washington, DC, *Russ Parr Morning
Show*, host, 1996–; TV ONE, *Get the Hook Up*, host,
2004.

Awards: Top Comedic Video, MTV, 1987.

would eventually sign with Eazy E's Ruthless Records.
Parr recorded under the name Bobby Jimmy, a character based on a childhood friend, and used the persona to rap his way through songs like "Big Butt,"
"Weave," and "Roaches." "Basically, I do it because it's
so much fun," Parr told Perkins, "it gives me a chance
to be creative in writing and, hey, it's like playing the
lottery. You really don't know if a song will be the one
that hits." Parr's creative streak also won him a MTV's
Top Comic Video award in 1987.

Parr recorded several Bobby Jimmy and the Critters
albums and multiple singles, and sold 100,000 copies
of "Hair Weave" and 300,000 of "Roaches." While
these parodies proved popular, many fans failed to
realize that Parr and Bobby Jimmy were the same
person, even though Parr made no secret of his double
identity. This, however, proved less problematic than
attacks on his songs' lyrics from feminists, African-
American groups, and even speech therapists. The Los
Angeles branch of the National Origination of Women
(NOW) threatened to boycott KDAY because of the
sexism of "We Like Ugly Women." "In hindsight," Parr
told Perkins, "I agree. It wasn't done with feelings for
the women's movement. I thought I was being funny,
and it totally slipped my mind that I could offend some
people." African-American groups were angered at
Jimmy's "jive talk," and when Parr explained that his
persona had a speech impediment, speech therapists
also weighed in with criticism.

Criticism failed to stall record sales, and Parr was soon
able to use his profits to found *Flava TV*, a variety/
video program. He quickly brought his radio sidekick,
Alfredas, on board, and honed his skills as a writer,
actor, and producer. In 1989 Parr accepted the position of morning host on KJMZ (later KRBV) in Dallas,
Texas, a position he held for nearly seven years. In
1994, however, the station switched to a nationally
syndicated morning show and moved Parr to an
evening slot, eventually leading to his departure. "We
hate to see him go," R.W. Schmidt told *Arts Beat*, "but

he's a great guy and a great talent, and he's going to go
do what he loves the most, and that's being a morning
man."

In 1996 Parr moved to Radio One's WKYS-FM in
Washington, D.C., where his program was syndicated
throughout the United States. The *Russ Parr Morning
Show* won listeners by adhering to a freewheeling style
that included live calls, song parodies, and unscripted
monologues. "Watching Parr and crew do their thing is
a refreshing journey back in radio time, back to an era
when satellites and computers didn't call the shots,
back to a place in which talents were left free to create
their own world of sound" noted Marc Fisher in the
Washington Post. "They do not employ comedy writers. They walk into the studio at 5:59 for the 6-to-10
a.m. shift. And they pull it off."

Parr also reserves time for serious issues. "For all its
bawdy banter and crackling fun," wrote Fisher, "Parr's
show is also a running commentary on class, a daily
conversation in which Washington's economically rising black population questions itself and pokes fun at its
willingness and even eagerness to conform to majority
expectations." Parr is quick to criticize double standards
and hypocrisy, including ridiculing certain rappers for
their use of non-standard English. His program is also
unusual because its target audience is women. Popular
subjects on the call-in program include relationships
and parenthood, and Parr frequently allows his audience to set the agenda. "If you allow people access to
your radio show," he told Fisher, "they start to take on
your personality."

Parr's philosophy produced results at WKYS, making
his show the number one morning program in the
Washington, DC area in the spring of 1997. His
weekend program pursues another track, featuring a
countdown of the week's most popular songs, while a
Dallas television program features videos. Parr, however, no longer made his own records and videos,
noting that the record industry was too ruthless. Even
while widely successful, Parr's radio career has been no
stranger to controversy. In one early radio interview, he
was confronted by controversial author Shahrazed Ali
while on the air. "You're only trying to get ratings!" she
accused him, while he answered, "You're only trying to
sell books." One of Parr's practical jokes also backfired
when he pretended to be Tom Joyner, a radio competi-
tor, and convinced the IRS on live radio that he had not
paid his taxes in years.

The success of Parr's radio program can also be
attributed to the strength of co-anchors like Olivia Fox.
Fox joined *The Russ Parr Morning Show* in July of
1996. In 1998 the team was nominated in *Billboard*
for Personality of the Year. Together, Parr and Fox
garnered laughs and ratings by shocking audiences with
audacious skits. "The show is a guilty pleasure that kept
morning audiences in stitches," noted *Black Press*.
The partnership came to an abrupt end in 2002 when
Radio One failed to renew Fox's contract. "Olivia Fox

is one of the most talented people I have ever worked with in radio," Parr wrote in a statement on his Web site. "I will miss working with her." Some commentators even predicted the demise of Parr's radio program without Fox, but he continued to be competitive in the crowded Washington, D.C., market.

Parr has worked hard to promote community involvement and he practices what he preaches. He remains active in the Russ Parr's Kids Klub, an organization that promotes a number of activities including attending movies and museums. The club also boasts of an active chapter in every city that Parr broadcasts from. In 2001 he led an effort to raise $700,000 for the restoration of Dr. Martin Luther King Jr.'s former church. "Radio One is a company that serves African-American communities across the country," Parr was quoted in PR Newswire, "and we feel that it is our obligation to try to help save Ebenezer Baptist Church. Dr. King tragically lost his life and devoted his time to making this world a better place for everyone to live in."

In January of 2004, Parr and Alfredas started Get the Hook Up, a dating game show/beauty pageant for TV One. "Russ Parr and Alfredas will essentially serve as the voice and face of TV One," noted Jonathan Rodgers in PR Newswire, "and we are delighted to make use of their tremendous talents." Parr also continued to interview athletes, recording artists, and politicians on his radio program, keeping his fingers on the pulse of current events. During the 2004 election season, he interviewed presidential candidate John Kerry, asking tough questions that many interviewers skirted around. "Russ's appeal is a little older, more adult...," Steve Hegwood told Fisher. "He's an adult who has children he can talk about. And he's married. He talks about real life."

Sources

Periodicals

Arts Beat, March 5, 1996, p. 19A.
Dallas Morning News, May 9, 1991, p. 1C.
PR Newswire, September 4, 2001; January 9, 2004.
Washington Post, August 12, 1997, p. D1; February 5, 2003, p. E1.

On-line

The Official Russ Parr Website, www.uptoparr.com (March 23, 2005).
"Out Foxed?" Black Press, www.blackpress.org/olivia fox.htm (January 3, 2005).

—Ronnie D. Lankford, Jr.

Harold Perrineau, Jr.

1968—

Actor

Whether playing a character from Shakespeare or a contemporary felon, actor Harold Perrineau, Jr., has demonstrated a wide-ranging talent over the course of his two-decade career. With recent prominent roles in the *Matrix* films as well as the 2005 TV series *Lost*, Perrineau has achieved recognition as one of the country's new generation of important African-American actors.

Began as a Dancer

Perrineau, Harold, photograph. Frederick M Brown/Getty Images.

A native of Brooklyn, New York, Perrineau studied music and theater at the Shenandoah Conservatory in Winchester, Virginia, and later worked at a variety of odd jobs—including bartending and busing tables—while trying to establish himself as a performer. He began his professional career dancing with the prestigious Alvin Ailey Company, with which he performed for a year and a half. But his interests gradually shifted to acting, and by the late 1980s Perrineau started to appear on stage. Among his early credits were performances in *Godspell* and *Avenue X*.

At the same time, the young actor had begun to land small roles in television, making appearances on *The Cosby Show*, *Law & Order*, and *I'll Fly Away*. He also obtained minor roles in films, including *Shakedown* and *King of New York*. His first important screen role came in 1995, when he appeared in Wayne Wang's acclaimed drama *Smoke*. Perrineau played Rashid Cole, a young man searching for his absent father, played by Forest Whitaker. The performance earned Perrineau an Independent Spirit Award nomination for Best Supporting Actor.

In 1996 Perrineau was cast as Mercutio in Baz Luhrmann's idiosyncratic film adaptation, *William Shakespeare's Romeo + Juliet*, starring Leonardo Di Caprio and Clare Danes as the star-crossed young lovers. The film included many shocking elements—including Perrineau's portrayal of Mercutio as a black drag queen. "Mercutio was just buggin' out, you know what I mean?" the actor responded when asked about the role in a *SPLICEDwire* interview. "He was just high, crazy, stoned. In a society where macho is the thing, for Mercutio to come out in a dress, that's ballsy. Mercutio is just off his...rocker and doesn't care. Then there was that thing about him maybe loving Romeo or not, well I guess that changes things."

Perrineau next appeared in *The Edge,* opposite Anthony Hopkins and Alec Baldwin. Though the role was

At a Glance . . .

Born Harold Williams on August 7, 1968 in Brook-lyn, New York; married Brittany Robinson; children: Aurora Robinson.

Career: Alvin Ailey Company, New York, NY, dancer, early 1980s; actor in stage, film, and television productions, 1988–.

Awards: Independent Spirit Award, for Best Supporting Actor, 1995.

Addresses: *Agent*—Larry Taube, Gersh Agency, 232 North Canon Dr., Beverly Hills, CA 90210.

not large, he appreciated the opportunity to work with these acclaimed actors. In 1999 Perrineau's performance in *The Best Man* earned him an Image Award nomination for Outstanding Supporting Actor in a Motion Picture. He went on to take increasingly prominent roles, including another drag queen (in the 2000 film *Woman on Top*, co-starring Penelope Cruz) and the character Link in *The Matrix Reloaded* and *The Matrix Revolutions*.

Played Paraplegic Prisoner in Oz

Perrineau's television career also expanded. His breakthrough role came in 1997 when he was cast as August Hill, a wheelchair-bound prisoner whose monologue introduced each episode of the gritty dramatic series *Oz*. The series, set in the fictional Oswald State Correctional Facility, a maximum-security prison, presented a world in which *everyone* is "on edge," according to *Boston Globe* writer Jim Sullivan. "It's a world of competing cliques and warring ethnic factions, tribe against tribe. Black thugs, black Muslims, neo-Nazis, the Italians, the Latinos, a couple of Irish, a couple of old-guy lifers."

Oz attracted significant critical attention for its uncompromising approach to the subject of incarceration. Caryn James in the *New York Times* described the series as "intelligent, ambitious and determined to shock," but also "gruesome and claustrophobic." Though the series had many stars, Perrineau earned much recognition for the role of Augustus Hill. He parodied the character on a *Saturday Night Live* episode in 1999, and the character even provided the basis for a spin-off book. In 2003 HBO published a volume purporting to be the character's "secret journal" of prison life: *Oz: Behind These Walls: The Journal of Augustus Hill*. Containing plot synopses

and other information about the series, the book is held together by Hill's thoughts and observations about freedom, violence, responsibility, and other issues.

Perrineau's next major television project, after *Oz* completed its run in 2003, was a starring role in the ABC series *Lost*. Hailed as "one of the best new series" of the fall 2004 season by *Boston Globe* critic Matthew Gilbert, *Lost* followed the experiences of the 48 survivors of a plane crash on a remote tropical island. Perrineau played Michael, a father who had just obtained custody of his estranged son; other characters included a doctor, a former member of the Iraqi Republican Guard, a Korean couple who speak no English, and an aging rock star. "We needed a huge cast," explained a series executive to Thelma Adams in the *New York Times*. "It's like a petri dish. You need as many protozoa as you can to begin with." The premise, as another executive commented, allowed for an intelligent treatment of a several important themes. "Certainly, race is an issue of the show," he noted, "as well as issues of society, leadership, trust, responsibility and personal destiny. You're on an island—how do you live, how do you survive?"

As Perrineau noted to *Zap2It* writer Daniel Fienberg, playing Michael has again made him a familiar face to audiences—though they may not remember his name. "I'm one of those guys that whenever I'm doing a project, people will notice me then," he said. "People will walk up to me and go 'Oh my God, you're the guy from *Oz* or 'Oh my God, *The Matrix*' or something like that, so now it's just 'Oh, *Lost*.' It stays the same, which is fortunate for me, because I guess I'm working." Explaining that he enjoys choosing unusual roles, Perrineau explained that "it's really the thing I set out to do" but that such choices can also create difficulties because he resists any type-casting. "Clearly I can do many things, but because I do so many things, I always have to prove I can do the next thing as well."

Perrineau, who has one daughter, is married to actress and model Brittany Robinson. Among his non-acting interests is the sport of motorcycle racing.

Selected works

Films

Shakedown, 1988.
King of New York, 1990.
Smoke, 1995.
William Shakespeare's Romeo + Juliet, 1996.
The Edge, 1997.
The Best Man, 1999.
Woman on Top, 2000.
Prison Song, 2001.
On-Line, 2003.
The Matrix Reloaded, 2003.
The Matrix Revolutions, 2003.

Television

The Cosby Show, NBC, 1989.
Law & Order, NBC, 1990.
I'll Fly Away, NBC, 1992-1993.
Oz, HBO, 1997-2003.
ER, NBC, 1997.
Lost, ABC, 2004-2005.
Theater
Godspell, Lambs Theatre, New York, NY, 1988.
Avenue X, Playwrights Horizons Theatre, 1994.
Joe Fearless, Atlantic Theatre Company, New York, NY, 2000.
Blue/Orange, Atlantic Theatre Company, 2002-2003.

Sources

Periodicals

Boston Globe, July 11, 1999, p. N1; February 5, 2002, p. E1; September 22, 2004, p. E1.

Entertainment Weekly, November 8, 1996, p. 46; November 14, 2003, p. 31.
New York Times, September 19, 2004.
Newsweek, November 4, 1996, p. 73.
People Weekly, July 14, 1997, p. 15.
Variety, July 14, 1997, p. 34; December 14, 1998, p. 42.

On-line

"From Prison Blues to High-Heeled Shoes," *SPLICE Dwire,* www.splicedonline.com (February 4, 2005).
"*Lost* Helps Viewers Find Perrineau," *Zap2It,* http://tv.zap2it.com (February 4, 2005).

—E. M. Shostak

Waverly Person

1927—

Geophysicist

Person, Waverly, photograph. AP/Wide World Photos Reproduced by permission.

As director of the U.S. Geological Survey's National Earthquake Information Center (NEIC) in Golden, Colorado, Waverly Person is often one of the first experts called upon for information and advice when natural disasters strike. A veteran seismologist and geophysicist, Person has worked in the field of earthquake studies for half a century and is the first African American to hold such a prominent position in the U.S. Department of the Interior. "I'm probably the first African American ever to be an earthquake scientist," he noted in an interview with *Contemporary Black Biography* (*CBB*). "I came from the bottom and went up to the top."

As chief of the NEIC, Person is responsible for locating earthquakes, computing their magnitudes, and disseminating this information quickly and efficiently to emergency crews, government officials, and news media throughout the world. Satellites and a host of sophisticated measuring devices record the quakes—as many as 50 a day worldwide. Though it is estimated that millions of earthquakes occur throughout the world each year, the NEIC staff annually tracks approximately 20,000 events. Since the early 1970s, the NEIC has located and reported on more than a quarter million earthquakes.

It is up to Person and his staff to interpret the information and disperse it to the public. As official spokesperson for the NEIC, media briefings and interviews constitute a large part of his job. "Once you give people—even if they're in the middle of the situation, like in California—the facts in a way that they can understand, it calms them down much more than if you're talking over their heads," he told *CBB*. In 1988 his success in accomplishing this earned him a prestigious award from the National Association of Government Communicators. And in 2004, when the second most devastating tsunami in history ravaged the countries in the Indian Ocean, Person was on hand to offer advice and to help plan safeguards that would improve detection of future killer waves.

Worked Hard to Achieve Success

Having overcome considerable obstacles in the drive to become a geophysicist, Person sees himself as an important role model for minority students. He devotes much of his free time to visiting schools throughout the

At a Glance . . .

Born Waverly J. Person on May 1, 1927, in Blackridge, VA; son of Santee (a farmer) and Bessie (Butts) Person; married Sarah Walker, 1956. *Education*: St. Paul's College, Lawrenceville, VA, BS, 1949; completed graduate work in geophysics at American University and George Washington University, ?-1973. *Military Service*: U.S. Army, served in Korea, 1949-52.

Career: Earthquake Services, U.S. Department of Commerce, technician, 1962-73; National Earthquake Information Center (NEIC), U.S. Geological Survey, Golden, CO, geophysicist, 1973-77; National Earthquake Information Center (NEIC), director, 1977–.

Memberships: American Geophysical Union; Seismological Society of America; Colorado School of Mines (honorary member, 1991); Boulder County Crimestoppers; Flatirons Kiwanis Club.

Awards: Honorary doctorate in science, St. Paul's College, 1988; Outstanding Government Communicator Award, National Association of Government Communicators, 1988; Meritorious Service Award, U.S. Department of the Interior, 1989; Annual Minority Award, Community Services Department, Boulder, CO, 1990; Outstanding Performance Rating, U.S. Department of the Interior, 1990, 1991, 1992, 1993, and 1994.

Addresses: *Home*—5489 Seneca Place, Boulder, CO 80303. *Office*—National Earthquake Information Center, U.S. Geological Survey, Box 25046, DFC, MS-967, Denver, CO 80225.

Waverly Person was born in 1927 in Blackridge, Virginia. After completing high school, he enrolled at St. Paul's College in his hometown of Lawrenceville. Hoping to become a high school math and science teacher, he concentrated his academic work in the areas of general science and industrial education. He received his bachelor of science degree from St. Paul's in 1949, then spent the next several years serving in Korea with the U.S. Army.

Unsure of which career path to follow—funds were not available for further education—he moved to Washington, DC, to help a relative run a construction company. A series of odd jobs followed. Then, in the summer of 1962, he was offered a job as a technician with the U.S. Department of Commerce, which then operated the NEIC. "I was changing the record in the drums for recording earthquakes [and] became very nosey about why we were getting these wiggly lines on these recordings," he recalled in *Emerge*. "So I decided that I wanted to know more about this field."

During his college years, Person told *CBB*, the idea of a career in earthquake studies had never occurred to him. "There were no African Americans in the field—no one for you to look up to," he said. But once he had had a taste of geophysics, there was no turning back. As a technician, his career prospects were limited, so he decided to return to school to study the subject on an advanced level.

Person spent the next 11 years working as a technician in the department of earthquake services during the day and studying geology, geophysics, and differential equations at American and George Washington universities at night. Over the years, his supervisors assigned him a variety of projects, and he always "came up with flying colors," he told *CBB*. By 1973 Person had qualified as a geophysicist and was transferred to the U.S. Geological Survey's NEIC in Colorado. Four years later he was named director of the center.

Achieved Respect as Center Director

Person's climb was not an easy one, however. Along the way he encountered anger and skepticism from many sides. "Any time you're breaking ground, you've got to take a lot, do a lot," he explained in his *CBB* interview. "People were always asking, 'Why do you want to get into this field?' They wondered how I would do as their colleague—on the same level as they were. Anything I did that was professional or scientific, I was always expected to do better, or more. But I was one who never gave up. No matter what anyone would say, I had my goals set as to what I was going to do. Nothing was going to stop me." Today Person supervises a staff of 26. "Once you get to respectability, people don't see your color anymore," he added. "They see you as an individual who knows what you're doing, and they accept you for that."

state of Colorado and encouraging black youngsters to consider careers in the earth sciences. "I try to show them that this is the kind of thing they can do if they want to do it," he commented in his *CBB* interview. "I tell them that the barriers are not there now the way they were, and that if they prepare themselves, they can make it." Person is editor of "Seismological Notes," a regular feature in the *Bulletin of the Seismological Society of America*, and he writes for the USGS's Earthquake Information Bulletin, "Earthquakes." Person also contributes significantly to professional journals, and his articles and picture appear in countless science textbooks.

Although the systems Person used when he first started working as a geophysicist would require days of measurement to predict an earthquake, advancements in technology now offer up-to-the-minute record keeping. Seismographs, computers, and other sophisticated instruments at the NEIC make it possible for Person and his staff to monitor earthquake activity all over the world, 24-hours a day. In the United States, even a tiny, insignificant quake can be detected, and a significant one—measuring at least 4.0 on the Richter scale—is enough to trigger an alarm system in the hall. If an earthquake occurs overseas, it must register at least 6.0 in order to be detected. No matter how sensitive the system, however, earthquakes cannot be accurately predicted, so the center relies on what it calls the Earthquake Early Alerting Service to help communities cope with the chaos and confusion that follow a significant tremor.

"The name of the game here is to try to get the earthquake located, compute the magnitude and give that location to the emergency people so that they can get into the area and start to rescue people and save lives," Person explained in *Emerge*. Thanks to a special hot line at the NEIC office, he and his staff are in direct communication with the North American Air Defense Command (NORAD) in Colorado Springs. "We tell them what state we want to go to and they hook us up with the state emergency people immediately," he elaborated in *Ebony*. "The state officials then get in touch with the fire departments, hospitals, etc."

If a destructive quake occurs in a foreign country, the NEIC forwards the information they have collected directly to the United Nations, as well as to the American embassy or consulate in that country. Person carries a special paging device for emergencies—it displays the location, time, and magnitude of major quakes—and two staff members maintain a 24-hour vigil at the center.

As soon as emergency personnel have been alerted and informed, Person turns to the media for assistance. "The media is our ally," he told *CBB*. "They get the information out to the public. What we try to do is inform the public as much as we possibly can about earthquakes—not only in the United States, but in the world. Our society today moves, and we have a lot of Americans everywhere."

Frequently Sought for Expert Commentary

When an earthquake occurs, however, it is often the media that get to Person first. He was not even out of bed on the morning of January 17, 1994, for example, when the ABC television news program *Good Morning America* called to ask his opinion about the deadly quake that had just shaken the San Fernando Valley in California. "I went straight for about seven hours after

I got to work giving interviews to the media on where the earthquake was, what did I think about damage, how aftershocks might come and this kind of thing," he related in *Emerge*.

Person continued: "And then the rest of the night, it was live TV interviews, locally and nationally. Then I got home, got a couple of hours of sleep and was able to change clothes. I got back the next morning at 5:00 because I was going to be on [NBC's] *Today* show. So it was pretty hectic. That's what happens when you have a large earthquake in the United States." Although Person has witnessed many more devastating tremors, the January, 1994, earthquake in Northridge, California, measuring 6.6 on the Richter scale, was "one of the most talked about, most interviewed quakes I've ever been on in my entire career," he told *CBB*. "I talked to everybody. You name them, I talked to them." When a 6.8 magnitude earthquake destroyed a survey reporting station in Washington state in 2001, Person told the *Rocky Mountain News* that "The phones here lit up like fireworks and lightning."

Person's nearly fifty years of experience as the bearer of bad news all came to call in 2004 when a magnitude 9.0 earthquake off the coast of Indonesia caused a huge tsunami that killed more than 275,000 people in the coastal areas of the Indian Ocean, ravaging huge portions of Indonesia, Malaysia, Sumatra, and Sri Lanka. The huge number of deaths prompted calls for better emergency warning systems to be put in place in the Indian Ocean.

In addition to giving interviews to U.S. newspaper, magazine, TV, and radio correspondents, when a major earthquake occurs, Person speaks to media representatives from around the world. He and his staff also field phone calls from panic-stricken citizens, anxious to know what to do and what to expect in the wake of a significant tremor. Even the mild quake that shook parts of the Midwest and Canada in June of 1987 was enough to tie up the NEIC's phone lines for three solid hours. "I had eight people here doing nothing but answering phones," Person recounted in *Ebony*. "We knew that the quake was not large enough to have killed thousands of people. But as far as those people in that area are concerned, they are being shaken by an earthquake and they want to know if they're going to have another."

Encouraged Minority Students to Study Earth Sciences

Although he still makes forays into the field to inspect earthquake damage, record aftershocks, and consult with emergency officials, most of Person's time is devoted to managerial work. This includes training and supervising staff, organizing the NEIC's budget, and producing hundreds of publications on earthquake activity worldwide. The center issues daily, weekly, and monthly reports on earthquakes, as well as pamphlets advising the public on what to do when a significant tremor occurs. "We have a database [at the World Data Center for Seismology] that's second to none," Person told *CBB*. "Builders and civil engineers want to know what kind of earthquake activity there's been in an area before they start to build dams, big buildings, and so forth." All of the publications produced by the office are available to the general public.

Discouraged by the desperate shortage of minorities in the field of geophysics and seismology, Person spends much of his time visiting middle schools and speaking with minority students about the challenges and rewards of a career in the earth sciences. In 1993 he traveled as far afield as Baltimore, Maryland, where nearly 400 students gathered to hear a presentation he gave at Dunbar Middle School. "I try to get them to understand that the easiest thing in school is not always the thing you want to do," he told *CBB*, "and that math and science are good no matter what field they go into. I try to stress the importance of being competitive in anything they go to do."

After several decades in the field, Waverly Person remained as fascinated by earthquake studies as he ever was. "No two earthquakes are alike," he pointed out in *Emerge*. "It's never a dull moment because earthquakes are occurring all over the world and we are working to find out where all the different seismic zones are. It's something that you just love to do because you continue to learn." Even on his golden anniversary of government service in 2005 Person related his love for his job, telling the *Denver Post* that "Well, I enjoy what I do, so it hasn't been a burden... but 50 years?" For all his years as the spokesperson for the world's worst disasters, Person had become something of a celebrity—both in his hometown of Boulder, Colorado, where he is active in community affairs, and around the globe. "Everywhere I go, people know me," he told *CBB*. "They keep looking at me, and then they come up close and say, 'Are you the earthquake man?'"

Sources

Periodicals

Boys' Life, September 1997, p. 50.
Denver Post, January 14, 2005, p. B5.
Ebony, September 1987, pp. 134-38.
Emerge, April 1994, pp. 9-10.
Rocky Mountain News, March 1, 2001.
Seattle Times, February 11, 2005, p. A10.

On-line

"Experts Say Tsunami Warning System Would Have Saved Lives," *Voice of America,* www.voanews.com/English/2004-12-28-voz5.cfm (April 29, 2005).

Other

Additional information for this profile was obtained from a feature story on Person aired on KCNC-TV, Denver, CO, February 16 and 23, 1994, and from an interview with Person on October 20, 1994.

—Caroline B. D. Smith and Sara Pendergast

Richard Price

1930(?)—

Mathematician

Dr. Richard L. Price—"Doc Price"—an associate professor of mathematics at Lamar University in Beaumont, Texas, has had a long and distinguished career in academics. He has devoted himself to recruiting black students to Lamar, to mentoring students, and to preparing them for careers in engineering, mathematics, and the sciences.

Price served 13 months of combat duty in Korea as a U.S. Army 2nd Lieutenant. He earned his Bachelor of Science degree in mathematics from Prairie View A&M University of Texas, a historically black university about 40 miles from Houston. He earned his master's degree in mathematics with a minor in philosophy from the University of Texas in Austin. Price began his teaching career at Prairie View A&M University in September of 1956. During a leave-of-absence from Prairie View, he studied at Iowa State University, the University of California-Los Angeles, and Ohio State University (OSU) with the assistance of National Science Foundation and Academic Year Institute grants. Price earned his doctoral degree in mathematics education from OSU.

In August of 1970 Price joined the Department of Mathematics at Lamar as an associate professor. During the early 1970s, he again took a leave of absence, this time to study religion at Yale Divinity School were he earned a master's degree in religion in 1972. During this period Price also served as associate director of the engineering program at the University of Bridgeport in Connecticut. At Lamar Price taught trigonometry, precalculus and calculus, and analytical geometry. Over the years he also taught at Central

State University, a historically black public university in Wilberforce, Ohio, at Ohio Northern University, and Michigan State University.

At Lamar, Price served as the College of Engineering's Director of Minority Recruitment and Retention. The *LU News* Website quoted Dr. Price: "The minority recruiting and retention program is committed to providing scholarships, internships, and other opportunities for traditionally under represented students." Under Price the program partnered with various companies and organizations—including the DuPont Corporation and the National Action Council for Minorities in Engineering—to provide educational opportunities for eligible students.

Although many black freshmen entered Lamar's engineering program, a large number dropped out by the end of their first year. Price helped his students found a chapter of the National Society of Black Engineers (NSBE) and served as the chapter's advisor. The NSBE is a 15,000-member organization that works to increase the participation of black Americans in the engineering professions. As the Lamar chapter raised scholarship funds for black engineering students, retention improved. Entrepreneur and businessman Paul Fregia, a 1981 Lamar graduate, told Lamar University's *Cardinal Cadence* in the spring of 2004: "People like Dr. Richard Price were pillars in my life—people who helped me to believe that I could take the next step, and that my dreams could be endless."

Dr. Price served on the National Advisory Board of the NSBE for 20 years. He advised NBSE student leaders

At a Glance . . .

Born Richard L. Price in 1930(?). *Education:* Prairie View A&M University of Texas, BS, mathematics; University of Texas, Austin, MA, mathematics; Iowa State University; University of California-Los Angeles; Ohio State University, PhD, mathematics education; Yale Divinity School, MA, religion, 1972. *Military Service:* U.S. Army 2nd Lieutenant, combat duty in Korea.

Career: Prairie View A&M University of Texas, 1956-(?); Lamar University, Department of Mathematics, associate professor, 1970–; University of Bridgeport, associate director of the engineering program, 1972(?); Lamar University, College of Engineering, director of minority recruitment and retention, 1979(?)–; Lamar University, long-range planning committee, 2003-05.

Memberships: Golden Triangle-Texas Alliance for Minority Engineering, chairman; National Society of Black Engineers, National Advisory Board, 1982-2002.

Awards: National Society of Black Engineers, Golden Torch Award for Lifetime Achievement in Academia, 2004; Golden Triangle-Texas Alliance for Minority Engineering, Lamar University Foundation, Dr. Richard L. Price Endowment Scholarship for Engineering Students, 2005.

Addresses: *Office*—Department of Mathematics, Lamar University, P.O. Box 10047, Beaumont, TX 77710.

institutions, and corporations who exemplify the NSBE's mission—as quoted on the NSBE Web site announcing the recipients—"to increase the number of culturally responsible black engineers who excel academically, succeed professionally and positively impact the community." Michele Lezama, the NSBE's executive director, was quoted on the Lamar NSBE Chapter web page: "As in past years, the Golden Torch Awards are NSBE's way of honoring and expressing its gratitude for the past and future accomplishments of its awardees, while also paving a path for young, aspiring black engineers to navigate toward their own personal and professional success."

In addition to his work with the Minority Engineering Program at Lamar, Price worked with the Golden Triangle-Texas Alliance for Minority Engineering (GT-TAME). In January of 2005, in honor of Dr. Price, GT-TAME announced the establishment of the Dr. Richard L. Price Endowment Scholarship for Engineering Students at Lamar University, to be administered by the Lamar University Foundation. The scholarship honored Doc Price's many years of service to Lamar students and others in the Golden Triangle—the Beaumont-Port Arthur area of Texas. The scholarship is earmarked for full-time Lamar undergraduates majoring in engineering, math, or science who have maintained a minimum overall-grade-point average of 2.75. The scholarship rotates among each of the departments on an annual basis. Janice Trammel, executive director of the Lamar Foundation, was quoted in a Lamar news release: "Scholarships are critical to the university's ability to attract and retain students. What better way to honor a faculty member who has devoted much of his time to recruit students to Lamar." The scholarship was endowed by Lamar parents, students, friends, faculty, and alumni. The *Lamar Mathematician* quoted Oscar Polk, a Lamar graduate: "Eastman Chemical Company would like to pay honor to Dr. Richard L. Price for the excellent job he has done over the years with the Minority Engineering Program at Lamar, his demonstrated commitment to the GT-TAME organization, along with his contributions as a National, Regional, and Chapter Advisor to the National Society of Black Engineers."

Between 2003 and 2005 Dr. Price was a member of the Lamar University long-range planning committee. As of 2005 he continued to serve as the Director of Minority Recruitment and Retention for Lamar's College of Engineering and as chairman of the Texas Alliance for Minorities in Engineering.

on membership issues and contributed significantly to the creation and development of NSBE's Pre-College Initiative for encouraging middle- and high-school African American students in math and science. In announcing Price's retirement from the board in 2002, Chairman Gary S. May said: "For Doc Price's unprecedented tenure on the National Advisory Board and his innumerable contributions to our growth as the premier organization for African American engineering students and professionals, each of us owe him a tremendous debt of gratitude." Following his retirement from the board, Price remained active in regional NSBE chapters.

Dr. Price received the 2004 Golden Torch Award for Lifetime Achievement in Academia from the NSBE. Golden Torches are awarded to individuals, academic

Sources

Periodicals

Cardinal Cadence (Lamar University), March-May 2004, p. 28.

On-line

"The Dr. Richard L. Price, I Minority Scholarship in Engineering, Mathematics, and Science," *Lamar Mathematician*, www.216.239.57.104/u/Lamar? q=cache:h3KcD-0rioAJ:www.math.lamar.edu/news letter/news_v3_n2.asp+%22lamar+mathematician %22&hl=en&ie=UTF-8 (February 24, 2005).

"Josephine Smalls Miller Esq. National Society of Black Engineers' National Advisory Board," *National Society of Black Engineers, The Multicultural Advantage*, www.multiculturaladvantage.com/contentmgt/ anmviewer.asp?a=350&z=80&isasp= (February 8, 2005).

"LU Engineering College Receives Dupont Grant," *News@LU*, www.lamar.edu/news/story.asp?ID= 222 (February 8, 2005).

"National Society of Black Engineers Announces 2004 Golden Torch Awards Winners," *National Society of Black Engineers*, www.nsbe.org/publicrelations/gta winners.php (February 24, 2005).

"National Society of Black Engineers 2004 Golden Torch Awards Winners" *National Society of Black Engineers*, www.nsbe.org/publicrelations/winner_ bios.php (February 24, 2005).

"Price Scholarship to Help Lamar Engineering, Math and Science Students," *Lamar University*, www. lamar.edu/news/story.asp?ID=898 (February 24, 2005).

"The 2004 Golden Torch Award Recipient," *Lamar University NSBE Chapter*, www.hal.lamar.edu/~ns be/advisor.html (February 24, 2004).

—Margaret Alic

Milous J. Reese, Jr.

1904—

Chiropractor, acupuncturist, herbologist

Reese, Milous, photograph. Courtesy Dr Reginald Hug.

Throughout his life Dr. Milous J. Reese, Jr., has been a soft-spoken, mild-mannered man, but a tenacious fighter for better healthcare practices and supporting legislation in Alabama. Before his phased retirement began in the 1980s he did not hesitate to lend his money, energy, and time to the people and organizations around the state that looked to him for support. Patients, civic groups, colleges, and medical groups all have been the recipients of Reese's good will. For his generous deeds he has earned many awards of recognition and deep respect from the city of Birmingham and the Alabama state legislature. To honor him the Alabama State Chiropractors Association presented him with a Lifetime Achievement Award on July 2, 1993. To further underscore his accomplishments on that day the State of Alabama designated July 2 as Dr. Milous J. Reese, Jr., Day.

In 1950 Reese founded the Alabama College of Drugless Therapy and was the first black chiropractor to meet the standard requirements to run a nursing home, opening a facility in Smithfield, Georgia, in June of 1952. He was the first black to become a member of the Alabama State Chiropractic Association and re-ceived a Certificate of Recognition for Outstanding Service from the Jefferson County Chiropractic Society in 1975. He was the first African American to serve on the United States Board of Acupuncture, and received a commendation form the Alabama legislature for public service work in 1983. Dr. Reese fought laws that forbade combining office and residential space in a common dwelling and supported passage of workers' compensation laws in the state. He also supported legislation that would allow chiropractic services to be covered by Medicare and Blue Cross Blue Shield in the state of Alabama.

Milous Reese, Jr., was born on a farm in Harris, Georgia, on October 17, 1904, to Milous Reese , Sr., and Ella Reese, the sixth of fourteen children. His father moved the family to Birmingham after selling the farm when Reese , Jr., was a teenager. But Birmingham held no interest for the young man at that time. He wanted to see the world while he was still young, so he took a job at the Pennsylvania Railroad as a porter on a sleeping car that ran between New York and Toronto. A chance meeting with Nelson Rockefeller on board the train became a life-changing event for Reese.

At a Glance . . .

Born Milous J. Reese, Jr., on October 17, 1904, in Harris, GA. *Education:* Standard Institute of Therapeutics, Chicago, IL, DC, chiropractic therapeutics, 1930; Indiana School of Chiropractic, Anderson, IN, DC, 1933; McCormick Medical College, MD, 1935; Indiana American Institute of Science, MS, philosophy, 1946; Ohio Christian College, PhD, psychology, (?); Villamoe University, BS, 1949; Mid-Western University, BA, 1953. Texas Chiropractic College, postgraduate studies, applied kinesiology and diagnostic roentgenology, 1972-76; Bissland Acupuncture Seminars, certified instruction, 1974; Emerson College of Herbology, MA, herbology, 1978. *Religion:* Methodist.

Career: Birmingham, Alabama, Chiropractor and Certified Acupuncturist, 1933–; Alabama College of Drugless Therapy, founder, 1950; Nursing home, Smithfield, Georgia, founder, 1952.

Selected memberships: Alabama State Chiropractic Association; Jefferson County Chiropractic Society; Acupuncture Society; Center for Chinese Medicine; U.S. Academy of Acupuncture.

Selected awards: Jefferson County Chiropractic Society Certificate of Recognition for Outstanding Service, 1975; Alabama Legislature Commendation for Public Service, 1983; Miles College Doctor of Humane Letters Award, 1989; Alabama Chiropractic Association, Lifetime Achievement Award, 1993; State of Alabama designation of Milous J. Reese, Jr., Day, July 2, 1993.

Addresses: *Office*—Dr. Milous Reese, Jr., 2117 18th Street, Ensley, Birmingham, AL, 35218.

When asked where the train was going, Reese told Rockefeller its destination. Later Rockefeller asked Reese how may pennies he had in his pocket. Reese responded that he only had a few. Rockefeller then pulled out his billfold and gave Reese a dollar for every penny Reese showed him. "This is to teach you the value of your pennies," Rockefeller told Reese, according to the *Birmingham News*. Then as the wealthy man turned away he said, "But you know, I'd give all my money up to get rid of my stomach problem." With that Reese decided to study medicine.

Dr. Reese studied as he traveled, completing high school in Las Vegas in 1926. He received chiropractic degrees from the Standard Institute of Therapeutics in Chicago in 1930 and the Indiana School of Chiropractic in Anderson, Indiana in 1933. Reese opened his practice soon after that and continued to learn in the field of chiropractic medicine and several other specialties for over 60 years. He earned a master's degree in philosophy from the Indiana American Institute of Science in Indianapolis and received a doctorate in psychology from Ohio Christian College. In 1956 his application was rejected when he applied for additional studies at the Texas Chiropractic College. At the time Texas law did not allow the enrollment of African Americans at the school. But Reese never lost sight of his goals: when the law changed, he applied again and was accepted to do post-graduate work there in applied kinesiology. He also studied internal medicine, acupuncture, herbology, and diagnostic roentgenology.

Prior to the 1950s many African Americans pursuing medicine did not consider becoming chiropractors due to the many obstacles to entering chiropractic schools. Because of the "Negroes not accepted" policy of white schools, those blacks that did had to study in northern white-run schools or schools that provided instructions to blacks only. Correspondence schools were an option also since one could hide his race more easily.

As late as 1979 the National Association of Black Chiropractors found the need to file discrimination complaints against the Council on Chiropractic Education (CCE), the professions accrediting group, along with its member colleges. The resulting action was a Recommendation by the Office of Civil Rights of the U.S. Department of Education to change or eliminate some admissions forms and statements that caused discrimination towards blacks. Since that time things have changed considerably for blacks in the field. Blacks are now graduating in greater numbers and working as administrators and faculty at many schools in the nation.

Dr. Reese worked side by side with colleagues and lawmakers to fight for the changes that came about. In a letter to the *African-American Health Week Special Edition* Alabama State Congressman Earl F. Hilliard stated, "Dr. Reese epitomizes that which is so needed in all our communities—a caring healthcare professional who is always accessible when there is a need. I can remember when Dr. Reese, as a young chiropractor, was the only primary care health professional willing to locate in his community—we could count on him in times of need."

In the 1930s when Dr. Reese began his practice he would charge each patient only one dollar. Some days he saw up to 300 patients. Christopher Elliott quoted Dr. Reese in the *Birmingham News* as saying, "They kept filing in and out every day until I became known. Then I started to ask for more money." Besides his dedication to his work they were fascinated by his collection of antique diagnostic equipment.

His early years in practice were tough but the times and people were all changing. In 1943 the Alabama Chiropractic Association started accepting blacks. Their Man of the Year award to Reese is the one he is most proud of. As he wiped a tear from his eye, Reese told Elliott, "If it weren't for some good white people and some good black people in the world we wouldn't get this far. Man is not judged by his color or his size, but his heart."

Sources

Periodicals

Birmingham News, July 17, 1989, p. 2D.
African-American Health Week Special Edition, March 31, 1994, p. 9.

On-line

"Challenges and Progress of Black Chiropractors," *Chiropractic Economics*, www.chiroeco.com/article/2004/issue10/10events6.html (December 28, 2004).
"Dr. Milous Reese: First Black Honored as Alabama's Chiropractor of the Year," *Chiropractic Economics*, www.chiroeco.com/article/2004/issue10/10people8.html (December 28, 2004).

Other

Additional information obtained through an interview with Dr. P. Reginald Hug on January 9, 2005, and through materials supplied by the Alabama State Chiropractic Association.

—Sharon Melson Fletcher

Cyrille Regis

1958—

British soccer player

Regis, Cyrille, photograph. Michael Fresco/Evening Standard/Getty Images.

Cyrille Regis is the best known of a trio of black players who appeared for the West Bromwich Albion team in the late 1970s, a time when there were very few black players in English soccer. At that time, to have three on one team was unique. A powerful striker with great pace, Regis joined West Bromwich Albion, also known as "The Baggies," in 1977 at the age of 19. In his first professional season, he scored 18 goals, appeared in a Football Association (FA) Cup semi-final, and became the Professional Footballers' Association Young Player of the Year. He joined Coventry City in 1984 and made almost 300 appearances, including being part of their FA Cup winning side of 1987. He played for England 14 times, including five full "caps," or appearances on the main team, as well as appearances in "B" internationals, and for the under-21 team. Regis was feared by defenders for his formidable pace, strength, and his ability to score goals from long range. He was also a fiercely competitive player, and though he faced a great deal of racist abuse on the pitch, he channeled his anger into a greater determination to play well. The efforts of Regis and the small number of other black players in Britain since the 1970s have changed the attitude of football fans and helped the English Football Association itself begin to take action against racism at games.

Cyrille Regis was born in Maripasoula, French Guyana, on February 9, 1958, to Robert Regis, a laborer from St Lucia, and Matilda Regis, from French Guyana. His first language was French, but he moved to Britain at age five and held a British passport because of his father's nationality. He grew up in London where he attended local schools; at age 16 he left school to begin an apprenticeship as an electrician. With obvious talent for soccer he also joined nearby amateur side Hayes Football Club where he stayed for two seasons, scoring a total of 45 goals, an impressive total for a teenager in a senior team. By then convinced he wanted to become a professional soccer player, Regis was spotted by West Bromwich Albion (WBA) scout Ronnie Allen and signed for £5000. It is claimed that Allen paid for Regis with his own money because he could not convince WBA about the player's ability.

Became a Professional Soccer Player

The move from London-based Hayes to West Bromwich, near Birmingham in the English West Midlands

At a Glance . . .

Born Cyrille Regis on February 9, 1958, in Maripasoula, French Guyana; married 1983 (divorced); children: Robert, Michelle. *Religion:* Catholic.

Career: Hayes Football Club, amateur soccer player, 1975-77; West Bromwich Albion Football Club, professional soccer player, 1977-84; Coventry City Football Club, professional soccer player, 1984-91; Aston Villa Football Club, professional soccer player, 1991-93; Wolverhampton Wanderers Football Club, professional soccer player, 1993-94; Wycombe Wanderers Football Club, professional soccer player, 1994-95; Chester Football Club, professional soccer player, 1995-96; West Bromwich Albion, reserve team coach, 1996-99; First Artist Corporation, football agent, 1999-2004; Stellar Group, football agent, 2004–.

Memberships: Professional Footballers' Association; Christians in Sport.

Awards: Professional Footballers' Association (PFA) Young Player of the Year, 1978; FA Cup Winner's Medal, with Coventry City, 1987; played for England's main team five times.

Addresses: *Office*—The Stellar Group Limited, 16 Stanhope Place, London W2 2HH, United Kingdom.

involved more than just relocating to another part of the country; the difference between the two clubs was immense. The professional WBA team was one of the founding clubs of the English Football Association and had been promoted to the English first division (now The Premiership) in 1976. WBA was considered one of the big football clubs of the time, regularly playing in front of large crowds. Regis debuted for WBA aged 19 in a League Cup game against Rotherham on August 31, 1977. Until then he had never played in front of more than 500 people, but the crowd that day numbered 13,000, an experience he described to *Contemporary Black Biography* (*CBB*) as "truly scary, but then you feel the passion of the fans as well." He endeared himself to the supporters by scoring in his first game, but gaining acceptance took longer than one game. Seventeen more goals were to follow that season, in which "The Baggies" made it to the FA Cup semi-final largely because of the goal scoring partnership of Regis with Ally Brown and Tony "Bomber" Brown.

Regis moved to WBA at the same time as another black player from the amateur leagues, Laurie Cunningham, and the pair became close friends. When manager Johnny Giles left the club in 1978 his replacement Ron Atkinson brought in a third black player, Brendon Batson, a surprising move at a time when racism was deeply ingrained in British soccer. Fielding three black players for the first time ever in English football, WBA came in for harsh treatment from opposition fans. Regis, Cunningham, and Batson were nicknamed "The Three Degrees" by Atkinson, after the popular black singing group of the time. Although it was meant affectionately, the nickname was in questionable taste; in 2005 it would not be acceptable to single out players that way. In fact many English fans at the time still believed that black players were lazy, lacked skill, and would not be able to play in cold weather. Some expressed their views by throwing bananas onto the pitch during games. But Regis told *CBB* that while racial abuse was certainly one of the "mind games" used by opposition fans inside the arena it was not part of his everyday experience. Even so he did once receive a bullet in the mail with a note warning him never to play at Wembley, the national stadium. He explained that on the pitch he was able to channel his anger into improving his performance: "the best answer to it was to score a lot of goals," he told *CBB*.

Built an Impressive Record

Regis's competitive mindset ensured that he put in many impressive performances at WBA and he became a favorite of the fans, who called him "Smokin' Joe." Having scored on his professional debut he went on to score 82 goals for the team in 237 league appearances, including 25 in the 1981-82 season alone. But by 1984 the exciting WBA side of the late 1970s had broken up. Cunningham left for Real Madrid in 1979, manager Atkinson departed for Manchester United in 1981 and then bought key players Bryan Robson and Remi Moses from WBA in 1982 for a record £2.5 million. Regis himself transferred to Coventry City in 1984, where he spent the next seven years, and where he won his only major medal as part of the FA Cup-winning team of 1987 when they beat his childhood team Tottenham Hotspur 3-2. By then Regis was a popular and well-respected player. His playing style was that of a typical English center forward: physical, courageous, and able to score goals on the slightest of chances. In particular he was renowned for his spectacular long-range shots.

Regis told *CBB* that in many ways he had a fairytale career. Starting out as a teenage hopeful, being spotted by a first division team, playing for England, and winning the FA Cup is the romantic backdrop to the dreams of many English boys. But he was at pains to point out that apart from hard work and talent his career benefited from a great deal of luck. And there were setbacks too. The problem of racism on the pitch was one, but Regis also described the problems that came with sudden wealth and fame at a young age. Then in 1988 his close friend Laurie Cunningham, with whom he had shared the experience of starting out in big-time soccer, was killed in a car accident in Spain, at age 33. Regis had been involved in a similar accident with Cunningham two years earlier and the pair had walked away unscathed. He told *CBB* that he and Cunningham had become "famous together and rich together" so Cunningham's sudden death made him reappraise his approach to life. It was shortly after this event that he became a Christian, and he remains a member of the organization Christians in Sport.

Regis's career at Coventry ended when he was bought in 1991 by Ron Atkinson who was then manager of another midlands team, Aston Villa. But his stay at Aston Villa was short; he moved to Wolverhampton Wanderers in 1993, then after a year and just 19 games he went to Wycombe Wanderers, where he became the club's oldest player to appear in a senior game at the age of 37 years and 86 days. His playing career ended with injury in 1996 while playing for Chester City.

Enjoyed a Twenty-Year Career

Regis's long playing career is testament to his huge enthusiasm for the game—the same enthusiasm and desire to play helped him through his difficult early days at West Bromwich Albion—and came across very strongly in the interview he gave to *CBB*. But he is also driven by an understanding of soccer as a community sport and expressed genuine admiration for the passion and commitment of football fans for their local team. In his twenty-year career Regis was an important figure in gaining acceptance for black players in the game, but as he explained, he never set out to do anything of the sort: he just wanted to play the best he could and win.

While at Wolverhampton Wanderers Regis took his coaching qualifications and was prepared to become a coach when his career ended. When that finally happened he took the job of reserve team coach at West Bromwich Albion, a job he described as "the worst in football" because no player wants to play or train with the reserves. After several changes of personnel at the club Regis finally left after three years and became an agent with First Artist Corporation where he trained and qualified as a FIFA football agent. He joined The Stellar Group in 2004 and acts as agent for several players, including his nephew, Jason Roberts.

Sources

Books

Bowler, Dave, and Jas Bains, *Samba in the Smethwick End: Regis, Cunningham, Batson, and the Football Revolution*, Mainstream Publishing, 2000.

Matthews, Tony, *Smokin' Joe: Cyrille Regis—25 Years in Football*, Britespot Publishing Solutions, 2002.

Periodicals

Observer (London), September 7, 2003.

On-line

"Black British Footballers—Cyrille Regis," *Black Presence in Britain*, www.blackpresence.co.uk/pages/sport/regis.htm (February 1, 2005).

"Cyrille Regis," *Hayes Men*, http://members.aol.com/mtofhayesfc/hayesfc/regis.htm (February 1, 2005).

"Cyrille Regis," *Dictionary of Athletes and Sports Personalities*, www.explore-biography.com/sports_figures/C/Cyrille_Regis.html (February 1, 2005).

Other

Additional information for this profile was obtained through an interview with Cyrille Regis on January 19, 2005.

—Chris Routledge

Will Robinson

1911—

Basketball coach, talent scout

Will Robinson made history in 1970 as the first African American to coach at a Division I school when he was hired as the head basketball coach by Illinois State University. Prior to joining the Redbirds, Robinson coached for 26 years in the Detroit public school system. In 1975 he became a scout for the Detroit Pistons, a position he held until 2003, when he retired at the age of 92.

Struggles of a Black Athlete

Robinson was born in the small town of Wadesboro, North Carolina, on June 3, 1911. Neither of his very young parents had reached their 15th birthday when he was born, and both had died before they turned 30. He was raised by his grandparents, who moved to Pennsylvania and then to Steubenville, Ohio, where Robinson attended junior high and high school. At the age of 12 he began to caddie at the Riverview Country Club, where professional golfer Bob Hillis taught him the game of golf. He learned to swim in the Ohio River that flows alongside Steubenville.

A versatile athlete, Robinson earned 14 letters in five sports—football, basketball, baseball, track, and golf—at Steubenville High School. Two days before the start of the 1930 football season, Robinson was moved to quarterback, becoming the first black to ever play the position at the school. The team went undefeated, never allowing an opponent to score the entire season. Robinson was also captain of the golf team, and despite not being allowed to play on the same course as the white players, he finished second in the state golf

tournament. Robinson recalled to the *Detroit News,* "We went to the state tournament in Columbus, and they wouldn't let me play with the others. I started alone at seven in the morning. I couldn't stay in the dormitory at Ohio State. I couldn't eat at the banquet they had that night. They gave me a sandwich. I finished second."

Robinson can tell many other stories of the struggles he encountered because of his race. "I remember when I went to a school counselor [in high school] and told her I thought I should take up typing, and she said: 'Typing? Why, you're going to be a janitor,'" he once told the *Detroit News.* Despite the many barriers in his way, Robinson's motivation was unwavering. After graduating from high school he moved to West Virginia to coach at a segregated black school, but it was during the Great Depression, and he received no salary. The school gave him a nickel for transportation to the school, which he put in his pocket and walked. After two years without pay Robinson requested a salary but was told that without a college degree, he was not qualified. As a result, Robinson enrolled in West Virginia State College. During his college career, Robinson earned 15 letters in four sports—football, baseball, basketball and gymnastics—and captained the football, baseball, and gymnastics teams.

The Road to Detroit

After earning his college degree in 1937, Robinson took a coaching job at the Central Avenue Recreation Center in Pittsburgh. He coached basketball in the

At a Glance . . .

Born on June 3, 1911, in Wadesboro, NC. *Education:* West Virginia State College, BA, 1937; University of Michigan, MA.

Career: DuSable High School, Chicago, coach, 1943; Miller High School, Detroit, coach, 1944-57; Cass Technical High School, Detroit, coach, early 1960s; Pershing High School, Detroit, 1960s-1970; Illinois State University, basketball coach, 1970-75; Detroit Lions, talent scout, 1960s(?); Detroit Pistons, talent scout, assistant to the president of basketball operations, 1975-2003.

Selected awards: Redbirds Athletics (Illinois State) Hall of Fame, 1980; Michigan Sports Hall of Fame, 1982; John W. Bunn Award, James Naismith Memorial Basketball Hall of Fame, 1992; Michigan High School Coaches Hall of Fame; West Virginia State Hall of Fame.

Addresses: *Office*—c/o Detroit Pistons, The Palace, 2 Championship Drive, Auburn Hills, Michigan, 48326.

YMCA league, taking his team to the national championship. He also arranged practices for the New York Rens, a hall-of-fame, all-black professional basketball team that barnstormed around the country (no professional league would accept an all-black team). Through the Rens, Robinson met many of the black stars of the day, including Paul Robeson and Marian Anderson, and honed many of his coaching skills. Robinson moved to Chicago and worked at a YMCA before beginning his high school coaching career in 1943 at Chicago's DuSable High School, where he coached basketball and swimming.

In 1944 Robinson, at the age of 33, began a 26-year stint in Detroit as a high school coach. Robinson arrived in Detroit a year after violent race riots that had resulted in the death of 25 blacks and nine whites, and racial tensions were still high. Robinson had been encouraged to go to Detroit by the Chicago school superintendent who believed that Robinson had demonstrated the ability to work with both blacks and whites. The second black in the school's athletic department, Robinson coached basketball and football at Miller High School for the next 13 years, winning six championships despite having neither a gym nor a home football field.

After a stint at Cass Tech, in the early 1960s Robinson began coaching at Pershing High School, where his teams won the state basketball championship in 1967 and 1970. Five players from the 1967 team, including Spencer Haywood and Ralph Simpson, went on to play professional sports. Robinson became a coaching legend, winning 85 percent of his games during his time as a coach in the Detroit school system. He also worked on the side as a scout for the Detroit Lions, becoming the first black professional sports scout. Most of the schools were still segregated, and Robinson's job was to cover all the black colleges in the South, where he discovered future hall-of-fame cornerback Lem Barney at Jackson State in 1967. Yet, because he was black, many opportunities passed him by. In 1969 he was promised the University of Detroit coaching job, but the school pulled out at the last minute, much to Robinson's disappointment.

First Black to Coach Division I

In 1970 Robinson became the first black to coach at a Division I school when he was hired by Illinois State University to head up the school's men's basketball program. At the time, Doug Collins, an All-American player who would be selected as the number one pick in the 1972 National Basketball Association draft, was a sophomore at Illinois State. "The first time I met him, I was blown away," Collins told the *Dallas Morning News* in 2004. "When you looked into his eyes, you saw a dignified, honorable man. He told me, 'You have talent, and I'll take you where you want to go.' To this day, I love him as a father." Robinson coached the Redbirds from 1970 to 1975, compiling a record of 78 wins and 51 losses, without posting a losing season.

Although Robinson's charismatic personality and superior coaching skills won the respect and adoration of his players, Robinson's groundbreaking role as a black coach in the college ranks was not as readily accepted by the public. Many wondered aloud if the team would change its name from the Redbirds to the Blackbirds. Robinson had trouble getting on the schedule with other teams, and he was often verbally abused with racial slurs at away games. Additionally, officials sometimes penalized the Redbirds with unfair calls.

Tired of the continual heckling and struggles with scheduling games, Robinson left Illinois State in 1975 to join the front office of the Detroit Pistons as a scout. Although he only coached Division I basketball for five years, Robinson opened the door for other black coaches. In 1972 George Raveling was hired by Washington State University and Fred Snowden became the coach at the University of Arizona.

For the next 28 years Robinson, whose official title was assistant to president of basketball operations, scouted talent for the Detroit Pistons. His many discoveries included Joe Dumars, Dennis Rodman, and John Salley. He retired in 2003 at the age of 92 as the oldest professional basketball scout. Robinson had plenty to be proud of in his long career, but one thing brought him particular pride: "The thing I like most about my life," Robinson told the *Detroit News*, "is that I have been instrumental in sending over 300 men and a few women to college at no cost to themselves. That's what I'm most proud of because those are the people that make this country strong."

Sources

Periodicals

Daily Vidette (Indiana State University newspaper), March 18, 2003; April 23, 2003.
Dallas News, February 23, 2004.
Detroit Free Press, February 14, 2002.
Detroit News, June 6, 2001; March 20, 2002; October 29, 2003.
PR Newswire, September 29, 2003.
Sports Illustrated, November 19, 2001.

On-line

"Pistons Scout Honored for 28 Years of Service," Detroit Pistons, http://nba.com/pistons/news/pistonshonor_willrobinson_040211.html (February 18, 2005).
"Will Robinson," Illinois State University, Redbird Athletics Hall of Fame, http://www.redbirds.org/HOF/Robinson.shtml (February 18, 2005).

—Kari Bethel

Johnathan Rodgers

1946—

Television executive

Johnathan Rodgers is among the nation's most influential television executives. He served as the highest-ranking black executive at an American television network from 1990 to 1996; then expanded Discovery Network into a multi-billion dollar success in the cable industry, and in 2003 helped launch a new black-oriented cable channel called TV One.

Throughout his career, Rodgers has held to the philosophy that a television station is in business to make money, but never at the expense of the community it serves. In fact, Rodgers believes that a station should be a member of the community. "He encourages the general managers to understand the neighborhoods and the people they serve," *Upscale* ZSL magazine wrote of his time at CBS. "He wants the stations to be advocates for good in the community." And Rodgers stayed true to his philosophy in 2004 as he described the success of TV One's first year, telling *Adweek*: "I am not only proud of the people here, but I am really proud of the industry…. It is those Berkeley leanings—accomplishing something not only in the right way, but for the right reasons."

Rodgers attributes his understanding of people—and of the importance of community—to his childhood as the son of a military officer. "I was born in Texas, went to grade school in southern California and lived in Rantoul, Ill., for four years," he told Steve Daley of the *Chicago Tribune*. "If you grow up that way, moving every couple of years, going to different schools, meeting new kids all the time, you have to develop some skills for dealing with people."

At the same time that Rodgers was developing his strong people skills, he was also deciding on a career in journalism. And so, after graduating from the University of California at Berkeley in 1967 with a bachelor's degree in journalism, Rodgers took a job as a reporter at *Sports Illustrated*. Two years later, he became a reporter for *Newsweek*.

Rodgers's journalism career was put on hold for a few years while he served in the armed forces. Once out of the army, he went back to school to get a master's degree in communications from Stanford University. With an advanced degree in his pocket, he went back to *Newsweek* in 1972 as an associate editor.

By the next year, Rodgers felt that his career in print journalism wasn't moving fast enough. He decided to try his hand at electronic journalism. "What happened was," a *Newsweek* colleague would later tell Cheryl Lavin of the *Chicago Tribune*, "he got into TV-land and cased the joint. He looked at himself and said, 'I'm never going to be the greatest reporter, but I think I could be a hell of a producer.'" Ironically, after only one year as a writer-producer for WNBC-TV in New York, Rodgers changed his mind and left that station to become an on-air reporter for WKYC-TV in Cleveland, Ohio.

While working at WKYC-TV, Rodgers became reacquainted with an old friend from his military days, Royal Kennedy, who was also an on-air reporter at the station. Eight months later, when she was offered a job in Chicago, Rodgers decided that he didn't want a long-distance romance, so he quit his job and followed her. After they were married, Rodgers spent nearly a

At a Glance . . .

Born Johnathan Arlin Rodgers on January 18, 1946, in San Antonio, TX; son of M. A. (an Air Force officer) and Barbara Rodgers; married Royal Kennedy (a television journalist), September 27, 1975; children: David and Jamie. *Education*: University of California at Berkeley, B.A., 1967; Stanford University, M.A., 1972. *Military Service*: U.S. Army, 1969-71.

Career: Television network executive. *Sports Illustrated*, reporter, late 1960s; *Newsweek*, reporter, then associate editor, 1972-73; writer-producer, WNBC-TV, New York City, 1973-74; reporter, WKYC-TV, Cleveland, OH, 1974-75; assistant news director, WBBM-TV, Chicago, IL, 1976-78; executive producer, news director, and station manager, KNXT-TV (now KCBS-TV), Los Angeles, CA, 1978-83; executive producer, CBS *Nightwatch*, weekend *CBS Evening News,* and *CBS Morning News*, all New York City, 1983-86; vice president and general manager, WBBM-TV, Chicago, 1986-90; president, CBS Television Stations Division, 1990-96; Discovery Networks, president, 1996-2002; TV One, president and CEO, 2003–.

Memberships: Alpha Phi Alpha; Procter and Gamble, board of directors, 2001; Children's Defense Fund, board member; University of California at Berkeley Foundation, board member.

Awards: Vanguard Award, 2005.

Addresses: *Office*—TV One, 1010 Wayne Avenue, 10th Floor, Silver Spring, MD 20910.

year making the rounds at all the local television stations looking for work. "It was awful," he told Lavin. "More awful for her than for me. People would say to her: 'So what's you husband doing now? Just living off your money?'" Nobody was interested in giving Rodgers a job in television, but he was offered a job as a sports reporter for the *Chicago Tribune*. He turned the job down, though, because he wanted to work in television.

One night while at a dinner party in 1976, Rodgers met Jay Feldman, then news director at WBBM-TV in Chicago. Feldman was impressed with Rodgers's intelligence and personality and later offered him a job as assistant news director. Their working relationship proved to be so successful that when Feldman was

appointed news director for KNXT-TV (now KCBS-TV) in Los Angeles, he took Rodgers with him to be his executive producer.

Rodgers's management training in Chicago paid off as he quickly rose through the ranks at KNXT-TV—from executive producer to news director to station manager in a few years. One of the people he worked under during his tenure at the station was Van Gordon Sauter, who would later become president of CBS News.

In November of 1983, Sauter, already president of CBS News, asked Rodgers to assume executive production duties for the network's pre-dawn newscast *Nightwatch*. Six months later, Rodgers was promoted to executive producer of the weekend edition of the *CBS Evening News*. "More than any other time in the business," he told *Broadcasting*, "I felt that I was doing good as opposed to doing well. To cover the world and put it in a cohesive, understandable fashion was the greatest thrill in the world."

Just when Rodgers thought he had found a niche where he could stay for a time, he was called upon in November of 1985 to help save the struggling *CBS Morning News*. As executive producer, Rodgers promised to expand the appeal of the program and improve its dismal ratings. Unfortunately, he never had the opportunity to put his plan into action. After only three months, he took what *Broadcasting* called "the most politically sensitive assignment of his career."

Back in October of 1985, CBS affiliate WBBM-TV in Chicago demoted its black weekday anchor, Harry Porterfield, to a weekend anchor position so that former *CBS Morning News* anchor Bill Kurtis, a white journalist, could have his old job back. This action, along with the station's dismal record on minority hiring, angered the black community. Together with Jesse Jackson and Operation PUSH (People United to Serve Humanity, a civil rights group), many African Americans in Chicago started picketing WBBM-TV's offices twice a week and urged black viewers to stop watching the station's programs.

PUSH officials vowed that they would urge a national boycott of the network unless station officials agreed to a proposal they had drafted. "The proposed agreement," Peter Boyer of the *New York Times* wrote, "which includes a provision for monitoring compliance, also asks the station, WBBM, to contract with minority-owned businesses and to donate $10 million to the United Negro College Fund and $1 million to black organizations chosen by PUSH." The station and its network owners felt that the demands were too high, but they also knew that they had to resolve the problem as soon as possible.

In March of 1986, Rodgers was offered the position of vice president and general manager of the station, making him the first black general manager of a network-owned station. Many felt that the network brass had given Rodgers the nod because he was black and the appointment might help ease tensions between the station and the black community. Rodgers accepted the job, but only after giving it careful consideration. "I came very close to not taking this job," he told Daley, "because of the linkage, because there might have been a perception by my friends and my family and the people of Chicago that I was given this job to solve CBS's problems with Jesse Jackson and Operation PUSH. I also wasn't crazy about being the second guy it was offered to, but what swayed me was the fact that the first guy they offered it to was white. That said to me that they weren't looking for just any black guy."

Almost immediately, Rogers took charge of the situation and tried to alleviate some of the station's biggest problems, namely the boycott by PUSH, a major slippage in ratings, and a newsroom in turmoil. His first order of business was to improve morale at the station, especially in the newsroom. Rodgers brought in some new talent for the newscasts, hired more blacks, and promoted women. In fact, by the time he left the station in 1990, everything that got on the air at WBBM-TV was controlled by one of several women, who held the posts of news director, program director, promotion director, and press director at the station.

It also didn't take long for Rodgers to strengthen the bottom line of the station. From 1986 to 1989, it is estimated that revenues at the station increased from $60 million to $80 million, mainly due to Rodgers's input on programming and scheduling. He was instrumental in acquiring programs like *Who's the Boss*, *Entertainment Tonight*, and *The Arsenio Hall Show* to attract the high-spending viewers that advertisers want: those in the 18-49 age group. Within a few years, WBBM-TV was either first or second in the ratings in all station-controlled time periods.

In the four years that Rodgers served as vice president and general manager of the station, not only did profits and revenues increase, but the boycott against the station was defused and the relationship with minority groups was strengthened. Therefore, it came as no great surprise when he was named president of CBS Television Stations Division in August of 1990.

Praised by his coworkers for his easygoing, amiable management style, Rodgers' friendly smile wasn't the reason he won the position as president of CBS Television Stations Division. At the time of his appointment, five CBS (Columbia Broadcasting System) television stations owned and operated by the network were not prospering. CBS executives knew that Rodgers, a 14-year CBS veteran, had a proven ability to increase ratings and revenue at the other television stations for which he had worked, so they called upon him to take command of their stations in five U.S. cities—New York, Los Angeles, Chicago, Philadelphia, and Miami.

Rodgers told Donna Whittingham-Barnes of *Black Enterprise* soon after his promotion that he believed there were three reasons he got the job. "First, as a Midwesterner…this will help minimize New York or Los Angeles bias and may be more reflective of the country as a whole. Second, a minority perspective to CBS strategy is vital because each of the stations serves a population that is more than 40% non-white. And third, a track record."

Even though these were the factors that management believed would be necessary for his role as the liaison between the five stations and the network's sports, news, and programming departments, CBS executives knew that his people skills would be an equally important asset. In fact, management was so sure of his success that shortly after he was hired, CBS acquired two more stations, one in Green Bay, Wisconsin, and another in Minneapolis, Minnesota. It didn't take CBS long to realize they had made the correct decision.

As the leader of nine network owned-and-operated stations that broadcast to over 20 million viewers, Rodgers used the same approach at the network level that he did at the local level. Whittingham-Barnes described his tasks at the time of his promotion: "managing an operating budget of over $200 million; formulating the stations' tone and priorities regarding programming, marketing and promotion; and carving out larger market share for the network." For some, the challenge would prove overwhelming, but for Rodgers it was just another job in an industry that he loved. According to *Black Enterprise*, "1992 was the most lucrative year in the division's history with analysts citing profits of $185 million, up 30% from 1991." In only three years, Rodgers managed to increase viewership, profits, and revenues at six of the seven stations. Rodgers was proud of the financial accomplishments he made in the television industry. However, he was equally proud of the social changes he had been able to make along the way. Rodgers left CBS in 1996 with a strong reputation for efficient management.

He immediately signed on to preside over a burgeoning cable network: Discovery. When Rodgers arrived at Discovery Networks it had only two channels and was valued at about $1 billion. For the next six years Rodgers set his sights on developing the network. As president, he expanded the distribution of Animal Planet and the Travel Channel and launched such channels as Discovery Health Channel and Discovery Kids, and ushered in such shows as The Learning Channel's *Trading Spaces*. When Rodgers left Discovery in 2002, the network had 11 channels and was valued at $20 billion.

In 2003, Rodgers accepted another challenge, to create a new cable channel for African-American adults aged 24 to 54. With Black Entertainment Television capturing the attention of younger viewers, TV One seemed a prime opportunity for the cable industry. Rodgers told *Adweek* that he toped to create TV One as a "home base" for older African-American viewers.

In describing his plan for the channel to *Business Week,* Rodgers said, "The two most important lessons I learned from my television experience is to build programming to attract an audience and to create an advertising environment that advertisers find the most beneficial. These are the two most critical objectives I bear in mind as I build everything else." By early 2005 Rodgers was well on his way to getting TV One to be carried in the top 60 markets, where 90 percent of the African-American viewers reside, according to *Broadcasting and Cable.* Praising the channel's first year, Rodgers told *Adweek,* "You walk around taller having accomplished something like this."

Sources

Periodicals

Adweek, April 4, 2005, p. SR40.
Black Enterprise, December 1990, p. 42; February 1993, p. 126.
Broadcasting, September 17, 1990, p. 95; January 21, 1991, p. 39; April 26, 1993, p. 14.
Broadcasting and Cable, April 4, 2005, p. 56.
Business Week, September 16, 2003.
Chicago Tribune, March 20, 1986, p. C1; March 31, 1986, p. E1; September 18, 1987, p. E5; October 3, 1990, p. E1.
Ebony, February 1991, p. 20.
Jet, April 8, 1996, p. 33.
Los Angeles Times, October 30, 1985, p. F1; January 20, 1986, p. F5; March 30, 1986, p. F10; August 29, 1990, p. D2.
New York Times, March 27, 1986, p. C26; August 30, 1990, p. C20.
TelevisionWeek, April 4, 2005, p. S7; May 10, 2004, p. 8.
Time, April 14, 1986, p. 88.
Upscale, March 1993, p. 130.
Wall Street Journal, August 29, 1990, p. B4.

On-line

TV One, www.tvoneonline.com (April 28, 2005).

—Joe Kuskowski and Sara Pendergast

Kenny Roy

1990(?)—

Pilot

Kenny Roy was just 14 years old when he flew his first solo flight over British Columbia in September of 2004, and made aviation history that day as the youngest African-American pilot licensed to fly a plane on his own in the world. Because Canadian aviation regulations allow 14-year-olds to earn their solo pilot's license, Roy journeyed with another young pilot and adult chaperone in a Cessna 172 aircraft from a Compton, California, airport to a flight-certification center in Vancouver, Canada, in order to earn his credentials. "I didn't want to stop flying because I knew I couldn't fly here solo," he told *Jet* writer Melody K. Hoffman.

The son of Everson and Linetta Esters, Roy's fascination with flight began when his parents bought him a flight-simulator game for his computer. He discovered a youth aviation program near his home. Roy joined the rigorous program at Tomorrow's Aeronautical Museum, run out of Compton/Woodley Airport. To do so, he had to sign a pledge statement promising not to miss class and to avoid drugs and gangs. In order to receive free flight instruction, he volunteered at the museum. Over time, he managed to log some 50 hours in the skies, and was soon a skilled pilot, according to Robin Petgrave, the museum's founder and the youth-aviation program director, as quoted in *Jet*. "We do landing contests for the kids to compete against each other," Petgrave told Hoffman in the *Jet* article. "I take a dime and put it on the runway. Their task is to take off, fly one traffic pattern and land as close to that dime as possible. And every year we do it, Kenny literally puts the main wheels on that dime. It's difficult for military pilots and this kid can land on the dime at will."

Roy was eager to earn his solo pilot's license, but in the United States the minimum age is 16; in Canada, however, 14-year-olds may qualify. Through the Compton youth-aviation program had Roy met eleven-year-old Jimmy Haywood, another enthusiastic young pilot who had some 20 hours' worth of flying experience. The two decided to make history with a flight to Canada in order for Roy to earn his solo license. They wrote to companies and private individuals, looking for sponsorship for their trip, and also had to submit a written flight plan before they began. With the support of museum officials and numerous well-wishers, the pair took off from Compton/Woodley Airport on a September day in 2004.

Their three-day trip was not a non-stop one: they landed and slept at hotels on the way. Nor were they alone: a certified flight instructor came with them, but the instructor did not fly the Cessna 172, allowing Roy and Haywood to log all the flight hours. At a Vancouver-area airport, Roy submitted to a physical, and then went aloft with a flight instructor. As part of the test, he had to demonstrate stalls, spins, and spiral dives in the plane; back on the ground he took a tough written exam, the Canadian Pre-Solo Aeronautical Test, for which he had studied over a lengthy two-day marathon session. "It was kind of hard, but I knew if I didn't I wouldn't have been happy with myself, because I would have come to Canada for nothing," he told *Jet*.

At a Glance . . .

Born 1990(?); raised in Compton, California; son of Everson and Linetta Esters.

Career: Trained as a pilot at Compton/Woodley Airport, Compton, CA; earned Canadian solo pilot's license, 2004.

Addresses: *Office*—c/o Tomorrow's Aeronautical Museum, 961 West Alondra Blvd., Compton, CA 90220. *Home*—Compton, CA.

Roy passed the exam, which made him the youngest black pilot licensed to fly solo in the world. When he earned his license, the other pilots at the Vancouver flight-training center tossed a bucket of water on him, a tradition there. He and Haywood returned home to Compton/Woodley Airport on Saturday, September 25. Haywood had set his own record, as the youngest African-American pilot to make an international round-trip flight. Their safe landing was a major event at the airport, with family, friends, and even more well-wishers gathered to greet them.

One member of their fan club was Oscar York, president of the Tuskegee Airmen's Los Angeles chapter. The Tuskegee Airmen were a group of World War II fighter pilots who flew missions for the Army Air Force at a time when the U.S. military was still a segregated institution. Roy and Haywood's feat, York said, "should fill them up with pride and confidence in themselves," a report on the *Black College View* Web site by Tiffany Settles quoted him as saying. "Even if they don't want to fly later in life, it shows you can do something; and they're on their way to a good career, because they have heads that are already turned to the future."

Both Roy and Haywood were impressed by the scenery they witnessed during their flight, which took them over the mountain ranges, lakes, and forests of the western United States and Canada. Back in Compton, Roy returned to his classes as a tenth-grader and focused on his career goal, to become a commercial jet pilot. "It's exciting," a *Grand Rapids Press* report quoted him as saying. "It helps other kids, too, because they're following me. I set an example for them."

Sources

Periodicals

Grand Rapids Press, September 27, 2004, p. A5.
Jet, November 8, 2004, p. 14.

On-line

"Young Black Pilots Make Flight History," *Blackcol legeview.com,* www.blackcollegeview.com/vnews/display.v/ART/2004/10/25/417d31518da61 (March 3, 2005).

—Carol Brennan

Bryce Salvador

1976—

Professional hockey player

By the time the players' strike and owners' lockout silenced the rinks of the National Hockey League (NHL) in 2004 and 2005, Bryce Salvador had become a defensive mainstay of the St. Louis Blues squad. Not a headline-grabbing offensive player, nor a natural talent who immediately shone in what was often a young man's game, Salvador developed his skills slowly but surely. A big, physical player with a straightforward approach to the game, Salvador could look forward to a long NHL career.

Bryce Salvador was born in Brandon, Manitoba, Canada, on February 11, 1976. Like many youngsters in Canada's prairie towns, he grew up playing hockey, putting on his first pair of skates at age three. Salvador's parents, though, were unusually devoted to his progress, ferrying their son to early morning practices and weekend tournaments whenever necessary. Off the ice, Salvador excelled in school and was a talented musician, mastering the violin, tuba, clarinet, and saxophone.

Drafted by Tampa Bay

Salvador took to the ice with the Brandon Kings of the Manitoba Hockey Association in 1991, at the age of 15, and the following year he won a defenseman slot with the Lethbridge Hurricanes of Canada's Western Hockey League (WHL). He was a team fixture from the start, playing in 64 games in the 1991-92 season and 61 the following year, when the Hurricanes won the WHL title. That got the attention of scouts from the NHL's Tampa Bay Lightning, which picked Salvador in the sixth round of the 1994 draft.

That promising beginning to Salvador's NHL career went nowhere, however, as he waited for two years for a summons to the Lightning or one of their minor-league teams. "I still don't know why they weren't interested," Salvador was quoted as saying on the St. Louis Blues Web site. "They had a lot of problems at the time. Maybe they just forgot." Whatever the reason, Salvador spent some time weighing his options. Prestigious McGill University in Montreal was impressed with Salvador's academic and musical accomplishments and wooed him as a student, suggesting that he consider a switch from hockey to football. Salvador also thought about giving up hockey and going into computer science.

Instead, he stuck with the game. He continued to play for Lethbridge, and his game began to solidify. Salvador won Canada's Scholastic Player of the Year award in 1996 and was signed as a free agent by the St. Louis Blues in December of that year. "I watched him stick up for his teammates one night playing for Lethbridge and I liked him right away," Blues scouting director Bob Plager was quoted as saying on the team's Web site. "He was tough in front of his own end and I liked his work ethic."

Developed Skills in AHL

Salvador was dispatched to the Worcester Ice Cats American Hockey League (AHL) team in the Blues' minor-league system and spent three seasons there, playing in 170 games and winning the team's Most

At a Glance . . .

Born on February 11, 1976, in Brandon, Manitoba, Canada; married April.

Career: Professional hockey player, 1992–. Lethbridge Hurricanes, Western Hockey League, Canada, professional hockey player, 1992-97; Worcester Ice Cats (a minor league team associated with the St. Louis Blues), American Hockey League, professional hockey player, 1997-2000; St. Louis Blues, National Hockey League, professional hockey player, 2000–; Jam 'n' Sal's Community Stars Program, co-founder (with Jamal Mayers).

Selected awards: Canadian Hockey League, Scholastic Player of the Year, 1996.

Addresses: *Home*—Worcester, MA. *Office*—St. Louis Blues, Savvis Center, 1401 Clark Ave., St. Louis, MO 63103.

Improved Player award in 1998. "Worcester was good for me," Salvador told the Worcester *Telegram & Gazette.* "Some guys say they don't need the minors, but I did. It was important for my career." Salvador and his wife April put down roots in that small Massachusetts city and continued to spend the off-season there after he joined the Blues in St. Louis.

Salvador first took to the ice as an NHL player on October 5, 2000, as the Blues took on Phoenix. It was the first of 75 regular-season games he would play in during his rookie season, and he also appeared in all 14 of the Blues' playoff games in the spring of 2001. He scored his first point, an assist, on October 29 as his father Eugene watched in the stands in St. Louis. But Salvador, although he surprised fans with some sudden goals in Blues playoff games and won the team's hardest shot competition in 2000, was never primarily an offensive threat. At six feet two inches tall and 215 pounds, he was a classic defenseman, strong, rangy, and physical.

In his first year with the Blues he had 142 hits, third-highest on the squad. "Crash and bang" was Salvador's succinct description of his playing philosophy, as quoted by Tom Wheatley of the *St. Louis Post-Dispatch.* "When the guy comes down to my wall, I've got to be hard to play against. I don't turn away from anyone, but I want to be killing penalties, not putting my team a man down and sitting in the box. There's a difference between being physical and being stupid."

Played Hard Despite Injuries

Indeed, Salvador's physical style of play resulted in a number of small injuries that kept him off the ice for short periods and in the penalty box for a career-high 95 minutes in the 2002-03 season. He was also briefly sidelined that year by whiplash resulting from an auto accident. Nevertheless, he became a key day-to-day component of the Blues' defensive backbone. In his early days with the Blues, noted Dan O'Neill of the *St. Louis Post-Dispatch,* he "soaked up knowledge.... The raw texture has given way to a resilient coating, tough and trustworthy."

"Salvy," as his teammates nicknamed him, played in over 65 games in each of his first four seasons with the team, and his plus-minus rating (a measure of a team's scoring ability when a particular player is on the ice) rose to a career-high plus-seven in 2002-03. He missed ten games due to wrist injuries during the 2003-04 season and was briefly sent to Worcester to recuperate, but he still got into 69 games and notched eight points on three goals and five assists.

Off the ice, Salvador made large donations to and became involved with the United Way organization in the African-American community. And he and fellow Blues player (and former Worcester Ice Cats teammate) Jamal Mayers started an innovative youth group called Jam 'n' Sal's Community Stars Program, which gave a total of 110 students per season the chance to attend a Blues home game for free and to attend a skating party with the two players. Students selected were nominated by teachers or school administrators in recognition of good deeds or acts of kindness toward others. Emerging as one of the NHL's most consistent defensemen as the 2004-05 strike halted play, Salvador seemed likely to have many more years ahead in the NHL after the game resumed.

Sources

Periodicals

St. Louis Post-Dispatch, April 21, 2001, p. Sports-7; September 21, 2000, p. B2; October 29, 2000, p. D11; February 10, 2001, p. 5; January 8, 2003, p. D4.
Standard (St. Catharine's, Ontario, Canada), April 20, 2001, p. C2.
Telegram & Gazette (Worcester, MA), January 22, 2002, p. D1.

On-line

"Bryce Salvador," *St. Louis Blues Hockey Club,* http://stlouisblues.com/team/players/salvador.html (March 10, 2005).

"Bryce Salvador," *TSN.ca*, www.tsn.ca/nhl/teams/
player_bio.asp?player_id=1915&hubName=STL
(March 10, 2005).

—James M. Manheim

Joe Sample

1939—

Jazz pianist

An artist who has flourished in both the artistic world of jazz and in the popular genres of funk and R&B, pianist Joe Sample has rejected artificial genre divisions. "I detest the separation that has gone on," he told the *San Diego Union-Tribune.* "[African-American musical styles] all came out of our spirituality, out of the church. When people say 'Are you a jazz musician?,' I say, 'No, I'm a jazz-gospel-and-blues musician." Whatever label was placed on his music, Sample had a down-to-earth style that both attracted wide audiences and commanded the respect of listeners focused on his musicianship.

Born on February 1, 1939, in Houston, Texas, Joe Sample grew up in a fertile musical crescent of the United States. "There was a migration from Louisiana into southeastern Texas during the 1920s because of flooding," he explained to the *San Diego Union-Tribune.* "So they moved over to the higher ground, and I grew up in a Creole neighborhood hearing zydeco and Louis Armstrong." He started playing the piano at age five, and he incorporated a range of local traditions into his music: jazz, gospel, blues, and even Latin and classical forms.

Escaped Realities of Segregation through Music

Sample explained a deeper motivation for his mastery of the piano in a statement reproduced on the Web site of agent Richard De La Font. "I grew up in a time and place where segregation was an acceptable way of life, and for me the piano was the only place I could run for an act of healing," he stated. "I still feel that expressing myself this way is my great sanctuary. I would like my legacy to be not only that I reflected the times in which I lived, but also that my music had the power to help heal people's pain the way it has healed mine."

In high school in the 1950s, Sample teamed up with two friends, saxophonist Wilton Felder and drummer Nesbert "Stix" Hooper, to form a group called the Swingsters. While studying piano at Texas Southern University, Sample met and added trombonist Wayne Henderson and several other players to the Swingsters. The Swingsters changed their name first to the Modern Jazz Sextet and then to the Jazz Crusaders, in emulation of one of the leading progressive jazz bands of the day, Art Blakey's Jazz Messengers. Sample never took a degree from the university; instead in 1960, he and the Jazz Crusaders made the move from Houston to Los Angeles.

The group quickly found opportunities on the West Coast, making its first recording, *Freedom Sounds,* in 1961 and releasing up to four albums a year over much of the 1960s. The Jazz Crusaders played at first in the dominant hard bop style of the day, standing out by virtue of their unusual front-line combination of saxophone (played by Wilton Felder) and Henderson's trombone. Another distinctive quality was the funky, rhythmically appealing acoustic piano playing of Sample, who helped steer the group's sound into a fusion between jazz and soul in the late 1960s. The Jazz Crusaders became a strong concert draw during those years.

At a Glance . . .

Born on February 1, 1939, in Houston, TX; married (divorced); children: Nicklas. *Education:* Attended Texas Southern University.

Career: Musician, 1950s–; Swingsters musical group (renamed Modern Jazz Sextet, Jazz Crusaders (early 1960s), then Crusaders (early 1970s)), co-founder and member, 1960s-1980s.

Addresses: *Label*—Verve Music Group, 1755 Broadway, New York, NY 10019.

Worked as Session Musician

While Sample and his band mates continued to work together, he and the other band members pursued individual work as well. In 1969 Sample made his first recording under his own name; the little-known *Fancy Dance* featured the pianist as part of a jazz trio. In the 1970s, as the Jazz Crusaders became simply the Crusaders and branched out into popular sounds, Sample became known as a reliable L.A.-studio musician, turning up on recordings by the likes of Joni Mitchell, Marvin Gaye, Tina Turner, B.B. King, Joe Cocker, and vocal divas Minnie Riperton and Anita Baker. The electric keyboard was fairly new at the time, and Sample became one of the instrument's pioneers. He switched to electric keyboard for his recordings with the Crusaders themselves, and the group hit a commercial high-water mark with the hit single "Street Life" and the album of the same name in 1979.

After a few more small-group releases, Sample made his true solo debut on the MCA label in 1978 with *Rainbow Seeker.* It was the first of nearly 20 solo albums he recorded, most of them falling under the umbrella of what would come to be known as contemporary jazz or smooth jazz—music with well-rounded edges and strong urban contemporary influences that featured jazz solos and, often, a vocal component. Sample's compositions became favorites of jazz-pop vocalists like Al Jarreau and Randy Crawford, and he toured with Lalah Hathaway, daughter of R&B legend Donny Hathaway.

Suffered from Chronic Fatigue Syndrome

The 1980s were a frustrating time for Sample, both personally and creatively. His marriage of over 20 years dissolved, and he suffered from chronic fatigue syndrome. The Crusaders, after losing several key members, broke up after recording the *Life in the*

Modern World album for the GRP label in 1987. The group's once-vital fusion of jazz and funk had fallen victim to music-industry pressures. "The most dangerous thing is to be convinced that you have to follow the rules of formula," Sample told the *San Diego Union-Tribune,* "and I realize that at certain times in my career (with the Crusaders) I've had to deal with formula or face consequences." Despite the disbanding of the Crusaders, the members would join each other to record periodically over the years; Felder, Hooper, and Sample recorded their first album, called *Rural Renewal,* as the reunited Crusaders group in 2003 and a live concert in Japan in 2004.

Sample, in fact, emerged as a strong critic of the recording industry in his later years. "We have totally departed from the origins and roots of our music, and that has happened because of businessmen," he told the *San Diego Union-Tribune.* "The reason music is made today is to make multimillion-selling albums. There's less and less music made for just the love of music…. The moguls will sugarcoat everything. It's time to speak out." Sample's musical philosophy had an idealistic tinge. Speaking to *Essence* about his 1991 *Ashes to Ashes* release, he said that the album "deals with the disintegration of both Black communities and America at large. What I am witnessing now is a total lack of love and self-respect. So I meant this album to be an inspirational factor in helping the Black community heal itself."

The pianist made a powerful spokesman for these ideas, for by the 1990s and 2000s jazz audiences had begun to refer to him as a legend. "I'm hearing that more and more," Sample told the *Chicago Sun-Times.* "It's flattering, but I think, gee, I had better play and create in a very special manner." His recordings, for the Warner Brothers, Universal, and Verve, continued to sell well; *Sample This* was produced in 1997 by jazz fusion giant George Duke, and the All Music Guide hailed the 2002 album *The Pecan Tree* for its "impressive musical style based upon his early appreciation for jazz, gospel, soul, bebop, blues, Latin, and classical music." Sample's live concerts, often in a trio format featuring percussionist Lenny Castro, could tap rhythmically into the Latin layer of his musical upbringing. His 2004 album *Soul Shadows* paid tribute to jazz musicians Duke Ellington and Jelly Roll Morton, and pre-jazz bandleader James Reese Europe.

Selected discography

Albums

(With Jazz Crusaders) *Freedom Sounds,* Pacific Jazz, 1961.
Fancy Dance, Gazell, 1969.
Try Us, Sonet, 1969.
The Three, Inner City, 1975.
Swing Street Café, MCA, 1978.
Rainbow Seeker, MCA, 1978.

Carmel, Blue Thumb, 1979.
(With the Crusaders) *Street Life,* MCA, 1979.
Voices in the Rain, MCA, 1980.
The Hunter, MCA, 1982.
(With the Crusaders) *Life in the Modern World,* GRP, 1987.
Roles, MCA, 1987.
Sermonized, Warner Brothers, 1984.
Oasis, MCA, 1989.
Spellbound, Warner Brothers, 1989.
Ashes to Ashes, Warner Brothers, 1991.
Invitation, Warner Brothers, 1993.
Did You Feel That? Warner Brothers, 1994.
Old Places, Old Faces, Warner Brothers, 1995.
Sample This, Warner Brothers, 1997.
The Song Lives On, GRP, 1999.
The Pecan Tree, Universal, 2002.
(With the Crusaders) *Rural Renewal,* Verve, 2003.
Soul Shadows, Verve, 2004.
(With the Crusaders) *The Crusaders: Live in Japan,* Verve, 2004.

Sources

Periodicals

Chicago Sun-Times, April 5, 1992, p. Show-2.
Essence, May 1991, p. 50.
San Diego Union-Tribune, August 23, 2001, p. 19; October 10, 2004, p. F4.
St. Louis Post-Dispatch, April 9, 1996, p. D3.

On-line

"The Jazz Crusaders," *All Music Guide,* www.allmusic.com (March 10, 2005).
"Joe Sample," *All Music Guide,* www.allmusic.com (March 10, 2005).
"Joe Sample," *Richard De La Font Agency, Inc.,* www.delafont.com/music_acts/Joe-Sample.htm (March 10, 2005).
"Joe Sample," *Verve,* www.vervemusicgroup.com/artist.aspx?ob=art&src=rslt&aid=2691 (March 29, 2005).

—Jim M. Manheim

Sonia Sanchez

1934—

Poet, playwright, activist, educator, lecturer

In her poetry, Sonia Sanchez has urged black unity and action against white oppression in addition to writing about violence in the black community, the relationships between black men and women, familial ties, and social problems. She is the foremost poet to use urban black English in written form. She also advocated the inclusion of black studies programs in institutions of higher learning and was the first professor to offer a seminar on literature by black American women while at the University of Pittsburgh. Many of her peers who began the Black Power movement in the 1960s later dropped out when they attained material wealth, but Sanchez continues her commitment to social justice. Now retired from teaching, Sanchez's artistic work remains a vital source of inspiration for generations of Americans.

Sonia Sanchez was born Wilsonia Benita Driver in Birmingham, Alabama, on September 9, 1934, to Wilson L. and Lena Driver. Her mother passed away when she was a baby, and she and her sister, Pat, resided with their paternal grandmother until her death, and then various relatives for several years before their father took them to live with him in Harlem. Because they lived in a cramped dwelling Sanchez felt constricted and isolated. Out of this feeling of isolation she began to write. In the city Sanchez went to public schools and later Hunter College, where she received her B.A. in political science in 1955. She also did postgraduate work at New York University and studied poetry with Louise Bogan, who encouraged her to make writing her career.

As a child, Sanchez was appalled by the ways in which lack people were treated in the South and in the North, but did not have the verbal means to express it. In *Black Women Writers at Work*, edited by Claudia Tate, Sanchez described herself as a "very shy child, a very introspective child, one who stuttered." All that changed when she became a vocal poet-activist in the Black Power and arts movement during the 1960s. With Nikki Giovanni, Etheridge Knight, and Don L. Lee, she created the "Broadside Quartet" of radical young poets. She became a leading voice in this group.

Although her first marriage (date unknown) to Puerto Rican immigrant Albert Sanchez did not last, Sonia Sanchez would remain her professional name. In 1968, Sanchez married poet-activist Etheridge Knight and they had three children: Anita, Morani, and Mungu, but later divorced.

During the 1950s and 1960s, she was affiliated with the black arts movement and the civil rights movement in New York City, and she believed at first in integration. Later, when she heard Malcolm X say that blacks would never become part of America's mainstream, she based her identity on her racial heritage. Her poetry focused on the black struggle for liberation from racial and economic oppression and used the language of the streets instead of the language of academe. She became one of the first poets to blend ghetto impressions with lower-case letters, slashes, dashes, hyphenated lines, unconventional spelling, abbreviations, and further untried uses of language and structure to reinterpret what a poem is, does, and for whom it is than any other poet for "legitimizing the use of urban Black English in written form."

William Pitt Root wrote about her early poems in *Poetry*, "Her poems are raps, good ones, aimed like guns at whatever obstacles she detects standing in the way of Black progress .... Her praises are as generous as her criticisms are severe, both coming from loyalties that are fierce, invulnerable, and knowing. Whether she's addressing her praises to Gwendolyn Brooks or to the late Malcolm X, to her husband or to a stranger's child, always they emerge from and feed back into the shared experience of being Black."

By the early 1970s Sanchez had left the "Broadside Quartet" to write and give poetry readings on her own. How her poems sound when read out loud has always been of importance to Sanchez. She has been sought out for her impassioned, bold readings which often create a spontaneous feeling, like that of a jazz solo. The poet has read in Cuba, China, the West Indies, Europe, and on over five hundred campuses in the United States.

Since the 1970s she has published a steady stream of poetry books, mainly for adults but also one for children, as well as plays which she had been writing since the 1960s. Her poetry books include, *Homegirls and Handgrenades*, which won the American Book Award in 1985; *We a BaddDDD People, Liberation Poems, It's a New Day: Poems for Young Brothas and Sistuhs, A Blues Book for Blue Black Magical Women, Love Poems, I've Been a Woman: New and Selected Poems, Under a Soprano Sky, Shake Down Memory, Continuous Fire, Wounded in the House of a Friend, Does Your House Have Lions?* and *Shake Loose My Skin: New and Selected Poems.*

Sanchez began writing plays while in San Francisco in the 1960s. Her first, *The Bronx Is Next,* was about the forces destroying community and individuals in Harlem. Sanchez recalled in *African American Review* that "Dr. Arthur P. Davis, that grand old man of letters down at Howard University, called it one of the great plays of the 1960s. I forever am grateful to him for putting that play into perspective for me." Among Sanchez's other plays are *Sister Sonji, Uh, Huh: But How Do it Free us?,* and *Malcolm Man/Don't Live Here No Mo'. Sister Sonji* was first produced in conjunction with other plays Off-Broadway at the New York Shakespeare Festival Public Theatre in 1972. *Uh, Huh: But How Do it Free us?* was initially staged in Chicago at the Northwestern University Theatre in 1975. *Malcolm Man/Don't Live Here No Mo'* was first produced in Philadelphia at the ASCOM Community Center in 1979.

Sanchez also has contributed to journals and anthologies as a poet, essayist, and editor. She has edited anthologies, including *Three Hundred and Sixty Degrees of Blackness Comin at You, An Anthology of the Sonia Sanchez Writers Workshop at Countee*

written. She also has written poems in ballad form, letters, and haikus.

Sanchez's initial volume of poems, Homecoming, published in 1969, addressed racial oppression in angry voices taken from street conversations. Haki Madhubuti noted in *Black Women Writers, 1950-1980: A Critical Evaluation* that she respected the power of urban street talk and was responsible more

Cullen Library in Harlem; and *We Be Word Sorcerers: Twenty-five Stories by Black Americans*. Also, she has written and edited stories for young readers, such as the compilation *A Sound Investment*, and the tale, *The Adventures of Fathead, Smallhead, and Squarehead*. In addition, Sanchez has contributed to a book on Egyptian Queens and written for the publications *Black Scholar* and *Journal of African Studies*. She also has recorded her poetry.

In her 1973 book of poems, *A Blues Book for Blue Black Magical Women*, Sanchez explores being a woman in a society that "does not prepare young black women, or women period, to be women," as she told Claudia Tate in *Black Women Writers at Work*. She also writes about politics and ethnic pride and uses parts of her life to illustrate a general condition. Although she still advocates revolutionary change she also focuses on individuals battling to survive and find love and joy in their lives. Her work has been called both autobiographical and universal. Critics have observed that while her early books address social oppression, her 1970s plays are about her personal struggles. In *Uh, Huh: But How Do it Free us?* a black woman participating in the movement against white oppression refuses to be mistreated by her husband. As Sanchez said to Claudia Tate, "If you cannot remove yourself from the oppression of a man, how in the hell are you going to remove yourself from the oppression of a country?"

Sanchez's books of verse include *Wounded in the House of a Friend* and *Does Your House Have Lions?* The first book, published in 1995, is a blend of poetry and prose in which she pays tribute to *Essence* magazine and presents memorial pieces for Malcolm X and James Baldwin. According to *Publishers Weekly*, "Sanchez is at her best…when she places her speaker in the furious center of criminal action: a raped woman's detailed account of her attack, a woman trading her seven-year-old daughter for crack ('he held the stuff out/to me and I cdn't remember/her birthdate I cdn't remember/my daughter's face'). A brilliant narrative is offered in the voice of a Harlem woman struggling with (and eventually hammered to death by) her junkie granddaughter."

In *Does Your House Have Lions?* (1997) Sanchez concerns herself with AIDS and familial estrangements and reconciliations. In the book she writes of her brother who left the South angry at his absentee father. He hurls himself into the gay world in New York City, "and the days rummaging his eyes/and the nights flickering through a slit/of narrow bars. hips. thighs./ and his thoughts labeling him misfit/as he prowled, pranced in the starlit/city," wrote Sanchez. But AIDS pursues him and the family is only brought together again because of his illness and hospitalization. As he dies, he hears the spiritual voices of his ancestors, who also are present. Kay Bourne stated in the *Bay State Banner*, "Stylistically, the 70- page heartfelt lyrical poem is a wonder. It is a triumph of skill with its

consistent rhyming pattern (ababbcc) that propels the reader forward. It is brilliant in its choice of words, which, while never sending the reader scurrying to the dictionary, is touchingly apt in plumbing the depths of her brother's experience and that of her other family members."

The author has won numerous awards for her work and activities, including the PEN Writing Award and the American Academy of Arts and Letters' $1,000 award to continue writing. She was given an honorary Ph.D. in fine arts by Wilberforce University in 1973 and received a National Education Association Award in 1977-78. She was named Honorary Citizen of Atlanta in 1982, and received an NEA award in 1984. More recent awards include a Pew Fellowship in the Arts in 1992-93, an honorary Ph.D. from Baruch College in 1993, a PEN fellowship in the arts in 1993-1994, and a Legacy Award from Jomandi Productions in 1995.

Throughout her distinguished teaching career, Sanchez taught and lectured at institutions across the country. As a teacher her legacy is as one of the pioneers of African-American Studies. She was the first professor to offer a course on the literature of African-American women (at the University of Pittsburgh in 1969). She began teaching in 1965 at New York's Downtown Community School. After teaching at several universities, including San Francisco State College (now University), the University of Pittsburgh, City College of the City of New York, Amherst, Spelman College, and the University of Pennsylvania, she became a professor of English and Women's Studies at Temple University where she remained until her retirement in 1999.

Though retired from teaching, Sanchez did not quit writing. She kept to her discipline that she started as a youngster. She attributes her desire to keep writing to her "love of language," as she told *African American Review*. "It is that love of language that has propelled me, that love of language that came from listening to my grandmother speak black English. I would repeat what she said and fall out of the bed and fall down on the floor and laugh, and she knew that I was enjoying her language, because she knew that I didn't speak black English. But I did speak hers, you know. It is that love of language that, when you have written a poem that you know works, then you stand up and you dance around, or you open your door and go out on the porch and let out a loud laugh, you know."

With the 2004 publication of the spoken-word album, *Full Moon of Sonia*, Sanchez is continuing her legacy as the poet who brought black English to the world. As put by *Black Issues Book Review*: "It is refreshing to see a legend, a respected artist, come forward and show all of us how to do it right. *Full Moon of Sonia* does more than give us good poetry set to music; it galavants through an amazing formal and stylistic range that reminds us all how Sonia Sanchez finally got to this place."

Selected works

Poetry

Homecoming Poems, Broadside Press, 1969.
We a BaddDDD People, Broadside Press, 1970.
Liberation Poems, Broadside Press, 1971.
It's a New Day: Poems for Young Brothas and Sistuhs, (Juvenile) Broadside Press, 1971.
A Blues Book for Blue Black Magical Women, Broadside Press, 1973.
Love Poems, Third Press, 1973.
I've Been a Woman: New and Selected Poems, Black Scholar Press, 1981.
Homegirls and Handgrenades: Poems, Third World, 1985.
Under a Soprano Sky: Poems, Africa World Press, 1987.
Shake Down Memory and Continuous Fire, Africa World Press, 1991.
Wounded in the House of a Friend, Beacon Press, 1995.
Does Your House Have Lions?, Beacon Press, 1997.
Shake Loose My Skin: New and Selected Poems, Beacon Press, 1999.

Plays

The Bronx is Next, Tulane Drama Review, 1968.
Sister Sonji, New Plays from Black Theatre, 1970.
Malcolm/Man Don't Live Here No Mo', Black Theatre, 1972.
Uh, Huh: But How Do it Free us? 1975.
I'm Black When I'm Singing, I'm Blue When I Ain't, OIC Theatre, 1982.
Black Cats Back and Uneasy Landings, 1995.

Recordings

Sonia Sanchez, Pacifica Tape Library, 1968.
Homecoming, Broadside, 1969.
We a BaddDDD People, Broadside, 1979.
A Sun Lady for All Seasons Reads Her Poetry, Folkways, 1971.
Sonia Sanchez and Robert Bly, Blackbox, 1971.
Sonia Sanchez: Selected Poems, Watershed Intermedia, 1975.

IDKT: Capturing Facts about the Heritage of Black Americans, Ujima, 1982.
Full Moon of Sonia, 2004.

Sources

Books

Black Women Writers at Work, ed. by Claudia Tate, Continuum, 1983, pp. 132-148.
Black Women Writers, 1950-1980: A Critical Evaluation, 1984.
Contemporary Authors, Gale, Vol. 49, New Revision Series, pp. 349-355; Vols. 33-36, First Revision, 1973, p. 691.
Contemporary Black American Poets and Dramatists, ed. by Harold Bloom, Chelsea House Publishers, 1995, pp. 171-172.
Contemporary Literary Criticism, Gale, Vol. 5, 1976, pp. 382-383.
Ijala: Sonia Sanchez and the African Poetic Tradition, Third World Press, 1996.
Notable Black American Women, Gale, 1992, pp. 976-977.
Sanchez, Sonia, *Does Your House Have Lions?* Beacon Press, 1997 p. 9.
Sanchez, Sonia, *Wounded in the House of a Friend*, Beacon Press, 1995.

Periodicals

African American Review, Winter 2000.
American Visions, August-September, 1996, p. 36.
Bay State Banner, October 23, 1997, pp. 22, 24.
Black Issues Book Review, March-April 2005.
Booklist, February 15, 1997.
Chicago Sun-Times, April 18, 1997.
Nation, April 17, 1972, p. 508.
New Yorker, April 8, 1972, pp. 97-99.
Poetry, 1973, pp. 45-46.
Publishers Weekly, July 15, 1974, p. 77; February 27, 1995, p. 97; February 24, 1997.
Time, May 1, 1972, p. 53.
Vibe, August 1997, p. 136.
World, May/June 1999.

—Alison Carb Sussman and Sara Pendergast

Milton Scott

1956—

Entrepreneur, executive

Milton Scott's appointments in corporate America have few parallels. As the first African American to become a partner in the audit practice at the international accounting firm of Arthur Andersen he influenced multi-million dollar deals and made important decisions that affected large segments of the telecommunications, technology and energy arenas at a time when the economy saw tremendous growth in those sectors. At Dynegy he was executive vice president and chief administrative officer responsible for several key divisions including Risk Management, Internal Audit, Supply Chain Management, and Human Resources, reporting to one of the most important players in the energy industry. As a managing partner of Complete Energy he uses his 25 years of accounting, finance and business experience to close deals on the purchase of multi-million dollar power plants.

Navigating deftly in the high-powered corporate waters of Houston, Texas, Scott's achievements have led him a long way from his childhood in Louisiana. Scott was born on November 21, 1956, in New Orleans and raised on a farm in St. Francisville, LA. He was one of eight children born to Bennett and Melnor Scott. He realized at an early age that he did not want to live on a farm for the rest of his life. "My father worked in a paper mill from 6:00 a.m. until 3:30 p.m. each day, changed his clothes, and worked on the farm until 10 at night," Scott said in an interview with *Contemporary Black Biography* (*CBB*). "I learned an incredible work ethic from him and I started from the bottom. My father had a seventh grade education and spent a lot of time teaching us that education was the way out. He

always made sure we had food on the table and he gave a lot of what he raised to others." Because of this Scott says, "I believe in giving a lot back to the community and I understand how success in life should allow you to help others." About his mother Scott says, "She created a strong home environment and made sure we attended church."

Never Gave Up Despite Misgivings

When he was a young child, Scott mentioned to his father that he might want to some day drive a construction truck. Clearly his father was disappointed. "I remember the look in my father's eye," Scott told *CBB*. Scott then developed an interest in law. He'd sometimes leave school and go to the local courthouse to watch the lawyers in action. In 1974 Scott graduated from St. Francisville High with plans to attend Southern University in Baton Rouge, earn a degree, and go on to law school.

Scott's plans changed when a congressman he had campaigned for suggested he complete the bachelor's degree and then get practical business experience before entering law school. In 1977 Scott received an accounting degree and landed a job at Arthur Andersen, the largest accounting firm in the country. He planned to work for two years, pass the CPA exam, and then tackle the law books.

At Andersen he was the only African American in his orientation class. Many of the new-hires there had attended prestigious schools and come from back-

At a Glance . . .

Born Milton Scott on November 21, 1956, in New Orleans, LA; married Yava Williams, 1982; children: Kirsten, Kameron. *Education:* Southern University, BS, accounting, 1977.

Career: Arthur Andersen, LLP, Houston, TX, partner, 1977-99; Dynegy Inc., Houston, TX, chief administrative officer and executive vice president, 1999-2002; The StoneCap Group LP, Houston, TX, managing director, 2003; Complete Energy Partners, LLC, Houston, TX, managing director, 2004–.

Selected memberships: University of Texas at Austin McCombs School of Business, trustee; Greater Houston Community Foundation, board member; WH Energy Services, lead director; Museum of Fine Arts, Houston, board member; River Oaks Baptist School, trustee.

Addresses: *Office*—Complete Energy Holding, LLC, 1221 Lamar, Suite 1020, Houston, TX 77010.

grounds very different from Scott's. "I remember not being very confident at the time; I began doubting myself and thought I had made a major mistake taking the job," Scott said. "But I remembered what my father taught me; nobody was going to make me quit." This difficult time in Scott's career taught him a valuable lesson about perseverance and raising his own kids. "As a result I instilled in my own children three important things: they belonged, they could compete, and they were always cared about," Scott told *CBB*.

Grew Telecom Division

Two years passed and Scott revised his plans about law school. "I was doing well at the firm," he said. "I was promoted to senior accountant and was preparing to become a CPA, but I did a cost-benefit analysis and determined that I hadn't put enough money away. If I stayed at Andersen for three more years I could become a manager and earn more." Scott was promoted to senior accountant in 1979. He became an audit manager in 1982, earned several other promotions through the years, and in 1990 he became the first African-American partner in the audit practice at Arthur Andersen.

One of Scott's many accomplishments at Andersen was the creation of the Technology and Communications division. Many other accounting firms had a large

presence in this sector and were way ahead of Arthur Andersen in the region. Scott had responsibility for building the southwest region. "We opened an office in Austin, Texas, and grew the regional practice to a very large P & L and a staff of 150 in three years," Scott told *CBB*.

Scott never planned to leave Arthur Andersen. But some offers are difficult to refuse. As he chaired a dinner one evening, Chuck Watson, CEO of Dynegy, one of the fastest-growing energy companies in Houston, heard Scott speak and was impressed. He submitted Scott's name to a search firm he had hired to find an African American for the position of chief administrative officer at his company; Scott declined the offer. Watson then contacted Scott personally. Realizing it would be diplomatic to at least discuss the matter since Dynegy was a client of Arthur Andersen, Scott met with Watson. "What I didn't know at the time was Chuck Watson doesn't take 'no' for an answer, and I realized it was a great opportunity," Scott said. "Here was a chance to go in as an executive vice president at a Fortune 500 company reporting directly to the chairman and CEO. I ended up being the highest-ranking African American in corporate Houston. I didn't see any downside to it; there was a huge upside."

Gained Entrepreneurial Experience at Dynegy

Joining Dynegy in 1999, Scott headed several areas: risk management and credit, corporate planning, compliance and internal audit, insurance, human resources, global facilities management, corporate security, supply chain management, and was liaison to the board of directors. "It was a fast-paced, entrepreneurial company that Chuck Watson had grown from scratch to a Fortune 500," Scott said. "There were not a lot of processes and controls, and it was a very close-knit group that had been together for a long time. I was an outsider; but I love challenges." Scott also attributes his success to the fact that he was well connected in the community. He knew it was a high profile position that was well chronicled in the press. "I had an opportunity to put my stamp on it; so I went in with ambitious objectives," he told *CBB*. "One of the first things I did was to help restructure the board. We added three women and two African Americans. We had no women in senior management and ended up having more than anyone in Houston in a matter of three years. We helped transform the company in a very short period of time."

Although he never made it to law school it all worked out well. He told CBB that in order to make the right career moves, "it's important for young people to surround themselves with mentors. They should try to get them early on. I believe you need three to be successful in corporate America: One inside the division you're working in, one outside the division who works for your company, and someone totally objective outside of the company." Scott highlighted other important qualities for success: "If you want to be influential you better know what you are doing and you must produce," he said. "Go beyond what is expected of you and you cannot have a chip on your shoulder. You can't whine, you can't assume anything, you must be willing to establish a rapport with others in the company who are rising; don't wait for them to come to you. Be aggressive. If you don't do these things you will be labeled early on; then it will be difficult to shake the label even if you change."

Scott left Dynegy in 2002 and became a managing director at The StoneCap Group LP. The company acquires power generation assets. In 2004 with three partners Scott formed Complete Energy Partners, LLC, a start-up investment boutique that also purchases power plants. Their work involves raising capital, arranging financing, and using the relationships the partners have built over the years to "open doors with sellers," he said. "Our first deal was a $330 million dollar transaction. If I had not been prepared to do this because of all of my previous work, no one would take us seriously. I'm taking on a lot more risk; but quite frankly I am not nervous. I am quite comfortable with what I can do."

Sources

Periodicals

Houston Business Journal, November 5, 1999, p. 5A.
Power, Finance, and Risk, September 20, 2004, p. 3.

Other

Additional information for this profile was obtained through an interview with Milton Scott on January 5, 2005.

—Sharon Melson Fletcher

Kimora Lee Simmons

1975—

Model, fashion business executive, entrepreneur

A towering 6-foot, 4-inches in heels, Kimora Lee Simmons began a successful career as a model when she was 14 years old, working under exclusive contract with Chanel. Then, in 1998, she married hip-hop media mogul Russell Simmons and entered the fashion design business. Expanding her husband's Phat Farm men's clothing line, Simmons became the creative genius behind Baby Phat, which offers urban, chic clothing and accessories for women and children. Outspoken and with a definite flair for high-end extravagance, Simmons has created a brand-worthy name for herself that has overflowed into jewelry, cosmetics, and shoes. She also has a fledgling career in film and television.

Simmons, Kimora Lee, photograph. Vince Bucci/Getty Images.

Modeled as a Teenager

Simmons was born on May 3, 1975, in St. Louis, Missouri. Her Japanese-born mother, Joanne Perkins (who is also known as Joanne Kyoko Syng) came to the United States in the aftermath of the Korean War when her mother, who had fled Japan for Korea during World War II, married a U.S. serviceman. Kyoko Syng, who never married Simmons's father, worked as a

district manager for the Social Security Administration and raised Simmons in the lower-middle class St. Louis suburb of Florissant. Simmons's African-American father, Vernon Whitlock, Jr., a native of St. Louis, spent three years in prison on drug trafficking charges while Simmons was in grade school. Whitlock was previously estranged from his daughter but did attend her wedding in 1998.

Simmons attended public school, but when she grew to 5-foot, 8-inches by the time she was ten years old, she became the easy target of schoolyard taunts and teasing. With no Asian population in her community, she also had difficulty fitting in with other African-American students who accused her of being white. Hoping to boost her confidence, Simmons's mother enrolled her daughter in a modeling class when she was eleven years old. Two years later, at the age of thirteen, Simmons was awarded an exclusive modeling contract with Chanel, and just after her fourteenth birthday, she boarded a plane for Paris to work under the tutelage of famed Chanel designer Karl Lagerfeld. Simmons quickly gained attention in the fashion world when Lagerfeld closed his haute-couture show with Simmons, who strutted down the runway decked out as a

At a Glance . . .

Born on May 3, 1975, in St. Louis, Missouri; daughter of Joanne (Perkins) Kyoko Syng and Vernon Whitlock, Jr.; married Russell Simmons, 1998; children: Ming Lee. Aoki Lee. *Education:* Attended University of California, Los Angeles.

Career: Model, 1989–; Baby Phat, president and creative director, 1999–; *Life&Style,* television host, 2004–; actor, 2004–.

Selected awards: Tony Award, for *Russell Simmons Def Poetry Jam* (executive producer), 2003.

Addresses: *Office*—Phat Fashions LLC, 530 7th Ave., 14th Fl., New York, NY 10018. *Web*—www.kimora-leesimmons.com.

child bride. "Everything people thought was weird about me before," Simmons told *People Weekly*, "was now good."

For the next two seasons, while working with Lagerfeld, Simmons developed her taste for expensive luxury items and, despite her mother's advice, at the age of 15 had spent part of her small fortune on such purchases as designer bags, a Rolex watch, and a BMW convertible. "She always had the new Prada bag and would laugh at me because mine was from Wal-Mart," friend and Chanel roommate Tyra Banks told *New York Magazine*. Shuttling back and forth between Paris and St. Louis, Simmons managed, with the help of an academic coach, to graduate from St. Louis's Lutheran High School North on time.

Met Russell Simmons

When Simmons was 17, and still working on finishing up high school, she met 35-year-old hip-hop entrepreneur Russell Simmons. He had become smitten with the six-foot-tall Simmons after seeing her on the runway during New York City's Fashion Week and had sent the young model a bouquet of flowers so large that it took two men to carry. She was impressed, but Banks, who had also received flowers from the mogul, initially warned Simmons to forget him for he was a self-professed and well-known womanizer and playboy.

Russell Simmons, once a New York City street hustler, had risen to the height of fame and fortune as the godfather of the hip-hop movement. He founded the Def Jam record label in 1984, which released the work of such influential artists and groups as Run-D.M.C., LL

Cool J, Slick Rick, Public Enemy, and the Beastie Boys. In 1991 HBO's *Def Jam Comedy Hour* became a forum for black comedians including Martin Lawrence, Chris Rock, Jamie Foxx, Steve Harvey, and Bernie Mac. In 1992 he created Phat Farm, which became a successful men's clothing line featuring hip fashions for the urban male.

Despite her friend's warning, Simmons allowed her suitor to pursue her, but his roaming ways strained the relationship, which was on-again, off-again for several years. When Simmons retreated to Milan, Russell Simmons took up yoga and reformed his lifestyle to the straight-and-narrow, and eventually convinced Simmons's mother to give him her daughter's phone number in Italy. Reconciling with her reformed king of hip hop, Simmons moved in to Russell's Beverly Hills home and attended classes at UCLA. With the relationship now on solid footing, in 1998 the couple were wed on the Caribbean island of St. Bart, vowing before a gathering of entertainment, music, and fashion elites to stay together "for richer or richer." The service was performed by Russell Simmons's brother, Pentecostal minister and rapper Joey "Rev Run" of Run-D.M.C. The elaborate reception was held on a 190-foot yacht.

Entered the Fashion Design Business

Following the wedding Simmons set up house in New York City, but her modeling career had tapered off (by some accounts because Simmons was reported to be difficult to work with) and the new bride found herself bored. "Manicures, sleeping all day—it wasn't fulfilling," she told *VIBE Magazine*. "Being around someone as driven as Russell rubs off on you." When her husband started passing out Phat Farm baby tees to some of his celebrity friends to promote his menswear, Simmons took hold of the project, and in 1999 Baby Phat was born.

As the company's creative director and president, Simmons expanded the Baby Phat line beyond its humble t-shirt beginnings to include an offering of bold, high-end urban-inspired womenswear. The Baby Phat label also appears on denim separates, leather, outerwear, and handbags. Simmons received accolades for her designs as well as the highly anticipated annual Baby Phat fashion shows, which were as hip and urban as the clothing they touted.

In January 2004 the Simmons sold the apparel and licensing of Phat Farm and Baby Phat to Kellwood Company for $140 million, but they retained the rights to peripheral items such as cosmetics and fragrances. As a result 2004 was a busy year of expansion into new arenas for the Baby Phat brand. The Simmons created the Simmons Jewelry Company to market jewelry items under the Phat Farm and Baby Phat labels, which resulted in Simmons's "Diamond Diva" line of jewelry. The couple also signed a license deal with Coty, Inc., to produce fragrances under the Baby Phat by Kimora

Lee Simmons brand. In the same year Simmons also partnered with Vida Shoes International, Inc. to create a new shoe line for Baby Phat to include stilettos, wedges, boots and toddler shoes, and in December 2004 she introduced a pink diamond-encrusted limited-edition Baby Phat i833 Motorola cell phone that retailed for $699.

Led an Extravagant Lifestyle

The Simmons, who have two daughters, Ming Lee, born in 2000, and Aoki Lee, born in 2002, live in a 49,000 square-foot home with 20 bathrooms on four acres in Saddle River, New Jersey, serviced by five maids, four assistants, two live-in nannies, a full-time chef, and two drivers. Simmons, who sports a 25-carat diamond ring, owns a fleet of luxury cars including a platinum extended-base Bentley, and brags about her extensive collection of Manolo Blahnik shoes, admits that she has a taste for the finer things of life.

Although her husband donates over a $1 million annually to some 70 charities and sports a Timex, he sometimes finds himself defending his wife's extravagant tastes against scrutinizing media attention. "Every other week it's the same thing, and I'm upset about it and she's upset about it," Russell Simmons told the *New York Daily News.* "This is all because Kimora is an African-American Asian woman. It's as if they think she's undeserving." Simmons did not help her public image in July 2004 when she faced drug and motor vehicle charges after failing to stop her Mercedes when police attempted to pull her over for driving erratically. When she did stop just outside her home police reportedly found marijuana in the car. Simmons denied the charges at her municipal court hearing in August.

Married to one of entertainment's biggest names, Simmons has proven her place alongside her husband as a trendsetter and fashion guru, but her sights are not just set on the fashion world. She is also carving out a place in the entertainment industry. In 2003 Simmons earned a Tony Award as the executive producer of the critically acclaimed *Russell Simmons Presents Def Poetry Jam.* She has hosted *MTV's Fashionably Loud,* served as a judge on Tyra Banks's talent-search series *America's Next Top Model,* and appeared on *MetroChannels' Full Frontal Fashion.* In the fall of 2004 she began co-hosting the *Life & Style,* a talk show produced by Sony Television based on *The View,* but aimed at a younger audience. She also appeared in the film *The Big Tease* and has parts (as herself) in the film *Beauty Shop* and as a reporter in *Rage Control,* a 20th Century Fox comedy starring Martin Lawrence.

Sources

Books

Newsmakers, Gale Group, 2003.

Periodicals

Adweek, March 8, 2004, p. 30.
Black Enterprise, May 2004, p. 24.
Broadcast & Cable, January 5, 2004.
Crain's New York Business, January 27, 2003, p. 29.
Jet, March 4, 2003, p. 44; August 16, 2004, p. 58.
New York Magazine, June 21, 2004.
The Observer (U.K.), October 10, 2004.
People Weekly, July 5, 1999, p. 105; July 1, 2002, p. 97+.
PR Newswire, September 10, 2004.
VIBE Magazine, September 2002.
WWD, June 8, 2000, p. 10B.

On-line

"Baby Phat," *WE: Women's Entertainment,* www.we.tv/article/0,,key=344&tzOffset=0,00.html (March 2, 2005).
"Designers: Kimora Lee Simmons of Baby Phat," *Factio Magazine,* www.factio-magazine.com/Designers/des_KimoraLeeSimmons.htm (March 2, 2005).

—Kari Bethel

Richard Smith

1957—

Firearms analyst

Richard Smith is an expert firearms analyst for the Los Angeles Police Department's Scientific Investigation Division. Possessing an uncanny ability to remember microscopic detail, keen eyesight, patience, and tenacity, Smith helps the department crack difficult cases. Unassuming, thoughtful, and articulate, Smith once sought to dedicate his life to the ministry but his talents afforded him another means to help his community. He has earned the awe and respect of many experts in his field who consider Smith to be gifted, comparing his work to that of a master jeweler.

Smith was born in Salisbury, North Carolina, on June 21, 1957, to Percy Smith, Jr., a Methodist minister, and Lucy Gilliam Smith. Because of his father's work the family lived in several cities around the South. Despite the constant uprooting he has memories of a happy childhood. "Most of my memories are visual or artistic," Smith said in an interview with *Contemporary Black Biography* (*CBB*). "But I'm terrible with names." This visual memory would later serve him well with his ballistics work for the Los Angeles Police Department.

Family Faced Racism and Death Threats

For a while Smith lived in Williamston, North Carolina, when his grandfather became ill with cancer. With the beginning of desegregation, Smith felt the sting of racism in the second grade when he began attending what had traditionally been an all-white school. "En route to school there was name calling and rock throwing by some older white kids," Smith said. "It lasted a few weeks and then settled down, except for one kid who attacked me during a dodge ball game. I knocked him down and then I cried because I thought I'd get in trouble for fighting. But I had a teacher who was a very nice Christian lady. She defended me and punished the other student. Things got better and that teacher made the difference."

Once civil rights marches began in the South, Smith's father wanted to get involved, seeking out a church in Montgomery, Alabama. In the summer of 1966 his father was assigned to the largest Methodist church in the city: Mount Zion. Percy Smith joined other blacks in forming a local chapter of the Southern Christian Leadership Conference (SCLC) and became a leading member of the National Association for the Advancement of Colored People (NAACP), working closely with Rev. Martin Luther King, Jr. "My father's church took on quite a reputation," Smith told *CBB*. "I remember 1966-67 when ministers met at our church. Dr. King came. As the ministers met we played with his kids in front of the church."

In 1969 Smith's father became the first African American to run for congress in Alabama. "Our family started to get threats from the Ku Klux Klan by phone and through the news media," Smith said. His father did not win the election but the loss did not deter him from running for mayor of Montgomery a few years later.

"Father had fought in World War II, so he knew how to use a firearm," Smith told *CBB*. "We are lucky that he

At a Glance . . .

Born Richard Smith on June 21, 1957, in Salisbury, NC; married Karen Lyday, 1993; children: Cameryn, Taylor. *Education:* College of Wooster, psychology and religion, 1975-79; Pierce College, literature, 1998-2001. *Religion:* Christian.

Career: Los Angeles Police Department, Los Angeles, CA, patrol officer, narcotics officer, training officer, undercover vice and narcotics officer, gang enforcement training officer, firearms analyst, 1980–.

Awards: Los Angeles Police Department Chief's Commendation Award, 2004; Los Angeles Career Service Award, 2005.

Addresses: *Office*—LAPD, 3401 San Fernando Road, Los Angeles, CA, 90065.

did. During his campaign for mayor I remember people coming to our home and shaking my father's hand. One day a white guy came and as my father reached out to greet him the man tried to pull a gun from his pocket. As the man fumbled he dropped the gun and my father pulled a gun from his own pocket, chasing the man out of the house. He never caught him; the man jumped the fence and drove off. It was a traumatic incident for the family, but it affirmed our faith in my father. That may have been when I first considered police work, because of what my father had done to protect his family. I felt he was a strong person." Smith also felt that because of what the movement accomplished, things got better. The schools were integrated and race relations improved. His father had not won the mayoral race but his two opponents courted him for his support during the primary.

Pursued Police Work Instead of Ministry

Smith excelled in high school and earned many awards in sports and academics, receiving a scholarship to the College of Wooster in 1975. From the time he was 15 years old Smith thought he might follow his father into the ministry. "I prepared for it by going through the preliminary rituals," Smith said. "Once you decide, you can then become a youth leader and occasionally you are called upon to write a sermon. I loved speaking and the leadership aspect of it, being able to express myself about Jesus Christ and bringing my philosophy to the sermons I wrote and presented. The part I did not like was the politics you sometimes find in the church."

By 1980 Smith had moved to Los Angeles and received an ordination. "In LA I tried to establish a youth group and helped the church find a music director for the youth," he said. "I was also a youth minister. But several incidents caused me to decide against the ministry. I started looking for other ways that I might help the community. That's when I decided to become a police officer." Smith entered the Los Angeles Police Academy in 1981. In 1982-84 he began an assignment as a Narcotics Officer in Hollywood. From 1984-85 Smith worked as a training officer to new recruits. During the next two decades he worked undercover vice and narcotics details in South Central Los Angeles, did gang enforcement training, and began working for the Firearms Analysis Unit where he would distinguish himself as a ballistics expert with extraordinary skill.

Smith noticed some time before the ballistics assignment that he could see things in the distance a lot better than other officers. When he took a temporary assignment in ballistics to get off the street during a difficult time in his life, Smith found that his sharp eye was particularly suitable for that type of work. He was able to find matches between computer images, and shell casings culled from crime scenes much more often than other ballistics experts. Finding more matches allows police to back up witness testimony and get more convictions. One case in point that Smith helped crack was the murder of 12-year old Gregory Gabriel, a victim of a gang shooting, earning Smith a commendation from the LAPD Chief William Bratton.

Earned Accolades from His Peers

Every Wednesday detectives from around the city jump at the chance to bring their difficult cases to Smith. This has resulted in a 40 percent match rate for the department, a remarkable number. As a result the LAPD posts more hits than any police department in the country. Smith's work has earned him monikers like "Guru" and "a one-man weapon against crime." When asked about his eye for detail Smith says, "I think it has a lot to do with my memory as well." This combination of keen eyesight and almost photographic memory allows Smith to see minute similarities between guns, cartridge casings, and bullets in a database housing three-quarters of a million images. Although the computer is able to produce a slew of possible matches, the human eye is needed to make the final match.

Despite the inevitable monotony of such work, Smith says there are two reasons that he continues to find the work rewarding. He says, "It's satisfying to be able to do it well, and because I do it well my family, my friends, and the people I see every day on the street with their kids who are trying to make it and trying to enjoy a piece of this American way of life, it makes them safer to do that. In one respect it sounds corny but if I couldn't do that I would have left this job. What keeps me here is that. And if I ever feel like—at least here in LA—that if the rest of the people who I've trained are able to do it or do it as well as I can—and I'm sure they will one day—then I can leave it in their hands and go on and do other things. Right now I feel like if I do leave there is someone out there who is going to go unseen. But at least I feel like I'm doing my part to make it a little bit safer so that when my wife and kids go to visit there grandmother or when their grandmother goes out to work in her yard there is a less likely chance of her being hit by some stray bullet because of what I do. That is where I get satisfaction."

Sources

Periodicals

Los Angeles Times, May 5, 2004, p. 1.
People Magazine, October 11, 2004, p. 125.

Other

Additional information for this profile was obtained through an interview with Richard Smith on February 21, 2005.

—Sharon Melson Fletcher

Zadie Smith

1975—

Writer

Smith, Zadie, photograph. David Levenson/Getty Images.

One of the most exciting and successful British writers of the twenty-first century, Zadie Smith published her first novel, *White Teeth*, in the year 2000, at age 25. An immediate success, her debut novel garnered acclaim from critics around the world. The book went on to win the prestigious Whitbread Award for a first novel and the *Guardian* first book award; Smith herself became a well-known literary celebrity in Britain. She followed up her success when her second novel, *The Autograph Man,* was nominated for the Orange Prize for Fiction and won the *Jewish Quarterly's* Wingate Prize in 2003. That same year she was named one of *Granta* magazine's "Best of Young British Novelists." Smith has cemented her place among the most talented writers of her generation with many articles and short stories published in magazines and journals in Britain, the United States, and elsewhere.

Born Sadie Smith in Willesden area of North London on October 27, 1975, to a British father and a Jamaican mother, Smith changed her name to "Zadie" when she was a child, because it seemed more exotic. Her parents, a photographer and a child psychologist, divorced when she was 15 years old, and she has two younger brothers as well as an older half brother and sister. Smith began writing stories at the age of six, but it was dance, not literature, that inspired her as a child. In an interview posted on the Random House (Smith's publisher) Web site, she remarked that it took some time for her to realize that the old-fashioned MGM musicals were not being made any more and from that point onwards, "Slowly but surely the pen became mightier than the double pick-up timestep with shuffle." She attended Hampstead Comprehensive School until the age of 18, then King's College, Cambridge, where she studied English literature and harbored ambitions of becoming an academic.

She began making serious attempts to write fiction for publication while at Cambridge, where she published the short story "The Newspaper Man" in the 1997 *May Anthologies*, an annual collection of work by students at the universities of Oxford and Cambridge, which attracted the publisher HarperCollins. On the advice of a friend Smith, who was still a college student at the time, signed with the Andrew Wylie Literary Agency, who negotiated her a reported advance of £250,000 for her first two books. An extract of her first

At a Glance . . .

Born Sadie Smith on October 27, 1975, in London, England, changed name to Zadie as a child. *Education:* University of Cambridge, England, BA, English, 1998; University of Harvard, Radcliffe Institute for Advanced Study, 2002-03.

Career: Author, 2000–.

Awards: British Book Awards, Newcomer of the Year, for *White Teeth*, 2000; Frankfurt eBooks Award, Best Fiction Work, 2000; Guardian First Book Award, for *White Teeth*, 2000; James Tait Black Memorial Prize, 2000; Commonwealth Writers' First Book Award, 2000; Whitbread Book of the Year Award, for *White Teeth*, 2000; Betty Trask Award, Debut Novel, Author Under Age 35, 2001; *Jewish Quarterly*, Wingate Prize, for *The Autograph Man*, 2003.

Addresses: *Publisher*—c/o Author Mail, Random House, 299 Park Ave., New York, NY 10171-0002.

novel, entitled "The Waiter's Wife" appeared in *Granta 67* in 1999 and was followed by the novel itself, *White Teeth*, in January 2000.

White Teeth was an impressive debut for a 25-year-old writer. Set in Willesden and centering on the lives of two men, Archie Jones and Samad Iqbal, *White Teeth* has been read as a portrait of multicultural Britain, but Smith has denied that it is "about" race as such. She told the *Los Angeles Times*: "Race is obviously a part of the book, but I didn't sit down to write a book about race…. So is [it that] a book that doesn't have exclusively white people in the main theme must be one about race? I don't understand that."

The novel was generally well received, though even favorable reviews, such as Daniel Soar's hint at a lack of realism behind the coziness of her multiracial communities, and point out a lack of sophistication in the plotting; Smith herself has since agreed that the novel needs redrafting. After publication Smith became an instant celebrity, appearing on television and radio, and criss-crossing the Atlantic on book tours and media junkets. Her high visibility in the media was undoubtedly attributable at least as much to her youthfulness, and her appearance, as her talent as a writer. But she also came to embody a particular, but important strand of British culture that is polyethnic, forward-looking, and alienated from the idea of "heritage" for which the country has become known elsewhere. Smith's confident, humorous, and inventive style also makes the

novel an engaging read and perhaps for these reasons *White Teeth* became a defining literary focal point at the beginning of a new century.

Soon after *White Teeth* appeared Smith became writer in residence at the Institute of Contemporary Arts in London and by 2001 she was working on her second novel, having withdrawn from the media gaze. The BBC commissioned a £5 million TV adaptation of *White Teeth* which aired in 2002. After the success of *White Teeth*, which was showered with awards, Smith was under pressure to follow it up with a second novel of similar weight. *The Autograph Man* was less well received than *White Teeth*, but is in many ways an answer to the media pressure Smith had suffered. It tells the story of a Chinese-Jewish autograph hunter and is set in London and New York; the widening of its geographical scope is matched by Smith's willingness to engage with issues in a more serious way than before. *The Autograph Man* also won several awards, including the *Jewish Quarterly's* Wingate Prize in 2003.

In what many in the British media saw as a further attempt to escape press attention, Smith accepted a position at Harvard in 2002, becoming a fellow in creative arts at the Radcliffe Institute of Advanced Study. There she began working on a book of essays about the morality of the novel and the way novelists engage with the ideas of moral philosophy; a book that is a marked change of direction from the novels that made her a celebrity in the popular, as well as the literary press. In 2003 Smith was named one of *Granta* magazine's best British novelists under 40. Since her dramatic debut Smith has been compared with Charles Dickens, Virginia Woolf, Salman Rushdie, and Martin Amis, as one of her generation's major literary talents. Few young writers live up to that kind of hype, but in her refusal to surrender herself to fame at the expense of her writing, Smith seems well equipped to do so.

Selected writings

Novels

White Teeth, Hamish Hamilton, 2000.
The Autograph Man, Hamish Hamilton, 2002.

Sources

Periodicals

Black Issues Book Review, Vol. 2, No. 5, September-October 2000, p. 26-27.
Daily Telegraph, February 19, 2000.
Guardian (London and Manchester), December 11, 2000; September 8, 2002.
London Review of Books, September 21, 2000.

Los Angeles Times, June 26, 2000, p. 1.

New Statesman (London), January 29, 2001.

New York Times Book Review, April 30, 2000, pp. 7-8; October 6, 2002, p. 13.

New Yorker, Vol. 75, No. 31, October 18-25, 1999 p. 182.

Time, September 30, 2002, p. 92.

Women's Review of Books, 18, No. 1, October 2000, p. 19.

On-line

"Bold Type: A Conversation with Zadie Smith," *Random House*, www.randomhouse.com/boldtype/0700/smith/interview.html (February 25, 2005).

"A Writer's Truth," *Boston Phoenix*, www.bostonphoenix.com/boston/news_features/qa/documents/03028816.asp (February 25, 2005).

"Zadie Smith," *Biography Resource Center*, www.galenet.com/servlet/BioRC (February 24, 2005).

"Zadie Smith," *100 Great Black Britons*, www.100greatblackbritons.com/bios/zadie_smith.html (February 25, 2005).

—Chris Routledge

Frank Thomas

1968—

Baseball player

Frank Thomas was quite possibly the most exciting major league baseball player to emerge in the 1990s. The six-foot-five-inch, 257-pound Thomas wears his nickname "The Big Hurt" well. It aptly describes his devastating talents as a power hitter for the Chicago White Sox. Thomas won back-to-back American League Most Valuable Player citations—in 1993 and 1994—after he put together outstanding seasons as a leader in a number of offensive and defensive categories. *Chicago Tribune* reporter Skip Myslenski described Thomas as "a major star, a supernova in his game's constellation of stars." For his part, the hard-working Thomas has only this to say: "I want to make a dent in the game." Indeed, by 2005 Thomas had made a "dent," becoming his team's all-time leader in home runs (436) and runs batted in (1,439).

Thomas's performance has brought comparison to some of baseball's biggest names. Between 1991 and 1997, Thomas became the first player in history to put together seven consecutive seasons where he bat over .300 with 20 or more home runs, 100 runs batted in, 100 runs, and 100 walks. Only four other players have come close to his record—Lou Gehrig, Ted Williams and Jason Giambi, each accomplished that feat for as many as four consecutive seasons—and they are all in the Baseball Hall of Fame. Small wonder that Thomas earned his first Most Valuable Player award by unanimous vote from the Baseball Writers' Association of America in 1993. As Jerome Holtzman noted in the *Chicago Tribune*, Thomas is "among the very best hitters in baseball history, probably the best of his generation, which is flooded with strong-arm sluggers hitting for both distance and average."

For Thomas, baseball is a serious business. Although he performs at the highest levels he continues to set even higher standards for himself, and diligently works toward them. "I'm a competitive person," he explained in the *Chicago Tribune*. "I've been involved in athletics all my life, and I don't handle failure well. That's why I try to outwork everyone else." In another *Chicago Tribune* profile, he concluded: "I've learned this much. A player can't take anything for granted. I have a gift. But that means I have to work extra hard to get better."

The fifth of six children born to Frank and Charlie Mae Thomas, Frank Edward Thomas Jr. was admittedly spoiled by his doting parents and older siblings. Growing up in Columbus, Georgia, he was called "Big Baby" and was encouraged to develop his gift for athletics. His parents never pushed him into sports, but they knew that if he was not at home he was playing ball somewhere nearby. As he grew he made little secret of his ambitions to play professional ball—even though his working-class family could hardly imagine such a life. "When I was a kid, probably around 12, I already knew I wanted to be a player," Thomas told the *Chicago Tribune*. "So I was just telling [my parents] what I wanted, and I followed my dream, and I worked hard enough to get it. A lot of people nowadays won't dedicate themselves like that.... I was a little different."

Thomas was just nine years old when he convinced his father and the local coaches that he could play football in the Pop Warner league, which catered to 12-year-

At a Glance . . .

Born Frank Edward Thomas Jr. on May 27, 1968, in Columbus, GA; son of Frank (a bail bondsman) and Charlie Mae (a textile worker) Thomas; married Elise Silver, 1992 (divorced); children: Sterling (son), Sloan (daughter), and Sydney (son). *Education*: Attended Auburn University, 1986-89.

Career: Professional baseball player with Chicago White Sox organization, 1989–. Class A Sarasota White Sox, 1989; Birmingham Barons, member, 1990; Chicago White Sox debut, August 2, 1990, White Sox, full-time first baseman, 1991. Big Hurt Enterprises (sports marketing company, founder, 1994-99; Un-D-Nyable Entertainment (recording company), founder, 1990s(?).

Awards: Southeastern Conference Most Valuable Player and All-SEC Tournament selection (baseball), 1989; named American League Most Valuable Player, 1993 and 1994. Member of American League All-Star Team, 1994 and 1995.

Addresses: *Home*—Burr Ridge, IL. *Office*—Chicago White Sox, 333 W. 35th St., Chicago, IL 60616.

olds. Sure enough, he easily made one of the teams and won the job of starting tight end. He was equally successful in Little League baseball, where he began seeing the frequent intentional walks that put him on base to this day. His success in sports was put into perspective by a family tragedy. In 1977 his two-year-old sister Pamela died of leukemia. Recalling those days many years later, Thomas told the *Chicago Tribune*: "It was sad. It affected me. But it's something you don't look back on. The way I've dealt with it is to totally forget about it. As the years went by, it got easier and easier." Thomas has not really forgotten his baby sister, however. For years he has worked closely with The Leukemia Foundation, helping to raise money for research into a cure for the disease.

Thomas's skills won him a scholarship to The Brookstone School, a private college preparatory institution in his hometown. He stayed only three years, opting to return to the local public school and its more competitive sports teams. There he lost little time in making his mark. As a Columbus High School sophomore he hit cleanup for a baseball team that won a state championship. As a senior he hit .440 for the baseball team, was named an All-State tight end with the football team, and played forward with the basketball team. He

wanted desperately to win a contract to play professional baseball, but he was completely overlooked in the 1986 amateur draft. Baseball teams signed some 891 players on that occasion, and Thomas was not among them.

"I was shocked and sad," Thomas recalled in the *Chicago Tribune*. "I saw a lot of guys I played against get drafted, and I knew they couldn't do what I could do. But I've had people all my life saying you can't do this, you can't do that. It scars you. No matter how well I've done. People have misunderstood me for some reason. I was always one of the most competitive kids around."

In the autumn of 1986, Thomas accepted a scholarship to play football at Auburn University. Even so, his love of baseball drew him to the Auburn baseball team, where the coach immediately recognized his potential. "We loved him," Auburn baseball coach Hal Baird told *Sports Illustrated*. "He was fun to be around—always smiling, always bright-eyed." He was also a deadly hitter, posting a .359 batting average and leading the Tigers in runs batted in as a freshman. During the summer of 1987 he played for the U.S. Pan American Team, earning a spot on the final roster that would compete in the Pan American Games. The Games coincided with the beginning of football practice back at Auburn, so he left the Pan Am team and returned to college—only to be injured twice in early season football games.

Thomas might have lost his scholarship that year because he could no longer play football. Instead the school continued his funding, and baseball became his sole sport. He was good enough as a sophomore to win consideration for the U.S. National Team—preparing for the 1988 Summer Olympics—but he was cut from the final squad. Stung and misunderstood again, he fought back. By the end of his junior baseball season he had hit 19 home runs, 19 doubles, and had batted .403 with a slugging percentage of .801. With another amateur draft looming, the scouts began to comprehend that the big Georgia native could indeed play baseball.

The Chicago White Sox picked Thomas seventh in the first round of the June 1989 draft—after his home state team the Atlanta Braves had chosen someone else. While he would have liked to have played in Georgia, Thomas was thrilled to be with Chicago. He made his minor league debut with the Sarasota, Florida Class-A White Sox. The following year, 1990, he was named Minor League Player of the Year by Baseball America magazine after hitting .323 with 18 home runs, 71 runs batted in, and a league-best 112 walks as a member of the Class-AA Birmingham Barons.

Finally prepared to admit that they might have a future star on their hands, the White Sox organization called Thomas to the major leagues on August 2, 1990. Thomas jumped into a tight pennant race and batted

.330 with seven home runs and 31 runs batted in over the following two months. He never saw another inning of minor league baseball after that. By the spring of 1991 he had won a position as regular first baseman for Chicago. In his first full season with the White Sox, Thomas batted .318 with 32 home runs and 109 runs batted in. He led the majors in walks, with 138, and on-base percentage (.453). At a stage when most young players are struggling to establish themselves, he finished third in the American League Most Valuable Player voting, behind veterans Cal Ripken Jr. and Cecil Fielder. Chicago fans quickly dubbed Thomas "The Big Hurt," based on his size and his ability to punish opposing pitchers.

Prior to the 1992 season, the *New York Times* released an article about the relative worth of active major league players. Using a formula based on several statistics, the paper declared that Thomas was "the biggest bargain in the majors," based on his 1991 salary of $120,000. The White Sox lost little time in placating their emerging star, issuing Thomas a new three-year contract with a base salary more than $1 million, not including performance bonuses. Thomas responded in 1992 by leading the American League in extra- base hits, on-base percentage, walks (a tie at 122), and doubles. Thomas promised that he could do even better if he could avoid the distractions of super-stardom. "Concentration is the key," he explained in the *Chicago Tribune*. "I try not to be distracted. Lately, I've been blowing a lot of people off because they've been getting in the way. I don't like to do that. But to be successful, I've got to have time for myself."

Both Thomas and the White Sox turned in stellar years in 1993. For Thomas it was the unanimous Most Valuable Player award. For the White Sox it was a division title in the competitive American League West. Although the White Sox were beaten in the American League playoffs by the Toronto Blue Jays, Thomas emerged as his team's focal point. He was rewarded accordingly with a four-year contract estimated to be worth $42 million, as well as lucrative product endorsement deals with Reebok, Pepsi-Cola, DonRuss, and Bausch & Lomb. The financial security Thomas achieved with the deal did little to dim his competitive spirit. "I can't afford...not showing up at the ball park mentally," he told the *New York Times*. "I have to be on every night to be a force in the lineup. I'm a humble guy; I've always been humble. But I realize my place."

White Sox fans might always moan for what might have been. Frank Thomas was on his way into the history books—and the 1994 baseball season was ended prematurely by a players' strike. No one felt the sting of the strike more than Thomas, who stood poised to achieve one of baseball's most prestigious honors: the Triple Crown. Not since 1967 had any player finished the regular season first in average, home runs, and runs batted in. Thomas was contending for the honor when the strike occurred, and his

numbers were good enough to earn him a second American League Most Valuable Player award. Pressed by the media to comment on his accomplishments—and his future—Thomas told the *Atlanta Journal and Constitution*: "I'm not into being known as the best by fans or the media. I care how I'm perceived by my peers. I can settle for the label 'one of the best' because that means you're considered an elite player."

This "elite player" has let it be known that baseball comes first and off-the-field activities rank a distant second. For years Thomas has tried to avoid the kind of fish bowl existence that plagues fellow Windy City superstar Michael Jordan. This dedication to his game as a serious business has led to some misunderstandings in Chicago for Thomas, but as the White Sox continue to fare well, he has earned respect for his workmanlike attitude. Thomas is such a lethal hitter that he draws walks—intentional and otherwise—with stunning regularity. Some observers have even speculated that he will some day be walked with the bases loaded, so tremendous is his home run potential. At the close of the 2003 season, Thomas had "joined the 400-home run club and surpassed 2,000 hits," according to *Baseball Digest*.

In 1993, Thomas had expressed no interest in leaving Chicago. "I see myself with the Sox my whole career," the slugger told *Sports Illustrated,* and in 2005, near the end of his career, he remained with the club. Before retirement he had two remaining goals, he told *Baseball Digest* that he aspired to win a World Series title and to reach the 500-homer, 3,000-hit plateau held by baseball greats Hank Aaron, Willie Mays, and Eddie Murray. And although he achieved more in his first few years in the major leagues than many players do in a lifetime, he continued to pursue higher goals. "I relish the opportunity to rise to the top," he told the *Chicago Tribune*. "When you see the Jordans and guys like that who love that type moment, it takes a special guy to want that. I want to be the guy there with two out and the bases loaded trying to get a hit. I love that situation." Asked what final mark he would like to leave on the game, Thomas paused and concluded: "I want to be able to...when I leave here, I want people to say, 'Hey, I don't know if some of the things he did can ever be done again.'" If injuries don't derail his plans, Thomas may get to hear those words. Whether or not he does, he seems destined for the Baseball Hall of Fame.

Sources

Periodicals

Atlanta Journal and Constitution, July 30, 1994, p. D7.
Baseball Digest, June 2004, p. 50.
Chicago Tribune, March 25, 1992, p. 1 (Sports); November 11, 1993, p. 6 (Sports); March 23, 1994, p. 1 (Sports); August 7, 1994, p.1 (Sports); September 17, 1995, p. 3 (Sports); April 16, 2005.

New York Times, March 12, 1992; October 5, 1993, p. B13;October 28, 1993, p. B15; November 11, 1993.

Sports Illustrated, September 16, 1991, p. 30-34; September13, 1993, pp. 40-44.

On-line

Chicago White Sox, www.chicago.whitesox.mlb.com (April 28, 2005).

—Mark Kram and Sara Pendergast

Cicely Tyson

1933—

Actress

In the minds of many, Cicely Tyson is the embodiment of black womanhood. A naturally gifted actress, she nonetheless worked diligently to learn all the nuances of her craft. Although strikingly beautiful, she has refused to get by on her looks, demanding instead to be judged on her professional abilities. Tyson is often given credit for inspiring black American women to embrace African standards of beauty, rather than trying to make themselves over in the image of white America.

In selecting scripts, she has consistently searched for those that will offer a positive image of people of color to the public, and in the process, she has "developed an artistic identity that does not ignore, but actively challenges the two major stereotypes of the black woman in film and drama: the roly-poly, desexed black mammy and the 'high yaller' femme fatale," according to *Ms*. Because of her choosiness, Tyson has not been a prolific actress, especially in the latter part of her career; few scripts meet her discriminating standards. But the quality of her work—particularly in the landmark films *Sounder* and *The Autobiography of Miss Jane Pittman*—has assured her of a reputation as one of America's finest dramatic performers.

Tyson was born in the borough of East Harlem, New York, to parents who had emigrated from Nevis, the smallest island in the Caribbean's Windward Island chain. The move to America brought no prosperity to the Tyson family. Cicely's father worked at carpentry, house painting, and whatever other odd jobs he could find; her mother worked as a housekeeper; and Cicely herself stood on the street-corners selling shopping bags to supplement the household income.

Nevertheless, they were forced to rely on welfare to survive, and the actress remembers that more often than not, they ate corn-meal mush for breakfast, lunch, and dinner. Her mother sought to protect Cicely and her two siblings from the harshness of their environment by keeping them in church as much as possible and forbidding them to associate with the neighborhood children. But young Tyson loved to wander the city and explore its many possibilities, and she frequently hopped onto a bus or subway train and rode to the end of the line, just to see what was there.

Career Began in Modeling

After graduating from Charles Evans Hughes High School in Manhattan, Tyson landed a job as a secretary for the American Red Cross. The monotony of the work soon frustrated her, however. As she told Louie Robinson of *Ebony*, the day came when she stood up and shouted to her fellow office workers: "I know that God did not put me on the face of this earth to bang on a typewriter for the rest of my life!" Fate intervened a few days later. Tyson, who had always been meticulous about the care of her hair, was asked by her hairdresser to model one of his styles at a fashion show. Her striking presence prompted several onlookers to encourage her to look into a modeling career. Before long she was enrolled in the Barbara Watson Modeling School and was engaged in photo shoots during her lunch breaks from the Red Cross.

At a Glance . . .

Born on December 19, 1933, in New York, NY; daughter of William and Theodosia Tyson; married Miles Davis (a jazz musician), November 1981 (divorced). *Education*: Studied drama at New York University, Actors Studio, and with Vinnette Carroll and Lloyd Richards.

Career: Photographic model during the late 1950s; actress, 1959–; Jewels of Unity jewelry line, designer, 1999–.

Memberships: Co-founder, Dance Theater of Harlem; trustee, Human Family Institute, American Film Institute.

Awards: Vernon Rice Award, 1962, for *The Blacks*; Vernon Rice Award, 1963, for *Moon on a Rainbow Shawl*; Academy Award nomination for best actress, Atlanta Film Festival Award for best actress, and National Society of Film Critics Award for best actress, all 1972, all for *Sounder*; Emmy Awards for best actress in a television special, and best actress of the year, 1974, for *The Autobiography of Miss Jane Pittman*; Emmy Award, for outstanding supporting actress in a miniseries or a special, 1994, for *Oldest Living Confederate Widow Tells* All; Ellis Island Family Heritage Award for performance, 2003; also recipient of awards from NAACP, National Council of Negro Women, and National Federation of Black Women Business Owners in Washington. Name graces, Cicely Tyson School of Performing and Fine Arts, East Orange, NJ, 1995–.

Addresses: *Home*—Malibu Beach, CA. *Office*—c/o Larry Thompson, 345 North Maple Dr., Suite 183, Beverly Hills, CA 90210.

It wasn't long before she was able to leave office work behind, for she quickly became one of the top black models in the United States. She earned as much as $65 an hour—a considerable sum during the late 1950s—and graced the covers of mainstream publications such as *Vogue* and *Harper's Bazaar*, as well as those of magazines specifically geared toward a black audience. But for all her success, modeling brought Tyson little satisfaction. "I felt like a machine," she once told a reporter for *Time* magazine.

Once again fate stepped in to move her along. Tyson was waiting in the offices of *Ebony* magazine for an appointment with fashion editor Freda DeKnight when she caught the eye of Evelyn Davis, a black character actress. Tyson related the encounter to *Ms.*: "When I walked by, [Davis] took one look at me and said, 'Lord, what a face!' She said I'd be perfect for a movie then in production called *The Spectrum*. It was about the problems between light-skinned and dark-skinned blacks. I auditioned for the part and I got it. Actually, the film was never released because the money ran out—but here I am."

Tyson's decision to take up acting led to a two-year rift between her and her mother, who considered movies sinful and had always forbidden her children to see them. But with characteristic determination, Tyson ignored all opposition to pursue her chosen goal. She studied at various acting schools, and briefly at New York University, but she had difficulty finding teachers who measured up to her demanding standards. Two who did were Lloyd Richards and Vinnette Carroll. Carroll recalled to *Ms.*: "There was never any doubt in my mind that Miss Cicely—that's my pet name for her—was going to make it. She had all the qualities needed: an enormous capacity for work (she seemed utterly driven) and for criticism (she was never thrown by it or immobilized). The most noticeable thing about her was her sense of herself. She was her own measuring stick. And she didn't look to the left or the right or talk about how unfair it was for blacks in the arts."

Brought her Talent to the Stage

In 1959 Tyson appeared in Carroll's Off-Broadway revival of the musical *The Dark of the Moon*, and in a Broadway variety show called *Talent '59*; she also understudied for Eartha Kitt in the role of Jolly Rivers in *Jolly's Progress*. Tyson landed a small part in the film *Odds Against Tomorrow* and a larger one in the courtroom drama *Twelve Angry Men*, which starred Henry Fonda. When she first auditioned for *Twelve Angry Men*, Tyson was told she was too chic to play the part of a girl from the slums, and was turned away. "I went home and got myself up in a costume that was out of this world," she recalled to *Ms.* "I found a skirt that was too big and botched up the hemline. Then I put on a dirty raincoat, sloppy shoes, an old hat, and mussed up my hair." When Tyson returned to the auditions, the office secretary didn't even want to let her in the door, but the casting agent was suitably impressed, and she was hired.

In 1961 Tyson became one of the original cast members of the Off-Broadway production of Jean Genet's controversial drama *The Blacks*. She was in good company: that first cast also included James Earl Jones, Maya Angelou, Lou Gossett, Jr., Godfrey Cambridge, and Raymond St. Jacques. Tyson played a prostitute named Virtue, and her stunning performance won her a Vernon Rice Award in 1962. Her other New York theater work included *Cool World*, *God's Trombones*, *Tiger, Tiger, Burning Bright*, *The Blue Boy in Black*, and *Carry Me Back to Morningside Heights*. She was willing to try almost any sort of role, but steadfastly refused to sing or dance: although perfectly capable of both, she felt that blacks were never expected to do anything else, and wished to break away from that stereotype.

In the early 1960s, Tyson became one of the few black faces to be seen regularly on television. Actor George C. Scott had admired her work in *The Blacks* and asked her to play a continuing role in his television series *East Side/West Side*, a CBS-TV series about social workers. The short, natural hairstyle she wore in that show caused a sensation and is often singled out as the beginnings of the Afro trend. According to *Ms.*, "the first young black actress to face film and television cameras with hair unstraightened…provoked a not-too-minor earthquake within the American minds of young black women…. All black women needed was some public person to take the first step toward a more positive identification with African beauty. And that person was Cicely Tyson." Donald Bogle, author of *Blacks in American Film and Television*, commented: "Tyson was a striking figure: slender and intense with near-perfect bone structure, magnificent smooth skin, dark penetrating eyes, and a regal air that made her seem a woman of convictions and commitment. [Audiences] sensed…her power and range…. Watching the young Tyson, one often has the feeling that, through the turn of a line or a look or gesture, at any moment something extraordinary could happen."

Throughout the 1960s and early 1970s Tyson was a frequent guest star on television, appearing in *I Spy*, *Naked City*, *The Nurses*, *The Bill Cosby Show*, and many other programs. Her film career progressed more slowly. She played the love interest to Sammy Davis, Jr.'s jazz musician character in the 1966 movie *A Man Called Adam*, appeared in *The Comedians* in 1967, and turned in an affecting, if brief, performance as a doctor's rebellious daughter in *The Heart Is a Lonely Hunter* in 1968. But by then, the film industry was entering the period of so- called "blaxploitation" films, which Tyson considered depressing and demeaning. According to *People* Tyson said "she would rather be unemployed than act in exploitation films like *Shaft* and *Superfly*," adding that "The lesser of two evils for me is to wait, rather than do something that isn't right." For nearly six years, she hardly appeared before the cameras at all, with the exception of an occasional television guest spot. There were no parts being offered that she felt were worth taking—and she was even ready to forsake her acting career altogether, if it came to that.

Fortunately, it didn't. Some six years after beginning work on *The Heart Is a Lonely Hunter*, Tyson was offered the role of Rebecca Morgan in the film adaptation of William H. Armstrong's novel *Sounder*. The story was a major departure from standard Hollywood fare of that time in that it depicted a black family in the Depression-era South with dignity and sensitivity. Tyson's Rebecca is a sharecropper's wife who is forced to carry on alone after her husband is jailed for stealing a piece of meat to feed his family. "Cicely Tyson is superb," enthused Jay Cocks in his *Time* review of the film. "It falls to her not only to display warmth toward her family but also to show such shreds of defiance and muted fury [against] a world that has always threatened to grind her down. For its range and its richness, and for its carefully portioned power, it is an indelible performance."

Showed Audiences the Beauty of Black Women

As it had in *East Side/West Side*, Tyson's hairstyle provoked a great deal of comment. In *Sounder*, she appeared in cornrows, long associated with degrading caricatures of southern blacks, and she was praised for elevating this traditional style to a new level of acceptability. Ellen Holly, a reviewer for the *New York Times*, commented: "Tyson has always been a lovely actress, easily capable of enameled glamour when it is called for. But here…she passes all of her easy beauty by to give us, at long last, some sense of the profound beauty of millions of black women."

Ms. declared that Tyson had broken new ground in the portrayal of black motherhood: "Before Cicely Tyson's internationally acclaimed portrayal of Rebecca…the three major exceptions to the black mother as mammy were Louise Beavers and Louise Stubbs in the two versions of *Imitation of Life* in 1934 and 1959 respectively, and Ethel Waters in *Pinky*, a controversial film of 1949. Even these two stories were less than redeeming. In both, the black child was a fair-skinned daughter passing for white…. These celluloid mulattoes were often played by white actresses and interpreted as likeable, but doomed by that awful drop of black blood…. Cicely Tyson's Rebecca was different. Through her, the American audience was introduced to a typical black mother and wife; hard-working, resilient, vigilant, and above all, sensitive."

The critical acclaim over *Sounder* had not yet died away when Tyson turned in another world-class performance in the title role of the television drama *The Autobiography of Miss Jane Pittman*. This fictional account, adapted from the novel by Ernest J. Gaines, follows the life of a 110-year-old woman from her childhood in slavery to her old age, when she becomes an active participant in the civil rights movement. The role required Tyson to age some 90 years. An astounding make-up job helped her to achieve this feat, but it could not have been successful without her masterful acting skills. She showed her dedication to the project by enduring as much as six hours of make-up application, then working for up to seven hours in front of the cameras.

The finished film was a triumph that delivered a powerful statement about the struggle of African Americans to achieve economic and political self-determination. *Ms.* characterized Tyson's acting as "almost eerie in its accuracy. Every gesture was right on target—from the way she walked to the white drinking fountain, her head and hands trembling only from age, to the way she held her mouth as she drank, chewing slightly as if her bridge did not fit properly." *New Yorker* film critic Pauline Kael declared: "She's an actress, all right, and as tough-minded and honorable in her methods as any we've got."

Tyson's performances in *Sounder* and *The Autobiography of Miss Jane Pittman* won her many accolades, but the entertainment industry itself had changed but little. She continued to seek out challenging, meaningful roles, but few existed for a serious black actress. She gave a very brief performance in the television miniseries *Roots* as Kunta Kinte's mother, portrayed real-life Chicago educator Marva Collins in *The Marva Collins Story*, paid tribute to Martin Luther King in the mini-series *King*, and worked with several other top black actresses in *The Women of Brewster Place*.

Yet while television offered Tyson more topical material than that being treated in feature films, "sometimes the standard TV-ish quality of TV films...seemed to strand her," in the opinion of Bogle. He continued: "In some cases, too, she appeared either miscast as in *King* or stuck with a script's undeveloped character as in *Roots*. Other times as in *The Marva Collins Story* (1981), she...injected spirit into what was essentially a formula film.... It became distressing to see her cast in meaningless supporting roles in disappointing projects: *Acceptable Risks* (1986) and *Intimate Encounters* (1986). Still even here it was interesting and oddly compelling to watch her struggling to invest such material with some intelligence and dramatic flair. She remained a major American dramatic actress for whom the film and then television industries rarely provided the kind of support system (and acting plums) accorded such white stars as Jane Fonda and Meryl Streep." Tyson described her dilemma to the *Bergen County Record*: "I'm a woman, and I'm black. I wait for roles—first, to be written for a woman, then, to be written for a black woman. And then," she added, "I have the audacity to be selective about the kinds of roles I play. I've really got three strikes against me. So, aren't you amazed I'm still here?"

Continued Acting and Supporting the Arts

Even when a lack of good roles limited her work before the camera, Tyson continued to work diligently on behalf of the arts in the black community, devoting at least one month out of each year to touring colleges on speaking engagements, an activity that once prompted her to comment to an *Ebony* interviewer: "I'm appalled at the lethargy and the lack of incentive and motivation among the youth.... I feel there's a great need, especially for the youth, for positive images." One of her most significant contributions to black culture in America was the founding of the Dance Theater of Harlem, which she accomplished in cooperation with Arthur Mitchell. This organization recruits its members from local public schools, provides classical dance training, and gives students the opportunity to perform at national venues. For all her efforts, Tyson became a respected role model for youth. In honor of her dedication to her craft and to others, her name has graced a magnet school in East Orange, New Jersey, the Cicely Tyson School of Performing and Fine Arts, since 1995.

The 1990s and 2000s found Tyson back on the large and small screens in several highly acclaimed projects. She wowed critics and fans alike with her stunning portrayals of strong black women in the motion pictures *Fried Green Tomatoes, Hoodlum,* and *Because of Winn-Dixie,* and the television miniseries *Oldest Living Confederate Widow Tells All,* for which she won another Emmy. As with the early years of her career, Tyson found more television than film work, and appeared in such television features as *Sweet Justice,* in which she played a gutsy southern lawyer; *Road to Galveston,* in which she portrayed a fictionalized story of a woman who realizes her dreams after being widowed; *A Lesson Before Dying,* in which she portrayed the aunt of a man sentenced to death for a crime he didn't commit; and *The Rosa Parks Story,* in which she played Parks' strong, supportive mother.

Despite her many successes, Tyson refused to rest on her laurels. "I think of myself as a work-in-progress to this day," Tyson told the *Bergen County Record.* Well into her seventies, she continued to seek out interesting and challenging roles. Her reasoning, as she described to the *Bergen County Record,* was attributable to her belief that "the day I ever feel I have attained greatness I will be finished. It means I have in fact stopped myself from developing."

Tyson's personal life is marked by the same type of discipline that typifies her acting. She is dedicated to physical fitness and eats a strict vegetarian diet with no caffeine or alcohol. She was married to jazz musician Miles Davis for a time; rumors have also circulated for years that she has two children, but the actress herself has refused to confirm or deny them. On the whole, she has been unusually successful in keeping the details of her life private and in forcing the public to judge her solely on the value of her work. And her body of work has won her a place among the most important black performers of the twentieth century. The *Houston Chronicle* describes Tyson as "like a chicken fried steak smothered in cream gravy. She's Southern comfort food—familiar, delicious, searing, satisfying. Her performances always hit the spot," adding that "She holds the patent for portraying struggling black women who make successes of themselves." As *Ms.* concluded, "She has an image that spans not only race, but the ideological differences among blacks themselves."

Selected works

Films

Twelve Angry Men, 1957.
Odds Against Tomorrow, 1959.
A Man Called Adam, 1966.
The Comedians, 1967.
The Heart Is a Lonely Hunter, 1968.
Sounder, 1972.
The Blue Bird, 1976.
The River Niger, 1976.
Fried Green Tomatoes, 1991.
Hoodlum, 1997.
Because of Winn-Dixie, 2005.
Diary of a Mad Black Woman, 2005.

Plays

The Dark of the Moon, 1959.
Talent '59, 1959.
The Blacks, 1961.
Moon on a Rainbow Shawl, 1962.
Tiger, Tiger, Burning Bright, 1962.
The Blue Boy in Black, 1963.
Carry Me Back to Morningside Heights, 1968.

Television

East Side/West Side, 1963.
The Autobiography of Miss Jane Pittman, 1974.
Just an Old Sweet Song, 1976.
Roots, 1977.
Wilma, 1977.
A Woman Called Moses, 1978.
King, 1978.
The Marva Collins Story, 1981.
Acceptable Risks, 1986.
Intimate Encounters, 1986.

The Women of Brewster Place, 1989.
Duplicates, 1992.
House of Secrets, 1993.
Oldest Living Confederate Widow Tells All, 1994.
Sweet Justice, 1994.
Road to Galveston, 1996.
Bridge of Time, 1997.
Riot, 1997.
The Price of Heaven, 1997.
Ms. Scrooge, 1997.
Always Outnumbered, 1998.
Mama Flora's Family, 1998.
A Lesson Before Dying, 1999.
Aftershock: Earthquake in New York, 1999.
Jewel, 2001.
The Rosa Parks Story, 2002.

Sources

Books

Bogle, Donald, *Blacks in American Film and Television,* Garland, 1988, pp. 472-473.
Notable Women in the American Theater, Greenwood, 1989.

Periodicals

Ebony, May 1974; February 1981, pp. 124-132.
Houston Chronicle, January 24, 1996.
Interview, September 1997, p. 102.
Jet, October 28, 1985, pp. 60-62; December 19, 1994, p. 8.
Ms., August 1974.
New York, March 23, 1992, p. 62.
New Yorker, January 28, 1974.
New York Times, October 1, 1972; October 15, 1972.
People, May 31, 1999.
Record (Bergen County, NJ), August 27, 1997; March 11, 1998.
Time, October 9, 1972, p. 58.
Variety, March 23, 1992, p. 35.

—Joan Goldsworthy and Sara Pendergast

Mario Van Peebles

1957—

Actor, director

Van Peebles, Mario, photograph. AP/Wide World Photos Reproduced by permission.

Mario Van Peebles has established himself as one of a prolific new generation of black filmmakers. After the handsome actor appeared in films and on television for more than five years, he was asked to direct a small-budget movie about drug abuse in the New York City ghetto. The resulting work, *New Jack City,* was both a commercial and a critical success, earning huge profits for its studio and making a permanent name for Van Peebles. Over the next decade, Van Peebles solidified his position in the film industry by delivering a vast array of entertaining, challenging films, the most notable being 2003's *How to Get the Man's Foot Outta Your Ass,* about his father.

Few young artists bring more impeccable credentials to moviemaking. Van Peebles is the son of veteran actor-director-writer Melvin Van Peebles, whom critics once dubbed the "godfather of modern black cinema." This is not, however, a case where a son has ridden to fame on his father's coattails. Mario was strongly encouraged to forge his own career, and he did so by working hard, looking for opportunities, and perfecting his craft through study and practice. Although the younger Van Peebles does not make light of his famous name, he admitted in *Ebony* that "it can get your foot in the door.

But if you don't have the talent to keep the door open you're going to get your foot slammed off."

"I got special attention being the first-born and the ugliest," Van Peebles said of his unconventional childhood, as quoted by *Ebony.* The oldest of three children, Mario was born in Mexico City and grew up following his artistic parents from America to Europe and back again, as their jobs demanded. His white mother worked as a photographer while his father made movies and television specials. As a youth, Mario spent time in Paris, Morocco, Denmark, and San Francisco. Remembering those days in a *People* interview, Van Peebles said: "We were always broke. My room was usually a hotel closet. Mom was my schoolteacher." On the other hand, he noted, the gypsy life had its advantages. "I can speak four languages fluently," he continued in *People.* "French, Spanish, Uptown and Downtown."

Destined for Show "Business"

While Van Peebles was still young, his parents divorced. Thereafter he and his sister Megan lived in San

At a Glance . . .

Born Mario Cain Van Peebles on January 15, 1957, in Mexico City, Mexico; son of Melvin (a writer, director, and actor) and Maria Magdalena (a photographer) Van Peebles. *Education*: Columbia University, BS, 1978; studied acting with Stella Adler.

Career: City of New York, budget analyst, c. 1979-80; Elite and Ford agencies, New York City, model, 1982-85; actor, 1982–; film director, 1990–.

Awards: Image Award, for outstanding supporting actor, 1989, for *Heartbreak Ridge*; Black Reel Award, for best director, 2005, for *How to Get the Man's Foot Outta Your Ass*.

Addresses: *Home*—Los Angeles, CA. *Agent*—Chris Black, William Morris Agency, Inc., 151 El Camino Drive, Beverly Hills, CA 90212.

know how to manage money. Therefore, Mario enrolled at Columbia University as an economics major and earned his degree in 1978. The following year he worked for the City of New York as a budget analyst—a far cry from the glamorous world of films and television. Still, Van Peebles recognized in *Ebony* that "the degree has helped. With the business background you don't say, 'Would you put me in this movie,' you say, 'Let's do this movie.'"

By 1981 Van Peebles was firmly on his way to a career in his father's field. The two appeared together on Broadway in a 1981 play, *Waltz of the Stork*, written and directed by Melvin Van Peebles. When the play closed, Mario studied acting with Stella Adler and paid his bills by modeling and working as a photographer. Long before he made a name as an actor, Van Peebles earned excellent wages with the Elite and Ford agencies, appearing in the pages of *Essence, Gentlemen's Quarterly*, and other glossy magazines. He never lost sight of his original goals, though. He continued to take acting lessons and began to write screenplays, hoping to sell a feature film to a studio.

Van Peebles began to land major acting roles in 1984; he took a bit part in the film version of *The Cotton Club*, but he drew more notice for playing a menacing villain named X in *Exterminator II*. He also worked as a regular on the daytime television drama *One Life to Live* for several years. Van Peebles observed in *Jet* that when he finally began to make a decent living as an actor, his father told him, "Hey, now if you want to work together you can bring something to the pot and I'm not just carrying my son along." In recent years, the father-son collaboration has swung in Mario's favor—he has helped earn roles for his father and has found financial backing for some his father's projects.

Van Peebles's rise to the front ranks as an actor came after his performance in Clint Eastwood's well-received adventure-drama *Heartbreak Ridge*. In the 1986 film Van Peebles appeared as "Stitch" Jones, a marine recruit who becomes Eastwood's right-hand man during an invasion. In the meantime, Van Peebles also took a recurring role on the popular television show *L.A. Law*. Though he was offered a full-time position on that series, other obligations forced him to forgo the opportunity. One of his commitments was the portrayal of an off-beat scientist in *Jaws: The Revenge*, a role for which Van Peebles put on weight, grew dreadlocks, and adopted a thick Bahamian accent. The actor commented in *People* that he was willing to try any character part, however small, as long as it was interesting. "I'm one actor who will be on time, won't be high and won't want a star on his dressing room door," he promised.

Television was the next vehicle for expanding Van Peebles's acting talent. In 1987 he landed the lead role in *Sonny Spoon*, a comedy-drama about an unorthodox big city private detective. The show allowed Van Peebles many opportunities for displaying his versatility

Francisco with their mother, whom Van Peebles described in *People* as the "original hippie," a free-spirited woman who was open to the ideas of the day. Despite the divorce, Van Peebles's parents remained on cordial terms, so Mario saw his father frequently and even appeared in his landmark film, *Sweet Sweetback's Baadasssss Song*, in 1971. The youngster had only a small part in the motion picture, which his father wrote and directed, but—as would happen later with *New Jack City*—that low-budget enterprise ultimately earned a hefty profit at the box office.

As a teenager, Van Peebles knew he wanted to be an actor, and after finishing high school, he sought his father's help. To Mario's surprise, his father was unwilling to lend a hand or afford him special opportunities to acquire roles. Van Peebles recalled in *Ebony* that his father said, "'I'm going to give you some free advice: Early to bed, early to rise, work like a dog and advertise!' That was the end of the conversation." Offended at first, Van Peebles began to ponder just what his father was trying to tell him. He eventually realized that "that was my father's way of telling me I had to learn to do it for *myself*; that he loved me enough not to allow me to ride on his success by doing it for me," the actor related in *Ebony*. "Though it didn't seem like it then, it was the greatest gift he could have ever given me. So many kids of famous people never learned the value of *earning* something, or how sweet it is to have accomplishments to call your own."

Another piece of advice Van Peebles's father passed on was the notion that show business is a *business*, and anyone looking for a career in that market had better since his character frequently employed disguises. In one episode, for instance, he donned a wig and sang with a gospel choir in order to hide from maleficent pursuers. "One of the things I wanted to show was that here you have this young Black guy in the lead and he's able to cross every line," Van Peebles explained in *Jet*. "This guy's going to go from the church lady to the blond yuppie. They have me speaking French in the show, Spanish." Still, the actor added, "I really try to keep an eye on not letting

get too super human." *Sonny Spoon* was one of the first hour-long television dramas to star a black actor. It never quite found a large audience, though, and was canceled after one season.

From Acting to Directing

Having proven himself as an actor, Van Peebles went on to achieve his goal of working behind the camera. He began with television, directing episodes of *Wiseguys* and *21 Jump Street* and a *CBS Afternoon Special* for children called *Malcolm Takes a Shot*, in which a cocky high school basketball star suddenly develops epilepsy and can no longer play his favorite sport. With these projects to his credit, Van Peebles let it be known at the film studios that he was ready to try directing a feature-length production, and Warner Bros. approached him in 1990.

The studio had a hard-hitting script titled *New Jack City* about crack cocaine dealers in Harlem; the film was given a small budget and the studio had low expectations of those working on the project. "They expected us to not necessarily be on time and on budget," Van Peebles noted in *Jet*. "So, I think it was a nice surprise that we completed the movie on time and on budget." Van Peebles not only directed the film—which was shot in only 36 days for a fraction of the cost of most features—he played a role in it as well.

Starring Wesley Snipes, rapper Ice-T, and Judd Nelson, *New Jack City* tells the story of Nino Brown, a ruthless crack dealer who rules his small domain in Harlem by any means necessary. Van Peebles cast himself as a police officer who supervises undercover operations aimed at putting Brown's crack empire out of business. "There aren't too many movies around that take a fresh look at old problems, especially problems like gangs and drugs," wrote a *Jet* reviewer. " *New Jack City* is one of those rare exceptions.... The movie deals with the exploitation of youngsters as it follows the rise of a Black gang that builds a lucrative crack kingdom in Harlem. In addition to showing how horrifying and ruthless the world of drugs and gangs can be, it also shows the caring and compassionate side of its villains."

New Jack City was released the same weekend as *The Hard Way*, an action-comedy starring Michael J. Fox. The latter film cost more than three times as much as *New Jack City* to create, but was quickly eclipsed at the

box office by Van Peebles's film. In fact, riots broke out at some urban theaters, in part, because of the huge crowds that attended early screenings of the controversial film. In its first weekend of release, *New Jack City*— which cost $8.5 million to make—grossed more than $10 million. It has since become an extremely popular and best-selling home video.

The press was quick to cover the violence at theaters showing *New Jack City*, and some observers even blamed the movie's content for the incidents that occurred in several cities. Van Peebles responded to these charges in a *New York Times* editorial: "The film opened to positive reviews and is doing well at the box office, but its anti-drug, anti-violence message seems to be getting lost in controversy. People assume that the movie's content somehow inspired young people who see it to violence—give me a break. Was the rioting in Los Angeles caused by young people who had just seen *New Jack City* or because they couldn't get in to see it? Was it because they had seen the movie or because they had seen the video of a black man being beaten by members of the Los Angeles police department?"

The violence did indeed subside when more theaters agreed to show the film, and Van Peebles's talent as a director was not overlooked. The movie's success earned Van Peebles a spot on the "A" list of black directors in Hollywood, assuring that he will be considered for future projects. A writer in the *Economist* noted that "Mr.
Peebles is best known as a film and television actor. Inexperienced as well as black, he would have stood no chance of a studio contract as recently as five years ago. Times have changed." Van Peebles took advantage of every opportunity that his newfound celebrity afforded him. Over the next decade he would rise to the top of his industry as both an actor and director. But in doing so, he never lost his focus on the social messages of his work.

Continued in his Father's Footsteps

He followed his feature film directorial debut *New Jack City* with *Posse* in 1993. *Posse* depicts life in the Wild West from a black perspective. Van Peebles hoped the film would provide audiences the context needed to understand the choices early black Americans made. "Back in 1893 we couldn't rap our way out of the 'hood,' so a lot of us became outlaws," he told *Essence*.

Van Peebles relishes following in his father's footsteps, telling *Jet:* "There aren't a lot of second generation filmmakers. I love to see us passing it on.... You see us doing what some of the White families have never even done." In the *New York Times* Van Peebles publicly thanked his father for being a role model and a source of inspiration: "Thanks to you [Dad], I grew up seeing a black man direct, a black man in charge, so I didn't have a color chip on my shoulder.... It never occurred to me that I couldn't do it because of my color, if I had the talent. Like you said, 'Hollywood isn't as much black and white as it is ultra-green.'" Father and son collaborated on several films, including the co-direction of the 1996 film *Gang of Blue* about police brutality and corruption.

In 2003, he wrote and produced a film depicting his father's place as a pioneer in the film industry: *How to Get the Man's Foot Outta Your Ass*, a story of how his father made *Sweet Sweetback's Baad Assss* in 1973. When Melvin Van Peebles embarked on making *Sweet Sweetback's Baad Asssss Song* in the early 1970s, he hurtled some of the film industry's most difficult blockades. His intense desire and firm commitment to his vision for the film, weathered near financial ruin, police harassment, racism, and his own failing health. Van Peebles told *Interview* that his father "changed the dynamic in movies. Prior to *Sweetback* almost all films with minorities showed them as one-dimensional. And the subtext of that is that if you can reduce a people to one dimension, either cinematically or in the media, you can then make it easier to repress them. With *Sweetback* you started to see empowered black folks on the screen...." Van Peebles plays his father with sympathy and respect, offering audiences not only insight into the production of independent films but also a sense of affects the sweeping social changes of the time have had on the film industry. The film won Van Peebles a Black Reel Award.

Van Peebles sees his directing and acting as symbiotic; he can't do one without the other. "As a director I've made the films I have to make," he told *Jet,* adding "As an actor I've made the films I want to make." When he accepted the role of black action hero in *Solo,* he commented to *Jet* that "If I didn't do what I did as a director, I wouldn't be getting these kinds of offers as an actor. I'm in a unique position as a director and an actor. I can be what Rev. Jesse Jackson refers to as the tree shaker and the jelly maker," adds Van Peebles. "Those who shake the tree (make) the fruit fall down."

Selected works

Plays

Waltz of the Stork, 1981.
Champeen!, 1983.
Take Me Along, 1984.
Cotton Club, 1984.

Films

Sweet Sweetback's Baadasssss Song, 1971.
The Cotton Club, 1984.
Delivery Boys, 1984.
Exterminator II, 1984.
South Bronx Heroes (also known as *The Runaways* and *Revenge of the Innocents*), 1985.
Rappin', 1985.

3:15, the Moment of Truth, 1986.
Heartbreak Ridge, 1986.
The Last Resort, 1986.
Jaws: The Revenge, 1987.
Hot Shot, 1987.
New Jack City, 1991.
Posse, 1993.
Panther, 1995.
Gang in Blue, 1996.
Solo, 1996.
Love Kills, 1998.
Judgment Day, 1999.
Ali, 2001.
How to Get the Man's Foot Outta Your Ass, 2003.

Television

The Sophisticated Gents, NBC, 1981.
L.A. Law, NBC, 1986.
Sonny Spoon, 1987-88.
One Life to Live, ABC.

Screenplays

(With Marc Shmuger) *South Bronx Heroes,* 1985.
Identity Crisis, 1989.
Los Locos, 1997.
Love Kills, 1998.
Standing Knockdown, 1999.
How to Get the Man's Foot Outta Your Ass, 2003.

Sources

Books

Contemporary Theatre, Film, and Television, Volume 6, Gale, 1989.

Periodicals

Ebony, May 1987; November 1987; June 1988.
Economist, March 30, 1991.
Entertainment Weekly, June 4, 2004, pp. 42-44.
Essence, June 1993.
Interview, June 2004.
Jet, July 27, 1987; April 18, 1988; March 11, 1991; August 7, 1995; August 26, 1996; September 23, 1996.
New York Times, March 5, 1990; March 8, 1991; March 31, 1991.
People, June 20, 1983; March 2, 1987.
Premiere, June 2004, pp. 98-100, 124.

On-line

"Get the Man's Foot Out," *Hollywood Reporter,* www.thehollywoodreporter.com/thr/reviews/review_display.jsp?vnu_content_id=1978600 (April 29, 2005).

—Anne Janette Johnson and Sara Pendergast

Bobby Westbrooks

1930(?)-1995

Chiropractor

Dr. Bobby Westbrooks, a practicing chiropractor, founded the American Black Chiropractic Association (ABCA) in 1981 in St. Louis, Missouri. He served as its executive director until his death in 1995. The goals of the ABCA include increasing the awareness of chiropractic treatment within the black community and attracting black men and women into the profession. Westbrooks also was active in St. Louis politics and civic organizations and once ran for mayor on the Freedom Party ticket.

Born and raised in Memphis, Tennessee, Bobby West-brooks settled in St. Louis in 1952, following his discharge from the United States Army. For the next 12 years he worked as a clerk for the U.S. Postal Service in St. Louis. Westbrooks graduated from the Missouri Chiropractic College (now Logan College of Chiropractic) in 1967 as a doctor of chiropractic (D.C.). He maintained a private practice for the remainder of his life.

Westbrooks was active in his St. Louis community, serving as chairman of the Montgomery-Hyde Park Neighborhood Council. In this position he oversaw St. Louis's first Model Cities program, a cornerstone of President Lyndon Johnson's Great Society initiative. Westbrooks also served as president of the Water Tower Business Association and the East Grand Businessmen's Association. He was a board member of the North Side TEAM Ministry and a member of the St. Louis Police Community Relations Committee.

In 1969 Westbrooks ran for mayor of St. Louis on the ticket of the newly-founded Freedom Party, losing to incumbent Alfonso J. Cervantes. Following his run for mayor, Westbrooks remained active in the politics of St. Louis's Fifth Ward. His comments at a St. Louis hearing were quoted in the 1972 Democratic Party Platform: "All your platform has to say is that the rights, opportunities and political power of citizenship will be extended to the lowest level, to neighborhoods and individuals. If your party can live up to that simple pledge, my faith will be restored." Later Westbrook switched his affiliation from the Democratic Party to the Republican Party.

As a chiropractor, Westbrooks knew that the black community lacked information about the benefits of chiropractic. Furthermore, there were few black chiropractors. Together with a small group of chiropractors and chiropractic students, Westbrooks founded the ABCA. The association held its first convention in St. Louis with 17 people in attendance. Officers were chosen and bylaws established. The organization began reaching out to chiropractic students across the country and students and doctors began to network.

In 1982 Westbrooks published a seminal article on black American chiropractors. Until the 1950s blacks were largely barred from chiropractic schools. According to an article in *Chiropractic Economics* in July of 2004, chiropractic school bulletins generally included the phrase "Negroes not accepted." However, blacks studied chiropractic anonymously via correspondence schools. Beginning in 1979 the National Association of Black Chiropractors filed a series of formal racial discrimination charges against the Council on Chiro-

At a Glance . . .

Born Bobby Westbrooks in 1930(?) in Memphis, TN; died on January 13, 1995, in St. Louis, MO; married Elizabeth (separated); companion to Cecelia Piekarski, 1974(?)-95. *Education:* Missouri Chiropractic College, DC, 1967. *Religion:* Roman Catholic. *Military Service:* U.S. Army.

Career: U.S. Postal Service, clerk, 1952(?)-64; chiropractor in private practice, 1967-94.

Memberships: East Grand Businessmen's Association, president; Montgomery-Hyde Park Neighborhood Council, chairman; North Side TEAM Ministry, board member; St. Louis Police Community Relations Committee, member; Water Tower Business Association, president; American Black Chiropractic Association, founder and executive director, 1981-95.

Awards: American Black Chiropractic Association, Chiropractor of the Year, 1994, Bobby Westbrooks Scholarship Foundation, 1994.

practic Education—the profession's college-accrediting agency—as well as against its member colleges.

Dynamic Chiropractic quoted Westbrooks in 1993: "While chiropractic struggled for its existence as a profession, black people had to struggle for membership in the profession founded on the back of a black man." Westbrooks was referring to Harvey Lillard, a black man whose hearing was restored in 1895 when a magnetic healer named Daniel David Palmer readjusted his vertebrae. Lillard became known as the first chiropractic patient.

The ABCA has relied on education and community service to further its aims of uniting and empowering black chiropractors, promoting chiropractic within the black community, and securing scholarships for black chiropractic students. The organization has archived numerous historical documents and materials relating to blacks and the chiropractic profession. Its annual convention has provided a venue for personal and professional connections among current and prospective chiropractic students, doctors, and supporters within the community. ABCA members have mentored hundreds of chiropractic students.

Following Westbrooks's death, the ABCA has continued to carry out his visions of educating the black community about chiropractic and its benefits and nurturing and promoting black students and professionals. The campuses of most chiropractic schools in the United States have active student ABCA chapters and the organization reaches out to schools in this country and abroad. Student chapter members are eligible to apply for the ABCA's Harvey Lillard Scholarship and the organization holds annual fairs to encourage young blacks to consider chiropractic as a career. The ABCA works closely with other national chiropractic organizations, including the Association of Chiropractic Colleges.

In 1994 Westbrooks received the ABCA's Chiropractor of the Year Award for his many years as executive director. His wife received an appreciation award from the ABCA's spouse's auxiliary. That same year the ABCA created the Bobby Westbrooks Scholarship Foundation.

Westbrooks was long estranged from his wife Elizabeth. Cecelia Piekarski was his companion for the last 21 years of his life. Bobby Westbrooks died of lung cancer on January 13, 1995, at the John Cochran Veterans Administration Hospital in St. Louis and was buried at the Jefferson Barracks National Cemetery. He was 64 years old.

Selected writings

"The Troubled Legacy of Harvey Lillard: The Black Experience in Chiropractic," *Chiropractic History,* 1982, pp. 47-53.
"The Missing Element," *Today's Chiropractic,* March/April 1983, pp. 56-59.

Sources

Periodicals

Dynamic Chiropractic, April 9, 1993; November 14, 1994.
St. Louis Post-Dispatch, January 15, 1995, p. 11D.

On-line

"The ABCA: Its Start, its Status and its Future," *Chiropractic Economics,* www.chiroeco.com/50/bonus/abc.html (February 8, 2005).
"Challenges and Progress of Black Chiropractors," *Chiropractic Economics,* www.chiroeco.com/article/2004/issue10/10events6.html (February 8, 2005).
"1972 Democratic Party Platform," *Federalist Patriot,* http://federalistpatriot.us/histdocs/platforms/democratic/dem.972.html (February 14, 2005).

—Margaret Alic

Cedric Yarbrough

1971—

Actor

A talented comic actor with a flair for improvisation, Cedric Yarbrough is best known for his role as Deputy S. Jones in the reality cop show parody *Reno 911!* Debuting in 2003 the improvised show became an instant hit for cable network Comedy Central and has been compared favorably with the hit BBC offering *The Office*. But it took almost three years for the show to make it onto the air, and in the meantime Yarbrough worked on various other television shows and in theater, while making his living waiting tables. His notable TV appearances in-

Yarbrough, Cedric, photograph. Frazer Harrison/Getty Images.

clude the *Cedric the Entertainer Show*, and *Andy Richter Controls the Universe*, but he also appeared at the Pasadena Playhouse alongside Phylicia Rashad and Diahann Caroll in *Blue*. Since coming to the attention of a wider audience in *Reno 911!* Yarbrough began to break into movies, including the 2004 comedies *Meet the Fockers* and *Broken*.

Cedric Yarbrough was born on August 26, 1971, and raised in Burnsville, Minnesota. He has two brothers, Eni and Trevor, and a sister, Amber. He attended Burnsville High School and after graduation attended Minnesota State University in Minneapolis, where he studied drama and musical theater, graduating with a

bachelor's degree in 1996. He appeared in several student theater productions including playing the title role in *Sweeney Todd*. He worked with theater groups in Minneapolis and after graduation became heavily involved as a writer and actor. In particular he appeared with Mixed Blood Theatre, The Children's Theatre, Penumbra and The Brave New Workshop, where he showed a strong talent for improvisation.

Yarbrough moved to Los Angeles, California, in 2000 to look for work in television and movies and within a few months he was part of the team booked by Fox to shoot the show that several years later would become *Reno 911!*, a spoof of Fox's own long-running reality TV show, *Cops*. Then a sketch show called *Ugly Americans,* the spoof police reality show idea came up when producers Tom Lennon, Robert Ben Garrant, and Kerri Kenney tried to win over skeptical Fox executives, but the gamble failed. Yarbrough went back to waiting tables and picked up a little acting work here and there, including appearances on TV comedy shows *The Cedric the Entertainer Show* and *Andy Richter Controls the Universe*. In 2002 he also appeared in the play *Blue* at the Pasadena Playhouse. Then in

At a Glance . . .

Born Cedric Yarbrough on August 26, 1971, in Burnsville, Minnesota. *Education:* Minnesota State University, BA, drama, 1996.

Career: Actor, 1990s–; Mixed Blood Theatre, Minneapolis, 1990s; The Brave New Workshop, Minneapolis, 1990s.

Addresses: *Agent*—Arlene Thornton & Associates, 12711 Ventura Blvd., Ste. 490, Studio City, CA, 91604, USA; MBA Theatrical Agency, Concorde House, 18 Margaret Street, Hove, BN2 1TS, UK.

2003 Comedy Central decided to bring Lennon, Garrant, and Kenney together again to remake the pilot of *Ugly Americans;* the result was *Reno 911!* Kenney, who plays Deputy Trudy Wiegel, described the process of making the program to the *Denver Post:* "We know we have to get from point A to point B. The rest is improv."

A theater workshop veteran, Yarbrough's talent and experience are well suited to the approach, but he is also aware that *Reno 911!* is unusual. He told the Department of Theatre and Dance at Minnesota State University: "The network actually trusts us to come up with things. The executive producers trust us to come up with character development. What a novel idea! I wish more production companies (and directors for that matter) would allow their actors to have an opinion." His character, Deputy S. Jones, sees himself as a Billy Dee Williams type and spends much of his looking for "action" and acting "smooth." Yet despite the freedom Yarbrough and the other actors enjoy as a result of the format, making each show is a time-consuming and laborious process. Actor and producer Kenney explained to the *Denver Post* that a 29-minute take can yield as little as 30 seconds of usable footage. She said, "Tape is cheap, you know" and in some ways that attitude is exactly what the show parodies in its take-off of cheap reality-TV documentaries. Though the humor comes from the behavior of a bunch of inept cops patrolling Reno, Nevada, another of the show's targets is TV production values themselves. The success of *Reno 911!* was something of a surprise. Since debuting in July of 2003 it has become a favorite for the network and a third series will air in the summer of 2005.

Reno 911! provided a platform from which Yarbrough could extend his acting career into movies. In 2004 he appeared in the short comedy *Broken,* directed by Paco Farias, and as a prison guard in *Meet the Fockers,* the sequel to the 2000 film *Meet the Parents,* starring Dustin Hoffman and Robert DeNiro. In 2005 Yarbrough's career as a comic actor seemed to be on the rise. Having lived for years in some of Los Angeles' least desirable areas, including Korea Town, he moved to Beverly Hills following the success of *Reno 911!* But he remained realistic about his career as an actor. His experiences of Hollywood have taught him not to expect it to be easy, as he related in an interview the Department of Theatre and Dance at Minnesota State University: "But if you're not prepared to work and struggle and to be kicked down and to get up only to be kicked down 500 more times, don't come out here. It really isn't for the weak."

Selected works

Films

Mulligan, 2000.
Broken, 2004.
Meet the Fockers, 2004.

Plays

Blue, produced at Pasadena Playhouse, 2002.

Television

Reno 911!, 2003.

Sources

Periodicals

Boston Herald, June 9, 2004, p. 49.
Denver Post, July 14, 2003, p. F01.
Houston Chronicle, July 23, 2003, p. 8.
Maxim (USA), June 2004.
New York Times, July 23, 2003, p. E5.
Washington Times, October 18, 2004, p. B06.

On-line

"Cedric Yarbrough," *Comedy Central,* www.comedycentral.com/press/bios/bio.jhtml?f=Cedric_Yarbrough.xml (March 10, 2005).
"Former Student Cedric Yarbrough Is on Patrol in *Reno 911*," *Minnesota State University, Mankato, Department of Theatre and Dance,* www.mnsu.edu/theatre/index/feature.htm (March 10, 2005).

—Chris Routledge

Cumulative Nationality Index

Volume numbers appear in **bold**

Cumulative Occupation Index

Volume numbers appear in **bold**

Art and design

Adjaye, David **38**
Allen, Tina **22**
Alston, Charles **33**
Andrews, Benny **22**
Andrews, Bert **13**
Armstrong, Robb **15**
Bailey, Radcliffe **19**
Bailey, Xenobia **11**
Barboza, Anthony **10**
Barnes, Ernie **16**
Barthe, Richmond **15**
Basquiat, Jean-Michel **5**
Bearden, Romare **2, 50**
Beasley, Phoebe **34**
Biggers, John **20, 33**
Blacknurn, Robert **28**
Brandon, Barbara **3**
Brown, Donald **19**
Burke, Selma **16**
Burroughs, Margaret Taylor **9**
Camp, Kimberly **19**
Campbell, E. Simms **13**
Campbell, Mary Schmidt **43**
Catlett, Elizabeth **2**
Chase-Riboud, Barbara **20, 46**
Cortor, Eldzier **42**
Cowans, Adger W. **20**
Crite, Alan Rohan **29**
De Veaux, Alexis **44**
DeCarava, Roy **42**
Delaney, Beauford **19**
Delaney, Joseph **30**
Delsarte, Louis **34**
Donaldson, Jeff **46**
Douglas, Aaron **7**
Driskell, David C. **7**
Edwards, Melvin **22**
El Wilson, Barbara **35**
Ewing, Patrick A. **17**
Fax, Elton **48**
Feelings, Tom **11, 47**
Freeman, Leonard **27**
Fuller, Meta Vaux Warrick **27**
Gantt, Harvey **1**
Gilliam, Sam **16**
Golden, Thelma **10**
Goodnight, Paul **32**
Guyton, Tyree **9**
Harkless, Necia Desiree **19**
Harrington, Oliver W. **9**
Hathaway, Isaac Scott **33**
Hayden, Palmer **13**

Hayes, Cecil N. **46**
Hope, John **8**
Hudson, Cheryl **15**
Hudson, Wade **15**
Hunt, Richard **6**
Hunter, Clementine **45**
Hutson, Jean Blackwell **16**
Jackson, Earl **31**
Jackson, Vera **40**
John, Daymond **23**
Johnson, Jeh Vincent **44**
Johnson, William Henry **3**
Jones, Lois Mailou **13**
Kitt, Sandra **23**
Knox, Simmie **49**
Lawrence, Jacob **4, 28**
Lee, Annie Francis **22**
Lee-Smith, Hughie **5, 22**
Lewis, Edmonia **10**
Lewis, Norman **39**
Lewis, Samella **25**
Loving, Alvin **35**
Manley, Edna **26**
Mayhew, Richard **39**
McGee, Charles **10**
McGruder, Aaron **28**
Mitchell, Corinne **8**
Moody, Ronald **30**
Morrison, Keith **13**
Motley, Archibald Jr. **30**
Moutoussamy-Ashe, Jeanne **7**
Mutu, Wangechi **44**
N'Namdi, George R. **17**
Nugent, Richard Bruce **39**
Olden, Georg(e) **44**
Ouattara **43**
Perkins, Marion **38**
Pierre, Andre **17**
Pinderhughes, John **47**
Pinkney, Jerry **15**
Pippin, Horace **9**
Porter, James A. **11**
Prophet, Nancy Elizabeth **42**
Puryear, Martin **42**
Ringgold, Faith **4**
Ruley, Ellis **38**
Saar, Alison **16**
Saint James, Synthia **12**
Sallee, Charles **38**
Sanders, Joseph R., Jr. **11**
Savage, Augusta **12**
Sebree, Charles **40**
Serrano, Andres **3**
Shabazz, Attallah **6**

Simpson, Lorna **4, 36**
Sims, Lowery Stokes **27**
Sklarek, Norma Merrick **25**
Sleet, Moneta, Jr. **5**
Smith, Marvin **46**
Smith, Morgan **46**
Smith, Vincent D. **48**
Tanksley, Ann **37**
Tanner, Henry Ossawa **1**
Thomas, Alma **14**
Thrash, Dox **35**
Tolliver, William **9**
VanDerZee, James **6**
Wainwright, Joscelyn **46**
Walker, A'lelia **14**
Walker, Kara **16**
Washington, Alonzo **29**
Washington, James, Jr. **38**
Wells, James Lesesne **10**
White, Charles **39**
White, Dondi **34**
White, John H. **27**
Williams, Billy Dee **8**
Williams, O. S. **13**
Williams, Paul R. **9**
Williams, William T. **11**
Wilson, Ellis **39**
Woodruff, Hale **9**

Business

Abbot, Robert Sengstacke **27**
Abdul-Jabbar, Kareem **8**
Adams, Eula L. **39**
Adkins, Rod **41**
Ailey, Alvin **8**
Al-Amin, Jamil Abdullah **6**
Alexander, Archie Alphonso **14**
Allen, Byron **24**
Ames, Wilmer **27**
Amos, Wally **9**
Auguste, Donna **29**
Avant, Clarence **19**
Beal, Bernard B. **46**
Beamon, Bob **30**
Baker, Dusty **8, 43**
Baker, Ella **5**
Baker, Gwendolyn Calvert **9**
Baker, Maxine **28**
Banks, Jeffrey **17**
Banks, William **11**
Barden, Don H. **9, 20**
Barrett, Andrew C. **12**
Beasley, Phoebe **34**
Bell, James A. **50**

Bennett, Lerone, Jr. **5**
Bing, Dave **3**
Bolden, Frank E. **44**
Borders, James **9**
Boston, Kelvin E. **25**
Boston, Lloyd **24**
Boyd, Gwendolyn **49**
Boyd, John W., Jr. **20**
Boyd, T. B., III **6**
Bradley, Jennette B. **40**
Bridges, Shelia **36**
Bridgforth, Glinda **36**
Brimmer, Andrew F. **2, 48**
Bronner, Nathaniel H., Sr. **32**
Brown, Eddie C. **35**
Brown, Les **5**
Brown, Marie Dutton **12**
Brunson, Dorothy **1**
Bryant, John **26**
Burrell, Tom **21, 51**
Burroughs, Margaret Taylor **9**
Burrus, William Henry "Bill" **45**
Busby, Jheryl **3**
Cain, Herman **15**
CasSelle, Malcolm **11**
Chamberlain, Wilt **18, 47**
Chapman, Nathan A. Jr. **21**
Chappell, Emma **18**
Chase, Debra Martin **49**
Chenault, Kenneth I. **4, 36**
Cherry, Deron **40**
Chisholm, Samuel J. **32**
Clark, Celeste **15**
Clark, Patrick **14**
Clay, William Lacy **8**
Clayton, Xernona **3, 45**
Cobbs, Price M. **9**
Colbert, Virgis William **17**
Coleman, Donald A. **24**
Combs, Sean "Puffy" **17, 43**
Connerly, Ward **14**
Conyers, Nathan G. **24**
Cooper, Barry **33**
Cooper, Evern **40**
Corbi, Lana **42**
Cornelius, Don **4**
Cosby, Bill **7, 26**
Cottrell, Comer **11**
Creagh, Milton **27**
Cullers, Vincent T. **49**
Daniels-Carter, Valerie **23**
Darden, Calvin **38**
Dash, Darien **29**
Davis, Ed **24**

Woods, Sylvia 34
Woodson, Robert L. 10
Wright, Charles H. 35
Wright, Deborah C. 25
Yoba, Malik 11
Zollar, Alfred 40

Dance

Ailey, Alvin 8
Alexander, Khandi 43
Allen, Debbie 13, 42
Atkins, Cholly 40
Babatunde, Obba 35
Baker, Josephine 3
Bates, Peg Leg 14
Beals, Jennifer 12
Beatty, Talley 35
Byrd, Donald 10
Clarke, Hope 14
Collins, Janet 33
Davis, Chuck 33
Davis, Sammy Jr. 18
Dove, Ulysses 5
Dunham, Katherine 4
Ellington, Mercedes 34
Fagan, Garth 18
Falana, Lola 42
Glover, Savion 14
Guy, Jasmine 2
Hall, Arthur 39
Hammer, M. C. 20
Henson, Darrin 33
Hines, Gregory 1, 42
Horne, Lena 5
Jackson, Michael 19
Jamison, Judith 7
Johnson, Virginia 9
Jones, Bill T. 1, 46
King, Alonzo 38
McQueen, Butterfly 6
Miller, Bebe 3
Mills, Florence 22
Mitchell, Arthur 2, 47
Moten, Etta 18
Muse, Clarence Edouard 21
Nicholas, Fayard 20
Nicholas, Harold 20
Nichols, Nichelle 11
Powell, Maxine 8
Premice, Josephine 41
Primus, Pearl 6
Ray, Gene Anthony 47
Rhoden, Dwight 40
Ribeiro, Alfonso, 17
Richardson, Desmond 39
Robinson, Bill "Bojangles" 11
Robinson, Cleo Parker 38
Robinson, Fatima 34
Rodgers, Rod 36
Rolle, Esther 13, 21
Sims, Howard "Sandman" 48
Tyson, Andre 40
Vereen, Ben 4
Walker, Cedric "Ricky" 19
Washington, Fredi 10
Williams, Vanessa L. 4, 17
Zollar, Jawole Willa Jo 28

Education

Achebe, Chinua 6
Adams, Leslie 39
Adams-Ender, Clara 40
Adkins, Rutherford H. 21

Aidoo, Ama Ata 38
Ake, Claude 30
Alexander, Margaret Walker 22
Allen, Robert L. 38
Allen, Samuel W. 38
Alston, Charles 33
Amadi, Elechi 40
Anderson, Charles Edward 37
Archer, Dennis 7
Archie-Hudson, Marguerite 44
Aristide, Jean-Bertrand 6, 45
Asante, Molefi Kete 3
Aubert, Alvin 41
Awoonor, Kofi 37
Bacon-Bercey, June 38
Baiocchi, Regina Harris 41
Baker, Augusta 38
Baker, Gwendolyn Calvert 9
Baker, Houston A., Jr. 6
Ballard, Allen Butler, Jr. 40
Bambara, Toni Cade 10
Baraka, Amiri 1, 38
Barboza, Anthony 10
Barnett, Marguerite 46
Bath, Patricia E. 37
Beckham, Barry 41
Bell, Derrick 6
Berry, Bertice 8
Berry, Mary Frances 7
Bethune, Mary McLeod 4
Biggers, John 20, 33
Black, Albert 51
Black, Keith Lanier 18
Blassingame, John Wesley 40
Blockson, Charles L. 42
Bluitt, Juliann S. 14
Bogle, Donald 34
Bolden, Tonya 32
Bosley, Freeman, Jr. 7
Boyd, T. B., III 6
Bradley, David Henry, Jr. 39
Branch, William Blackwell 39
Brathwaite, Kamau 36
Braun, Carol Moseley 4, 42
Briscoe, Marlin 37
Brooks, Avery 9
Brown, Claude 38
Brown, Joyce F. 25
Brown, Sterling 10
Brown, Uzee 42
Brown, Wesley 23
Brown, Willa 40
Bruce, Blanche Kelso 33
Brutus, Dennis 38
Bryan, Ashley F. 41
Burke, Selma 16
Burke, Yvonne Braithwaite 42
Burks, Mary Fair 40
Burnim, Mickey L. 48
Burroughs, Margaret Taylor 9
Burton, LeVar 8
Butler, Paul D. 17
Callender, Clive O. 3
Campbell, Bebe Moore 6, 24
Campbell, Mary Schmidt 43
Cannon, Katie 10
Carby, Hazel 27
Cardozo, Francis L. 33
Carnegie, Herbert 25
Carruthers, George R. 40
Carter, Joye Maureen 41
Carter, Warrick L. 27
Cartey, Wilfred 47

Carver, George Washington 4
Cary, Lorene 3
Cary, Mary Ann Shadd 30
Catlett, Elizabeth 2
Cayton, Horace 26
Cheney-Coker, Syl 43
Clark, Joe 1
Clark, Kenneth B. 5
Clark, Septima 7
Clarke, Cheryl 32
Clarke, George 32
Clarke, John Henrik 20
Clayton, Constance 1
Cleaver, Kathleen Neal 29
Clements, George 2
Clemmons, Reginal G. 41
Clifton, Lucille 14
Cobb, Jewel Plummer 42
Cobb, W. Montague 39
Cobbs, Price M. 9
Cohen, Anthony 15
Cole, Johnnetta B. 5, 43
Collins, Janet 33
Collins, Marva 3
Comer, James P. 6
Cone, James H. 3
Coney, PonJola 48
Cook, Mercer 40
Cook, Samuel DuBois 14
Cook, Toni 23
Cooper Cafritz, Peggy 43
Cooper, Anna Julia 20
Cooper, Edward S. 6
Copeland, Michael 47
Cortez, Jayne 43
Cosby, Bill 7, 26
Cotter, Joseph Seamon, Sr. 40
Cottrell, Comer 11
Cox, Joseph Mason Andrew 51
Creagh, Milton 27
Crew, Rudolph F. 16
Cross, Dolores E. 23
Crouch, Stanley 11
Cullen, Countee 8
Daly, Marie Maynard 37
Davis, Allison 12
Davis, Angela 5
Davis, Arthur P. 41
Davis, Charles T. 48
Davis, George 36
Dawson, William Levi 39
Days, Drew S., III 10
Delany, Sadie 12
Delany, Samuel R., Jr. 9
Delco, Wilhemina R. 33
Delsarte, Louis 34
Dennard, Brazeal 37
DePriest, James 37
Dickens, Helen Octavia 14
Diop, Cheikh Anta 4
Dixon, Margaret 14
Dodson, Howard, Jr. 7
Dodson, Owen Vincent 38
Donaldson, Jeff 46
Douglas, Aaron 7
Dove, Rita 6
Dove, Ulysses 5
Draper, Sharon Mills 16, 43
Driskell, David C. 7
Drummond, William J. 40
Du Bois, David Graham 45
Dumas, Henry 41

Dunbar-Nelson, Alice Ruth Moore 44
Dunnigan, Alice Allison 41
Dunston, Georgia Mae 48
Dymally, Mervyn 42
Dyson, Michael Eric 11, 40
Early, Gerald 15
Edelin, Ramona Hoage 19
Edelman, Marian Wright 5, 42
Edley, Christopher 2, 48
Edley, Christopher F., Jr. 48
Edwards, Harry 2
Elders, Joycelyn 6
Elliot, Lorris 37
Ellis, Clarence A. 38
Ellison, Ralph 7
Epps, Archie C., III 45
Evans, Mari 26
Fauset, Jessie 7
Favors, Steve 23
Feelings, Muriel 44
Figueroa, John J. 40
Fleming, Raymond 48
Fletcher, Bill, Jr. 41
Floyd, Elson S. 41
Ford, Jack 39
Foster, Ezola 28
Foster, Henry W., Jr. 26
Franklin, John Hope 5
Franklin, Robert M. 13
Frazier, E. Franklin 10
Freeman, Al, Jr. 11
Fuller, A. Oveta 43
Fuller, Arthur 27
Fuller, Howard L. 37
Fuller, Solomon Carter, Jr. 15
Futrell, Mary Hatwood 33
Gaines, Ernest J. 7
Gates, Henry Louis, Jr. 3, 38
Gates, Sylvester James, Jr. 15
Gayle, Addison, Jr. 41
George, Zelma Watson 42
Gerima, Haile 38
Gibson, Donald Bernard 40
Giddings, Paula 11
Giovanni, Nikki 9, 39
Golden, Marita 19
Gomes, Peter J. 15
Gomez, Jewelle 30
Granville, Evelyn Boyd 36
Greenfield, Eloise 9
Guinier, Lani 7, 30
Guy-Sheftall, Beverly 13
Hageman, Hans and Ivan 36
Halliburton, Warren J. 49
Hale, Lorraine 8
Handy, W. C. 8
Hansberry, William Leo 11
Harkless, Necia Desiree 19
Harper, Michael S. 34
Harris, Alice 7
Harris, Jay T. 19
Harris, Patricia Roberts 2
Harsh, Vivian Gordon 14
Harvey, William R. 42
Haskins, James 36
Hathaway, Isaac Scott 33
Hayden, Carla D. 47
Hayden, Robert 12
Haynes, George Edmund 8
Henderson, Stephen E. 45
Henries, A. Doris Banks 44
Herenton, Willie W. 24

Government and politics-- international

Government and politics--U.S.

Cumulative Subject Index

Volume numbers appear in **bold**

Paige, Rod **29**
Thomas, Clarence **2**, **39**
Tribble, Israel, Jr. **8**

U.S. Department of Energy
O'Leary, Hazel **6**

U.S. Department of Health and Human Services (HHS)
See also U.S. Department of Health, Education, and Welfare

U.S. Department of Health, Education, and Welfare (HEW)
Bell, Derrick **6**
Berry, Mary Frances **7**
Harris, Patricia Roberts **2**
Johnson, Eddie Bernice **8**
Sullivan, Louis **8**

U.S. Department of Housing and Urban Development (HUD)
Gaines, Brenda **41**
Harris, Patricia Roberts **2**
Jackson, Alphonso R. **48**
Weaver, Robert C. **8**, **46**

U.S. Department of Justice
Bell, Derrick **6**
Campbell, Bill **9**
Days, Drew S., III **10**
Guinier, Lani **7**, **30**
Holder, Eric H., Jr. **9**
Lafontant, Jewel Stradford **3**, **51**
Lewis, Delano **7**
Patrick, Deval **12**
Payton, John **48**
Thompson, Larry D. **39**
Wilkins, Roger **2**

U.S. Department of Labor
Crockett, George, Jr. **10**
Herman, Alexis M. **15**

U.S. Department of Social Services
Little, Robert L. **2**

U.S. Department of State
Bethune, Mary McLeod **4**
Bunche, Ralph J. **5**
Keyes, Alan L. **11**
Lafontant, Jewel Stradford **3**, **51**
Perkins, Edward **5**
Powell, Colin **1**, **28**
Rice, Condoleezza **3**, **28**
Wharton, Clifton Reginald, Sr. **36**
Wharton, Clifton R., Jr. **7**

U.S. Department of the Interior
Person, Waverly **9**, **51**

U.S. Department of Transportation
Davis, Benjamin O., Jr. **2**, **43**

U.S. Department of Veterans Affairs
Brown, Jesse **6**, **41**

U.S. Diplomatic Corps
Grimké, Archibald H. **9**
Haley, George Williford Boyce **21**
Harris, Patricia Roberts **2**

Stokes, Carl B. **10**

U.S. District Court judge
Carter, Robert L. **51**
Diggs-Taylor, Anna **20**
Keith, Damon J. **16**
Parsons, James **14**

USFL
See United States Football League

U.S. Foreign Service
Davis, Ruth **37**
Dougherty, Mary Pearl **47**

U.S. Geological Survey
Person, Waverly **9**, **51**

U.S. House of Representatives
Archie-Hudson, Marguerite **44**
Ballance, Frank W. **41**
Bishop, Sanford D., Jr. **24**
Brown, Corrine **24**
Burke, Yvonne Braithwaite **42**
Carson, Julia **23**
Chisholm, Shirley **2**, **50**
Clay, William Lacy **8**
Clayton, Eva M. **20**
Clyburn, James **21**
Collins, Barbara-Rose **7**
Collins, Cardiss **10**
Conyers, John, Jr. **4**, **45**
Crockett, George, Jr. **10**
Cummings, Elijah E. **24**
Davis, Artur **41**
Dellums, Ronald **2**
Diggs, Charles C. **21**
Dixon, Julian C. **24**
Dymally, Mervyn **42**
Espy, Mike **6**
Fauntroy, Walter E. **11**
Fields, Cleo **13**
Flake, Floyd H. **18**
Ford, Harold Eugene **42**
Ford, Harold E., Jr., **16**
Franks, Gary **2**
Gray, William H. III **3**
Hastings, Alcee L. **16**
Hilliard, Earl F. **24**
Jackson, Jesse, Jr. **14**, **45**
Jackson Lee, Sheila **20**
Jefferson, William J. **25**
Jordan, Barbara **4**
Kilpatrick, Carolyn Cheeks **16**
Lee, Barbara **25**
Leland, Mickey **2**
Lewis, John **2**, **46**
Majette, Denise **41**
Meek, Carrie **6**
Meek, Kendrick **41**
Meeks, Gregory **25**
Metcalfe, Ralph **26**
Mfume, Kweisi **6**, **41**
Millender-McDonald, Juanita **21**
Mitchell, Parren J. **42**
Norton, Eleanor Holmes **7**
Owens, Major **6**
Payne, Donald M. **2**
Pinchback, P. B. S. **9**
Powell, Adam Clayton, Jr. **3**
Rangel, Charles **3**
Rush, Bobby **26**
Scott, David **41**

Scott, Robert C. **23**
Stokes, Louis **3**
Towns, Edolphus **19**
Tubbs Jones, Stephanie **24**
Washington, Harold **6**
Waters, Maxine **3**
Watson, Diane **41**
Watt, Melvin **26**
Watts, J.C. **14**, **38**
Wheat, Alan **14**
Wynn, Albert R. **25**
Young, Andrew **3**, **48**

U.S. Information Agency
Allen, Samuel **38**

U.S. Joint Chiefs of Staff
Howard, Michelle **28**
Powell, Colin **1**, **28**
Rice, Condoleezza **3**, **28**

U.S. Marines
Bolden, Charles F., Jr. **7**
Brown, Jesse **6**, **41**
Petersen, Franke E. **31**
Von Lipsey, Roderick K. **11**

U.S. Navy
Black, Barry C. **47**
Brashear, Carl **29**
Brown, Jesse Leroy **31**
Doby, Lawrence Eugene Sr. **16**, **41**
Fields, Evelyn J. **27**
Gravely, Samuel L., Jr. **5**, **49**
Howard, Michelle **28**
Miller, Dorie **29**
Pinckney, Bill **42**
Reason, J. Paul **19**
Wright, Lewin **43**

U.S. Olympic Committee (USOC)
DeFrantz, Anita **37**

U.S. Open golf tournament
Shippen, John **43**
Woods, Tiger **14**, **31**

U.S. Open tennis tournament
Williams, Venus **17**, **34**

U.S. Peace Corps
Days, Drew S., III **10**
Johnson, Rafer **33**
Lewis, Delano **7**

U.S. Register of the Treasury
Bruce, Blanche Kelso **33**

U.S. Senate
Black, Barry C. **47**
Braun, Carol Moseley **4**, **42**
Brooke, Edward **8**
Bruce, Blanche Kelso **33**
Dodson, Howard, Jr. **7**
Johnson, Eddie Bernice **8**
Obama, Barack **49**
Pinchback, P. B. S. **9**

U.S. Supreme Court
Marshall, Thurgood **1**, **44**
Thomas, Clarence **2**, **39**

U.S. Surgeon General
Elders, Joycelyn **6**

U.S. Virgin Islands government
Hastie, William H. **8**

U.S.S. Constitution
Wright, Lewin **43**

UVC
See Ultraviolent Camera/Spectrograph

UWUSA
See United Workers Union of South Africa

Vancouver Canucks hockey team
Brashear, Donald **39**

Vancouver Grizzlies basketball team
Abdur-Rahim, Shareef **28**

Vaudeville
Anderson, Eddie "Rochester" **30**
Austin, Lovie **40**
Bates, Peg Leg **14**
Cox, Ida **42**
Davis, Sammy Jr. **18**
Johnson, Jack **8**
Martin, Sara **38**
McDaniel, Hattie **5**
Mills, Florence **22**
Robinson, Bill "Bojangles" **11**
Waters, Ethel **7**

Verizon Communication
Gordon, Bruce S. **41**

Veterinary science
Jawara, Sir Dawda Kairaba **11**
Maathai, Wangari **43**
Patterson, Frederick Douglass **12**
Thomas, Vivien **9**

Video direction
Barclay, Paris **37**
Fuqua, Antoine **35**
Pinkett Smith, Jada **10**, **41**

Vibe
Jones, Quincy **8**, **30**
Smith, Danyel **40**

Vibraphone
Hampton, Lionel **17**, **41**

Village Voice
Cooper, Andrew W. **36**
Crouch, Stanley **11**

Violin
Murray, Tai **47**
Smith, Stuff **37**
Tinsley, Boyd **50**

VIP Memphis magazine
McMillan, Rosalynn A. **36**

Virginia state government
Marsh, Henry **32**
Martin, Ruby Grant **49**
Wilder, L. Douglas **3**, **48**

Virgin Records
Brooks, Hadda **40**
Carey, Mariah **32**

Cumulative Name Index

Volume numbers appear in **bold**